GAMBLING
with
TRUTH

An Essay on Induction
and the Aims of Science

GAMBLING

with

TRUTH

*An Essay on Induction
and the Aims of Science*

ISAAC LEVI

THE MIT PRESS
CAMBRIDGE, MASSACHUSETTS, AND LONDON, ENGLAND

First printed in 1967 by Alfred A. Knopf, New York, and Routledge &
Kegan Paul, Ltd., London

First MIT Press paperback edition, October 1973.
Manufactured in the United States of America.

Library of Congress Cataloging in Publication Data

Levi, Isaac, 1930-
  Gambling with truth.

  Original ed. issued in series: Borzoi books
in the philosophy of science.
  Bibliography: p.
  1. Science—Methodology. I. Title.
Q175.L445 1973   501'.8   73-3092
ISBN 0-262-62026-X

to SIDNEY MORGENBESSER

PREFACE

Scientific inquiry, like other forms of human deliberation, is goal-directed activity. Consequently, an adequate conception of the goal or goals of scientific inquiry ought to shed light on the difference between valid and invalid inference; for valid inferences are good strategies designed to attain these objectives.

However, knowing what one wants does not determine the best way to obtain it. Other items of information are required. What these items are is controlled in large measure by appropriate criteria for rational deliberation. To be told, for example, that science looks for true, informative, and simple answers to questions is of little help to an understanding of legitimate inference if an account of how legitimate inferences aid in obtaining such answers is lacking.

Contemporary work in decision theory provides one source from which the required account of rational decision-making might be fashioned. Unfortunately, those philosophers, statisticians, and decision theorists who have appreciated the relevance of decision theory to induction have tended to use decision theory to foster a distorted conception of science. Some writers seem to hold that science has no aims of its own different from the moral, political, economic, or prudential objectives of other types of deliberation. Others are inclined to reduce the role of the scientist to that of a statistician who organizes and analyses data in a manner helpful to the policy-maker without actually making policy recommendations.

Both of these views are rejected in this book. Scientists are not mere guidance counselors. Nor are the aims which they attempt to realize always practical ones. But insistence on the distinctive "cognitive" character of the objectives of science is compatible with the claim that the criteria for rational decision-making applicable where the goals are "practical" are operative also when the objectives are "cognitive." In an attenuated but, nonetheless, interesting sense, scientists do gamble. But the stakes are truth, information, simplicity, explanatory power, and the like. Consequently, an analysis of the character of these stakes together with a theory of rational gambling ought to lead to interesting conclusions about inductive inference. This book attempts to show that this is so.

The dedication to Sidney Morgenbesser is but a small indication of the profound debt I owe him. His encouragement and criticism, his readiness to share his ideas with me, and, above all, his friendship, have contributed to the development of the views presented here in a way that no number of scholarly footnotes could document. I have internalized so many of his suggestions and so much of his address to philosophical questions that it is often difficult for me to tell where his insight leaves off and my gloss begins.

To have been a student of Ernest Nagel's has always been for me a source of pride and good fortune. He first awakened in me an interest in probability and induction and his constructive suggestions and encouragement have been invaluable in writing this book.

Chapters VIII and IX present a reconstruction of G. L. S. Shackle's theory of potential surprise. I hope that I can partially repay my considerable debt to Professor Shackle by introducing some of his original and profound ideas to students of philosophy.

I owe the term "epistemic utility" to Carl Hempel. The account of epistemic utility offered here is largely the product of interaction between his published discussions and my own earlier views on the subject.

Henry Kyburg prompted me to worry about deductive closure. I have found close study of his work extremely helpful in writing this book.

I regret that the recent important contributions of Ian Hacking, Jaakko Hintikka, and Richard Jeffrey came to my attention too late for me to include a serious discussion of their work in this volume.

Henry Kyburg, Sidney Morgenbesser, Ernest Nagel, Robert Nozick, Frederic Schick, and G. L. S. Shackle have all seen earlier drafts of this book. I am most grateful for their comments. Of course, no one but myself is to blame for its deficiencies.

Some portions of Chapter I are reprinted from *The Monist*, Vol. 48, No. 2 (1964) by permission of the Open Court Publishing Co., LaSalle, Illinois. The first two pages of "Corroboration and Rules of Acceptance" which appeared in the *British Journal for the Philosophy of Science*, Vol. 13, No. 52 (1963) are reprinted by permission of the editors at the beginning of Chapter VII.

The National Science Foundation awarded me two summer grants which provided me with the leisure to write this book.

My wife Judith and our boys, Jonathan and David, have surrounded me with the love, warmth, and moral support without which the leisure time would have been useless. To them I owe the greatest debt of all.

I. L.

CONTENTS

GAMBLING
with
TRUTH

An Essay on Induction
and the Aims of Science

I

Belief and Action

1] *Global vs. Local Justification*

Philosophers and scientists have often arranged, either tacitly or explicitly, a rather delicate division of labor. In science, justification of belief is demanded only when the need for such justification arises in the context of specific inquiries. Philosophers have often been discontent with justification in this "local" sense. Like Descartes or some of the contemporary writers who worry about choosing between "conceptual schemes," many philosophers occupy themselves with efforts at the more "global" justification of the totality of beliefs held at a given time.

Consider an investigator who is puzzling over apparent cloud formations that have been recorded on pictures of the surface of Mars. He wants to know whether they are sandstorms, collections of moisture or mere illusions created by some malfunction of the camera. His specific question controls what is to count as a relevant answer. At the outset, he is in doubt as to which of the relevant answers to accept as true. He wishes primarily to remove this doubt; when he finally proposes an answer, however, he also feels obligated to justify his picking that answer rather than some alternative.

Supplying this justification requires an appeal to evidence, which will include observation reports and theoretical assumptions, as well as much of the apparatus of logic and mathematics. In short, evidence will consist of those of the investigator's findings and beliefs that are relevant to the problem at hand and are not likely to be questioned by any participant in the inquiry or by anyone who is qualified to evaluate its results. Evidence is not ruled out as illegitimate solely because of the possibility that in some future inquiry it may be shown to be false. Sleeping dogs are allowed to lie when there is no apparent reason, at the moment, for arousing them.

Global justification is more demanding. Following Descartes, the globalist wishes to show that all his beliefs (at least those he holds at a given time) are justified. Consequently, he seeks an evidential base in which all the evidence is evident; for the nature of evident beliefs is that they carry with them their own justifications, which render them impervious to legitimate question in further inquiry.

Evident beliefs are generally held to belong to one of two categories: (a) Belief in the truth of necessary propositions. To understand such a proposition is to recognize the justification of its truth. (b) Belief in the direct testimony of the senses. Here understanding conjoins with direct empirical confrontation to justify belief.

Efforts at global justification have historically foundered on three major difficulties. The domain of necessary truth, upon being subjected to close scrutiny, has been found to be restricted to the realm of logical truth. The incorrigible status of direct reports of experience, on the other hand, has been impugned. Finally, since Hume, even fairly accommodating conceptions of the scope of the evident have had trouble including within the confines of the evident presuppositions adequate to justify the multitude of nonevident beliefs that are supported by science and common sense. When two "conceptual schemes" both of which satisfy minimal requirements of logical consistency and empirical adequacy are brought face to face, the suspicion arises that no rational means is available for deciding between them on global terms.

Global skepticism does not, however, imply local skepticism. Evidence in local inquiry includes both necessary truth (whatever that may be) and observation reports. In short, it will contain whatever counts as evident from the global point of view. But the price of admission to evidential status is not global. The evident (if there be such) is evidence in local inquiry because all parties to the inquiry agree that such beliefs do not stand in need of justification. Beliefs that are nonevident can also meet this less rigorous standard: laws and theories can and generally will be taken as evidence even though they are not evident. To include H in the evidence requires that (a) at the time of the inquiry H be believed true, and (b) at that time, critical scrutiny of H in the light of new evidence be considered pointless. What cannot legitimately count as evidence consists of beliefs that are subject to question in the inquiry itself and beliefs which, while they are not actually questioned at the time of the inquiry, are recognized at that time as calling for further examination.

Satisfaction of the conditions for evidential status does not imply incorrigibility. Results of new experiments, new disagreements, and deeper curiosity can all provide the occasion for removing some item from the evidence. To regain evidential status, the truth of the hypothesis in question would have to be justified by an appeal to other evidence, which in turn would have to be shown to be sufficiently decisive to justify terminating further efforts at the collection of evidence.

Thus, the central problem of a theory of local justification or rational belief is the establishment of criteria for determining which of the relevant answers to a given question, on the evidence available, is the best. These criteria do not determine what questions are raised or what evidence is available. Rather they reveal features of legitimate inference that are invariant over broad categories of local inquiries, regardless of the questions and the evidence peculiar to each individual problem.

Admittedly some comments on questions and evidence will be in order. The presuppositions of questions and other evidential assumptions are often, during the course of scientific investigations, subject to critical review. But even here, local justification for accepting H as evidence requires local justification for taking H to be true on other evidence. A theory of evidence, insofar as one is needed, depends upon a theory of inference—not the other way round.

Interest in local problems does not imply disparagement of

global concerns. The sense in which justification is demanded by globalists is different from the sense in which justification is pertinent to local inquiries. The skeptical despair that threatens quests for global justification need not infect efforts at local justification. Whether that despair stands in need of alleviation in its own right, however, is an entirely separate matter.

This book is concerned with justification in the local sense. Some features of local justification will be considered that seem to remain invariant over a wide variety of investigations. This investigation, though broad in scope, is itself a local one. No attempt will be made to justify the criteria offered by deriving them in some globalistically impeccable manner from the incontrovertibly evident. Such justification as is possessed by the proposals to be made comes from their success in systematically accounting for more or less widely acknowledged features of local justification. These proposals are, it goes without saying, liable to error and subject to revision.

2] *Local Skepticism*

Skepticism appears in many forms. Although local justification appears to be immune to the variety that threatens global justification, a relatively recent strain has been bred in a culture brewed from contemporary reflections on the relations between rational belief and rational action. In reaction against certain oversimplifications that are to be found in classical models of this relation—especially when these are applied to risky situations—some writers have concluded that no beliefs can be justified, even locally, that are not deducible from the available evidence.

From the local point of view, the evidence available at a given time consists of assumptions that might and often will be subject to question at some later time. When they are so questioned, even local justification will require supporting belief by appeal to evidence via nondeductive inference. Consequently, once evidence has been questioned, it can never regain its status unless it is shown to be evident (or deducible from the evident). This new skepticism, which arises in the context of local justification, will lead an investigator who takes it seriously, over the long run, to restrict his stock of beliefs to the evident, to what is deducible from the evident and to those nonevident beliefs that to date he has not questioned. Local skepticism thus converges on global skepticism. The remainder of this chapter will be given over to a consideration of those features of rational belief and action that seem to imply this new skepticism and to some suggestions for its elimination.

3] *Naïve Cognitivism*

Most philosophers, in discussing the problem of selecting an optimal policy for realizing given ends, adopt a very simple model for dealing with this situation.[1] They view the decision-maker as confronted with a choice among several optional courses of action. If he is to make a rational choice among these options, he must form some judgment about the consequences of the alternative policies relative to his goals and compare these consequences in terms of the extent to which they constitute realizations of these objectives.

Let $A_1, A_2, ..., A_n$ be a set of alternative policies open to the decision-maker, $o_1, o_2, ..., o_n$ the set of relevant outcomes expected by the decision-maker to eventuate from adoption of these options, and $u(o_i)$ the "utility" or value attached to the ith outcome in the light of the decision-maker's goals.[2] The simple model just described may be represented as follows:

$$A_1 \qquad\qquad u(o_1)$$
$$A_2 \qquad\qquad u(o_2)$$
$$\cdot \qquad\qquad\qquad \cdot$$
$$\cdot \qquad\qquad\qquad \cdot$$
$$\cdot \qquad\qquad\qquad \cdot$$
$$A_n \qquad\qquad u(o_n)$$

[1] The view to be discussed here has apparently been considered too obvious to warrant detailed scrutiny by students of ethics. Writers like Dewey, Moore and Stevenson seem to share it. Those philosophers who, like Kant, attempt to minimize the relevance of consequences in typically ethical decision problems do, nonetheless, adopt this position with respect to questions of prudence and expediency. The subsequent discussion leaves open the question of the extent to which the problem of selecting an optimum policy for realizing given ends is typical of ethical decision problems.

[2] The notion of utility as used here may refer either to the position of a given outcome in a rank ordering of outcomes with respect to value relative

Given the information in this representation, the rational decision-maker is enjoined to adopt the A_i for which $u(o_i)$ is greater than any $u(o_j)$, where j is different from i. In case of a "tie," the acts involved are deemed equally optimal.

According to this simple model, two factors are central to determining a rational choice among a given set of options: the outcomes or consequences of these options and the utility or value attached to them. Most discussion by writers on ethics has been devoted to a consideration of the second factor. Determination of the consequences of action has been taken to be a matter for scientists to handle. Philosophical questions that pertain to the determination of consequences are, therefore, considered to be properly assigned to students of scientific method and inference and not to students of ethics.

The point of interest here has nothing to do with this division of labor. Rather what is involved is the assumption that science can help us ascertain the outcomes or consequences to which utilities or values are to be attached. This claim presupposes that part of the product of scientific investigation consists of predictions—i.e., statements about the future that are accepted as true. Such a view conforms well to the classical position that holds that at least one of the aims of science is to replace doubt by true belief. The result of efforts to attain this aim is a body of propositions divided into those accepted as true, those rejected as false and those still consigned to the limbo of doubt. Part of this output—to wit, that portion consisting of predictions of the outcomes of policies—is the scientific contribution to rational decision-making. Thus, the scientific quest for truth works hand in glove with the practical man's effort to attain his ends in the best way possible.

Many supporters of naive cognitivism (as we shall term the view just outlined) recognize that the conclusions reached in

to the goals of the decision-maker or, when the context calls for it, an interval measure of value—e.g., the interval measure based on postulates for rational preference of a Von Neumann-Morgenstern variety.

The utility assigned to an outcome can be understood to reflect all kinds of values, including conformity to or violation of moral laws, the goals of the decision-maker, prudential and aesthetic considerations, etc. The terms "goal," "objective," etc. could be interpreted as shorthand for the factors determining the decision-maker's utility function. The subsequent discussion attempts to remain neutral between this and narrower readings.

scientific investigations cannot be guaranteed to be true solely on the basis of the evidence that supports them. Hence, the scientist cannot assure the decision-maker that the predicted consequences of his actions will come true. The decision-maker has to realize that his policies may result in outcomes other than those predicted, and these outcomes may be far less desirable relative to his goals than the ones he anticipates. At the very least, therefore, the diagrammatic representation of the decision-maker's problem has to be modified in order to take into account these other outcomes.

	H_1	H_2	...	H_m
A_1	$u(o_{11})$	$u(o_{12})$	...	$u(o_{1m})$
A_2	$u(o_{21})$	$u(o_{22})$	...	$u(o_{2m})$
.	.	.	...	.
.	.	.	...	.
.	.	.	...	.
A_n	$u(o_{n1})$	$u(o_{n2})$	...	$u(o_{nm})$

In this representation, the H_j's are an exclusive and exhaustive set of hypotheses, which describe the possible "states of nature" under which the decision-maker may be acting. The outcome o_{ij} represents the result of adopting policy A_i when H_j is true.[3]

The naive cognitivist view may be restated in terms of this matrix representation as follows: The scientist aids the decision-maker by indicating which of the alternative hypotheses H_j we are entitled to accept as true on the basis of the available evidence. The selection of an H_j restricts the decision-maker's problem to considering the utilities of outcomes in the jth column of the matrix, according to the method previously described.

Although most philosophers who write in ethics seem to subscribe to some variant of naive cognitivism, this view has been

---

[3] Real-life decision-makers would usually consider the possible outcomes of each act to be available to them separately, without making them a function of a single set of exclusive and exhaustive hypotheses. However, insofar as the decision-maker is able to specify alternative outcomes for each policy considered, simple formal devices can be used to convert the representation of his problem into this form. Since it is both customary and convenient to use this scheme, it will be adopted here. It must be remembered, however, that real-life decision-makers are often vague in their ideas about alternative outcomes of options available to them. Hence, this discussion is infected with a certain (hopefully tolerable) amount of idealization.

almost universally rejected by those statisticians, social scientists and philosophers who in recent years have concerned themselves with decision theory. Certain elementary, almost commonsensical, considerations support this rejection. First, the evidence available to the scientist may oblige him to suspend judgment. In that event, his conclusions are of no help to the decision-maker, who still has to decide what to do. Thus, a physician may prescribe a certain therapy even though he cannot honestly predict what the outcome of the therapy will be. He may argue that, while he cannot make the prediction, the evidence available to him indicates that the chances of successful cure are greater through this therapy than through its alternatives. Second, the evidence may entitle the scientist to accept one of the H_j's as true, yet may not warrant the decision-maker's choosing the act that produces maximum utility when H_j is true. Recently certain medical groups temporarily suspended dispensing the birth control pill, Enovid, pending further examination of evidence regarding its safety. Several physicians endorsed this policy, even though they acknowledged that they believed the pill to be safe. The trouble here stems from the fact that no amount of evidence can provide an infallible guarantee of the safety of the pill. Conclusions reached regarding its safety run the risk of error. Similarly, the policies adopted concerning the use of the pill run the risk of leading to disastrous consequences. If moral considerations demand greater insurance against possible harmful side effects of use of the pill than our cognitive scruples demand against possible error, the available evidence could render it quite reasonable to predict the safety of the drug and still not to recommend its use.

These considerations suggest that naive cognitivists oversimplify the relevance of the conclusions of science to policy-making. If the conclusions reached by scientists about the consequences of policies are relevant to the choice among policies, they are relevant in a more indirect way than is indicated by naive cognitivists. For this reason, alternatives to naive cognitivism must be considered.

4] *Behavioralism*

The considerations just cited as reasons for abandoning naive cognitivism point to the conclusion that not belief but probability is the guide in life. This is not to say that decision-makers must rely on probabilities in a sense that conforms to the requirements of the calculus of probabilities. The point is that it is the degree to which evidence supports the alternative hypotheses, confirms them, renders them more likely, etc., that is relevant to selecting optimal policies. How and in what sense degrees of evidential support are to be measured remain open questions. Hence, if the scientist does contribute any guidance to the decision-maker, it is not through the prediction of consequences. Rather it is by indicating how likely various outcomes will be when given policies are undertaken, or how well the available evidence supports alternative hypotheses about the state of nature.

This thesis about the relevance of science to action has often been accompanied by a still stronger claim—namely, that scientists do not accept or reject propositions at all, unless such acceptance or rejection is reduced to action that is related to practical objectives. "Behavioralists," as supporters of this position may be called, sometimes deny outright that scientists either accept or reject hypotheses. Thus, Rudolf Carnap contends that the "conclusions" of nondeductive or inductive inferences are the assignments of degrees of confirmation to hypotheses. According to Carnap, the only statements that can be accepted are those that are directly confirmed by observation, logical and analytic truths, and the deductive consequences of these.[4] Other writers (e.g., Richard Rudner and C. W. Churchman) do assert that scientists accept hypotheses, but they seem to interpret "accepting a hypothesis as true" to mean the same as "acting or being disposed to act in the manner which would be best relative to a given objective if the hypothesis were true."[5] The significant dif-

[4] R. Carnap, *Logical Foundations of Probability* (2nd ed.; Chicago: University of Chicago Press, 1962), pp. 205–206.

[5] R. Rudner, "The Scientist *qua* Scientist Makes Value Judgments," *Philosophy of Science*, 20 (1953), 3 f. and C. W. Churchman, "Science and Decision Making," *Philosophy of Science*, 23 (1956), 248–249.

ference between these two versions of behavioralism is that the latter views the scientist as being actually a decision-maker, whereas the former relegates the role of the scientist in decision-making to that of a guidance counselor. Both positions agree, however, that insofar as scientific inquiry can be isolated from practical concerns, the output of such investigation consists of assignments to statements of degrees of probability, confirmation, likelihood, and so forth.

5] *Critical Cognitivism*

The considerations adduced in favor of rejecting naive cognitivism do not necessitate the adoption of a behavioralist viewpoint.[6] At least some scientific inquiries may be concerned with prediction, postdiction, explanation, and other activities that lead to accepting propositions as true, rejecting them as false, or suspending judgment on them. The force of the objections raised previously was directed against the assumption that the outcomes of such activities contribute to rational decision-making. If what scientists do is attempt to replace doubt by true belief, then the results of their efforts are not directly relevant to practical affairs.

To be sure, those "critical cognitivists" who affirm the antecedent of this conditional acknowledge that scientific inquiry bears some relevance to decision-making. An investigator who is engaged in the quest for truth will have to weigh evidence for and against alternative conclusions; the degrees of probability, confirmation, evidential support reflecting such weighings are relevant to decision-making as much as to truth-seeking. But critical cognitivists will insist—contrary to the behavioralist view —that these weighings are no more the end-products of scientific inquiry than they are of decision-making. They are rather pro-

---

[6] Rudolf Carnap has argued against the propriety of inductive rules of acceptance by way of considerations similar in all essential respects to the arguments described previously as telling against naive cognitivism. See R. Carnap, "Replies and Systematic Expositions," in *The Philosophy of Rudolf Carnap,* Paul A. Schilpp, ed. (LaSalle, Ill.: Open Court Publishing Co., 1964), pp. 972–973. He uses such arguments as a basis for defending his own behavioralist point of view.

cedures relevant to the attainment of two distinct types of objectives—practical and cognitive (theoretical) objectives.

Thus, critical cognitivism renders asunder, at least partially, what many philosophers have endeavored to join together—theoretical and practical wisdom. John Dewey, for example, found it possible to accommodate the view that scientific inquiry is disinterested inquiry with the thesis that the results of such inquiries are important as guides to action.[7] This accommodation is predicated on the naive cognitivist assumption that propositions accepted as true are appropriate guides. If this assumption is true, then an investigator can engage in a quest for truth without concern for any specific practical objective. His conclusions will nevertheless—pending further evidence—provide the basis for rational action relative to any practical objective for which the answers he obtains are relevant. Similarly, writers like Braithwaite, who are eager to uphold an action analysis of belief, can maintain, with the tacit aid of naive cognitivism, that belief that p entails a disposition to act as if p were true, in relation to any practical objective.[8]

The objections previously raised against naive cognitivism suggest that positions such as Dewey's or Braithwaite's are in need of drastic revision. Situations can be specified in which a rational agent would not act as if a proposition p were true unless he had an infallible guarantee of the truth of the proposition.[9] Evidence might warrant acting on the proposition relative to some objectives; owing to the seriousness of error, however, the same evidence might justify acting as if the proposition were false relative to other objectives. This situation cannot be avoided except by evidence that entails the proposition in question. Thus an action analysis of belief of the sort that Braithwaite at one time advocated entails the requirement that a rational agent believe

[7] John Dewey, *Reconstruction in Philosophy* (New York: Beacon, 1948), pp. 121–123.

[8] R. B. Braithwaite, "The Nature of Believing," *Proceedings of the Aristotelian Society*, 33 (1932–33), 129–146; and "Belief and Action," *Aristotelian Society Supplementary Volume*, 20 (1946), 1–19.

[9] See I. Levi and S. Morgenbesser, "Disposition & Belief," *American Philosophical Quarterly*, 1 (1964), 222–223. R. C. Jeffrey has used substantially the same argument to support a behavioralist viewpoint. See R. C. Jeffrey, "Valuation and Acceptance of Scientific Hypotheses," *Philosophy of Science*, 33 (1956), 245.

only those propositions to be true that constitute evidence. This would imply, as has already been argued, that rational belief will tend to be restricted to the evident—a consequence that neither Dewey nor Braithwaite would be prepared to accept.

Advocates of action analyses of belief can avoid this difficulty by abandoning the thesis that accepting a proposition as true entails a disposition to act as if the proposition were true, relative to *every* objective to which the proposition is relevant. Restrictions have to be imposed on the objectives. The most obvious suggestions are the following:

a) Equate "believes that p" with "being disposed to act as if p were true relative to objective O," where O is a specific practical objective. This view (which is at least implicit in the position advanced by Richard Rudner[1]) reduces attempting to replace doubt by true belief to practical decision-making. In short, it results in one version of behavioralism.

b) Equate "believes that p" with "believes that p to a certain degree." Since degrees of belief (at least in the sense in which they are understood to be subjective probabilities) are supposed to reflect the decision-maker's judgment with regard to how well evidence supports hypotheses, the obstacles cited above to an action analysis of belief do not apply. "Believes p to degree k" can be interpreted as characterizing a disposition to act as if p were true for those objectives relative to which evidential support for p to degree k rationally warrants such action. This analysis leads to that variant of behavioralism according to which the conclusions of science are degrees of probability, confirmation, evidential support, etc., which determine rational degrees of belief.

Thus, quite aside from various other considerations that have been adduced in favor of behavioralism, it is easy to see why writers who are committed to action analyses of belief, or adherents to the idea that knowledge is power, would opt for behavioralism rather than critical cognitivism. Critical cognitivism insists that both the scientist and the common man are frequently concerned to replace doubt by true belief in a sense that is not amenable to analyses either of type (a) or of type (b). It recognizes the quest for truth as a legitimate human activity whose

[1] Rudner, *op. cit.*, pp. 2–3.

aims and products are not directly relevant to practical concerns; it rejects action analyses of belief.

Yet, in spite of its inhospitability toward action analyses of belief, critical cognitivism deserves a hearing if for no other reason than the liabilities from which behavioralism suffers. Behavioralists must admit that in some instances scientists do accept propositions in a sense that is difficult to reduce to a disposition to act relative to practical objectives. Even the decision-maker must consider the range of possible outcomes of alternative policies; this requires that he accept as true statements that specify alternative outcomes. These disjunctive statements may in some instances be logical truths, such as a behavioralist might be prepared to admit are accepted as true. However, the decision-maker must also accept statements that describe the evidence on which assignments of probability, degrees of confirmation, etc. are based; as is usually acknowledged, such statements cannot be provided with an infallible guarantee. Finally, what counts as evidence is frequently a function of theoretical commitments.[2] Practical deliberation, like scientific inquiry, relies on evidence that is not evident.

Action analyses of belief are sometimes thought to be important to the clarification of obscurities that reside in the notions of belief, disbelief, and suspension of judgment. These notions are indeed in need of clarification; but then again, so are the notions of declaring war, taking a walk, making an omelet, writing a book, and so on. In particular, attempts to reconstruct such concepts in terms of language that describes publicly observable behavior seem to be no easier to carry through than analogous attempts in the case of belief. Critical cognitivists are free to regard belief predicates as theoretical, relative to language that describes overt behavior; they can also concede that such attributions are in need of clarification.

Such clarification must ultimately depend, however, upon advances in psychological theory. Proposals of criteria for rational belief need not wait for such advances. If it is reasonable (as indeed it is) to proceed with systematic studies of rational action without a fully adequate understanding of the notion of an act

---

[2] For further discussion, see C. G. Hempel, "Deductive-Nomological vs. Statistical Explanation," *Minnesota Studies in the Philosophy of Science*, 3 (1962), 161.

(rational or irrational), surely it cannot be unreasonable in itself
to attempt studies of criteria for rational belief with only a vague
understanding of the notion of belief.[3]

6] *Autonomy*

The critical cognitivist outlook is hostile not only to the more or
less familiar varieties of action analyses of belief attributions. By
insisting that scientific inquiry has objectives quite distinct from
those of economic, political, moral, etc. deliberation, it rejects
the point of view which holds that the scientific propriety of a
man's beliefs is dependent, at least in part, on the moral, political, economic, etc. consequences of his having these beliefs.[4]

Beliefs, being inner (psychological) states, are accessible to
public scrutiny only by way of their manifestations in overt behavior; these manifestations can on some occasions have psychological and social consequences of a morally, economically, etc.
relevant nature. On such occasions, it might be argued, justification of belief should take into consideration these consequences.

Consider, for example, an economist who is acting as advisor
to the government and is asked whether a tax cut will have sig-

[3] The view regarding belief predicates advocated by the author follows
lines similar in many respects to the position proposed with respect to want
predicates by Brandt and Kim (R. Brandt and J. Kim, "Wants as Explanations of Actions," *Journal of Philosophy*, 60 [1963], 425–435). However,
one important qualification ought to be mentioned here. Brandt and Kim
contend that common sense is committed to rudimentary psychological
theories which determine the conceptual content of want predicates in
ordinary language. Developments in psychology might lead to the supple-
mentation and revision of these theoretical assumptions and bridge laws, but
certain conditions (Brandt and Kim cite illustrations) would be revised only
at the expense of a radical alteration in the concept of "wants." In the case
of many psychological predicates, it seems doubtful whether families of
conditions of this sort can be furnished which are not extremely weak. What
can sometimes be done is to provide a system of principles of rationality—
e.g., of rational belief. Such principles are admittedly normative. The assumption that they are realizable or are realized to some degree, however,
may be taken as a theoretical postulate characterizing a "core" meaning for
the predicates involved—subject of course to modification through psychological inquiry. If this observation is correct, not only may an investigation of
rational belief proceed without benefit of a full-bodied analysis of belief,
it may contribute to the development of such an analysis.

[4] The view under consideration has been taken by Richard Rudner in
an oral reply to criticisms that I have levelled against him.

nificant inflationary effects. His beliefs will influence the answer he offers and thereby have an impact on the economy. Surely he ought to take the consequences of his beliefs into account in forming his opinion on this question.

Perhaps occasions do arise in which deciding what to believe brings forward serious moral, political, economic, etc. questions. And it is conceivable (but just barely) that on some occasions moral, political or economic considerations might carry sufficient weight to justify conclusions that scientific considerations would not by themselves justify. Perhaps, a person is justified in believing the earth to be flat if not to do so would do him great emotional harm. Cases such as this arise when there is a conflict between the interests of scientific inquiry and other human interests. How such conflicts are to be adjusted may indeed be an important and complex question, quite on a par with adjudicating between conflicting moral claims, moral and political claims, etc. Nevertheless, recognition of this fact does not rule out maintaining that scientific inquiry has its own objectives, in the light of which the results of such inquiry are to be judged qua scientific results. A person may be justified in believing the earth to be flat; but he cannot be justified in so believing according to scientific standards of fixing belief.

The main point to keep in mind here is that, when they are engaged in prediction, estimation, explanation, etc., the conclusions that scientists reach, insofar as they are put forth as conclusions justified by scientific standards, are to be judged in terms of the institutional objectives of scientific inquiry. The critical cognitivist point of view assumes that such standards are operative in the scientific evaluation of beliefs. It does not insist that the objectives of scientific inquiry are identifiable with the personal ends of scientific investigators but only that, insofar as the scientist (or average man) seeks to have his opinions appraised in a scientific or "rational" (in one of the many senses of that term) way, the appraisal is to be made with reference to these objectives.

One need not be dogmatic with regard to how the "cognitive" or "theoretical" aims of scientific inquiry are distinguished from the "practical" ends of moral, economic, political, etc. deliberation, in order to insist that they are different. Nor is it necessary to suppose that all scientific inquiry has a single type of cognitive objective. It might very well prove to be true that the objectives involved in explanation are different from those involved in prediction and estimation. Questions such as these are best postponed until some effort has been made to isolate the objectives that are characteristic of various kinds of inquiry and to compare them in a systematic way. Perhaps certain features can then be selected that will characterize the aims of scientific inquiry as contrasted with the ends of practical deliberation.

A full defense of such a position requires elaboration of a theory of scientific inference which will relate the criteria for legitimate inference to scientific objectives; a partial defense can be offered at the outset, however, in the light of at least two considerations.

First, scientific inquiries are often conducted in situations where no practical interests are visibly at stake—at any rate, none that are seriously considered relevant to assessing the results. (One can always cite the investigator's ego involvement in his work; but is that relevant to appraising the scientific value of his contributions?) In such cases, truth, relief from agnosticism, explanatory power, etc. seem to be desiderata, but these are precisely the sorts of values that are characteristic of theoretical as contrasted with practical concerns.

Second, it should be noted that scientific interests are public interests, in the sense that conclusions reached by scientists in order to further scientific ends are of value to the scientific community only insofar as they are communicated and subjected to scrutiny by that community. This implies that along with the cognitive objectives of science account should be taken of procedural norms that pertain, among other things, to honesty in reporting results and are intended to facilitate the furtherance of the cognitive ends of science.

Now, regardless of whether serious conflicts ever do arise between scientific and other interests with respect to belief, it is sometimes true that conflicts of a morally serious nature are occasioned when scientists reflect on whether they should communicate the results that they have obtained. From the legendary anguish of the Pythagorean community to the concern of Einstein and others over their responsibilities with regard to the atomic bomb, the history of science is replete with moral problems that have been occasioned by prima facie obligation to scientific procedures.

It is difficult to understand, however, why such conflicts are serious—indeed, are conflicts at all—unless scientists are understood to be committed to certain objectives distinctive of the scientific enterprise. If science is indeed the handmaiden of practice, as the behavioralists would have it, then all conflicts involving scientists would appear to be conflicts between moral, economic, political, aesthetic, etc. values.

Consideration of implications such as these suggests, if it does not establish, that scientific inquiry is part of an autonomous enterprise, which is engaged in pursuing special objectives, distinct from those that are found in other sorts of deliberate human activity.

7] *Statistical Inference*

Many of the observations that have been made in outlining the critical cognitivist viewpoint might appear to be philosophically commonplace. To be sure, the factor of risk, which is so damaging to the naive cognitivist viewpoint, has not until recently received from philosophers a fraction of the attention that it deserves. But hopefully it has been shown that to abandon naive cognitivism need not necessarily mean adopting a behavioralist viewpoint.

However, the strongest weapon in the behavioralist arsenal has yet to be considered. Since the work of Neyman and Pearson on the testing of hypotheses and interval estimation, the point of view adopted by writers on the theory of statistical inference has become increasingly a behavioralist one. The problems of statistical inference are, according to what is by now the orthodox position, problems of decision-making under risk or uncertainty. Such decision-making is generally understood to be practical decision-making, in the sense in which a production manager, a politician, a general is engaged in practical decision-making. Inductive inference is, in the language of Jerzy Neyman, reduced to inductive behavior.[5]

The authority of statisticians is not necessarily decisive in matters as controversial as behavioralism. However, the con-

[5] See J. Neyman, *Lectures and Conferences on Mathematical Statistics and Probability* (Washington: Graduate School, U.S. Department of Agriculture, 1952), p. 210.

tributions of mathematical statisticians are sometimes applied; some applications are made in psychology, the social sciences, and genetics, in situations where prima facie cognitive interests are at stake. Since these procedures have obtained whatever theoretical backing they possess from behavioralist assumptions, critical cognitivists have to acknowledge that in many cases procedures used in science for reaching conclusions have no rationale that they can find acceptable.

Two alternatives are open to the confirmed cognitivist: either he must scrap much scientific research, on the grounds that the procedures used were illegitimate, or else he must provide an alternative rationale for these procedures, which is compatible with cognitivist commitments. On the assumption that the first choice is a desperate measure, the proper course is to show that a decision-theoretic approach to inductive inference that conforms to cognitivist requirements is feasible.

The idea behind this alternative is that although scientific inquiry has its own objectives, they are, after all, objectives. As in the case of practical deliberation, the attainment of ends involves the selection of one option from among alternatives. And, as in much practical deliberation, there is no guarantee that the option chosen will not fail. Thus, in certain respects, justifying reaching a conclusion via nondeductive inference is comparable to making a practical decision under conditions of uncertainty or risk. If this is so, then the general criteria for rational decision-making might be operative both in practical deliberation and in scientific inference.[6] Yet, the standards for legitimate scientific inference will not be reducible *in toto* to decision-making criteria; for the distinctive commitments of the scientific inquirer will impose constraints upon him in addition to those that have already been imposed by the criteria for rational decision-making.

---

[6] Thus, critical cognitivism is capable of preserving many of the insights of the Peirce-Dewey tradition. The account of the occasion for development and termination of inquiry presented by that tradition can be understood as a characterization of certain features that are shared in common by inquiries into the truth and deliberations for the purpose of practical decision. What critical cognitivism rejects is the much stronger claim that the conclusions of scientific inquiry are either decisions to act relative to practical goals or aids to such decision-making, whose value is to be assessed in terms of their success as "guides in life."

The approach being proposed here has also been suggested by Hempel, *op. cit.*, pp. 149–159.

If it proved possible to develop such a decision-theoretic yet cognitivist approach to scientific inference, a rationale for current statistical practice would be forthcoming.

Note should be made in passing that adoption of a decision-theoretic approach to scientific inference commits no hostages to the view that men choose their beliefs. Whether they do so or not, their beliefs are appropriately subject to criticism, which evaluates beliefs in the light of alternative opinions that might have been held. Such opinions are evaluated in turn with reference to the ends of inquiry. In other words, there is a sufficient analogy between choosing how to act and reaching conclusions, to warrant exploring the possibility of subjecting both action and belief to similar conditions of rationality.

8] *The Aim of This Book*

These considerations, which are based on reflection on decision-making under uncertainty and risk as well as on recent developments in statistical theory, point to the desirability of initial efforts to construct an account of scientific inference that is frankly decision-theoretic while still remaining faithful to a cognitivist point of view. Removal of the threat of local skepticism that is implicit in behavioralism and better understanding of the relations between rational belief and rational action are not, however, the only dividends to be reaped from a successful attempt to achieve such a program. Scientific inquiry is often alleged to have ends whose generic traits control the criteria for fixing belief scientifically. This claim remains a barren commonplace, without philosophical fruit, unless a specification of these ends is accompanied by criteria for picking the best options by which to attain given ends on given evidence. To be informed that simplicity, informativeness, falsifiability, etc. are desiderata is of little help, even when these notions are precisely explicated, if a conception of the way in which these desiderata control the selection of a "best" conclusion is lacking. Similarly, the relevance of truth and probability (in its various statistical and inductive interpretations) to inductive inference stands in need of clarification. A decision-theoretic approach to inductive inference offers a promise of remedying these deficiencies.

Tentative and speculative first steps are taken in these directions in the following discussion. No pretense is made that the proposals to be introduced are immune against revision—even radical revision. They should be taken as constituting a first approximation to an adequate account of scientific inference sufficiently plausible to warrant further inquiry along the lines of the program being suggested.

II

****

Deductive Cogency

1] *Deductive Methodology*

Rational inductive inference and its relation to rational inductive behavior are the chief topics to be considered in this book. No matter what criteria for fixing beliefs are proposed, however, if they are to be judged adequate they must incorporate provisos that ensure the logical consistency of beliefs, as well as other stipulations that have to do with rational deductive inference. Some attention should be devoted at the outset, therefore, to questions of deductive rationality.

Consideration of deductive rationality does not mean, in this context, examining the deducibility relation, as it is articulated in the familiar formal systems of deductive logic. For our present purposes, notions of deducibility and consistency can be taken to be well understood. Of chief concern here is the application of principles of deductive logic in the evaluation of inferences, where an inference is understood to be an attempt to justify one belief or many by an appeal to others. Principles of deductive logic such as *modus ponens*, which states that Q is deducible from P→Q and P, do not of themselves indicate whether a man who believes that P→Q and also believes that P ought rationally to believe that Q. Determination of the conditions under which this normative pragmatic, or (in Carnap's language[1]) "methodological" principle is applicable proves not to be entirely trivial.

This chapter will be devoted to an examination of some problems of deductive methodology and their relevance to an account of inductive inference.

2] *Acceptance as True*

A commonplace practice in evaluating putative deductive inferences starts with a formulation of the premises and conclusions of such inferences in sentences and proceeds from there to a rephrasing of these sentences into sentences in some more or less artificial but standardized "language." This approach allows for the formulation of criteria for rational inference that are applicable to inferences expressed in certain standardized forms, and avoids thereby the necessity for settling questions of sentential synonymity prior to the formulation of these criteria. Synonymity does, nevertheless, become a problem when attempts are made to apply these criteria to inferences that find their articulation in "ordinary" language; for decisions have to be made regarding the propriety of paraphrases in natural languages of sentences that have appeared in the standardized language. The problem of finding an appropriate paraphrase can often be settled piecemeal, however, when the problem is to apply criteria for rational inference in real life. The deductive validity of arguments that are couched in ordinary language can often enough be decided even though systematic criteria for paraphrasing these arguments are unavailable. Since the central concern here is with the evaluation of inferences, attention can be restricted to those who use some standardized language L. Criteria for rational inference (both deductive and nondeductive) will be formulated in relation to such idealized languages, and questions of paraphrase for the purpose of applying these criteria in real life will be treated in the customary piecemeal fashion.

[1] Carnap's discussion of the distinction between deductive logic and deductive methodology can be found in R. Carnap, *Logical Foundations of Probability* (2nd ed.; Chicago: University of Chicago Press, 1963), pp. 202–205.

Very little will be said about the structure of the language L to be used. It will be required to have as an underlying logic the lower predicate calculus with identity and as many extralogical terms and axioms (including those of some set theory and some formulation of mathematics) as the occasion demands. Such a cavalier approach to matters of formalization may be defended in this context in view of the fact that most questions to be considered here are methodological in character. While the methodological principles to be proposed require the utilization of such logical notions as deducibility, consistency, and the like, these principles will, by and large, be applicable to any language with an underlying logic of the sort described. Excessive discussion of formal matters would complicate the exposition without paying any significant dividends in clarity.

Given an investigator A and a language L, "A believes that P" will be paraphrased by "A accepts the sentence S in L as true," where S is judged an adequate paraphrase of P in L. In many of the illustrations to be employed, both S and P will be the same English sentence and "A believes that P" and "A accepts P as true" will be used interchangeably.

This approach would undoubtedly require some modification if it were designed as an explication of belief-attributions useful for settling questions that have to do with the object of belief or interchangeability in indirect contexts. But neither of these matters is central here. An attempt to reach some resolution of them would complicate the discussion without contributing in any important way to the resolution of the problems under consideration.

For all intents and purposes, therefore, in this book an inference can be taken to be an attempt to justify accepting one sentence or a set of sentences in L on the grounds that one has accepted other sentences in L. Deductive methodology is concerned with the conditions under which such attempts are successful when the conclusions are deductively entailed by the premises. Inductive methodology, by contrast, is concerned with such conditions when the conclusions are not deductively entailed by the premises.

Let S be any sentence in L. An investigator might accept S. Alternatively he might accept not-S ($-S$). In that case, he rejects S. He might not, however, either accept or reject S. This may be based on his refusal to regard S as a relevant answer to the question posed. Such a possibility will be considered at greater length later on. In many cases, on the other hand, while S is deemed relevant, it is still neither accepted nor rejected. The investigator will then be said to be agnostic, to have suspended judgment regarding the truth of S.

Acceptance, rejection, and suspension of judgment are here taken to be psychological conditions, whose relations to overt behavior can be adequately understood only in terms of some articulated psychological theory. However, as was noted in the first chapter, an account of rational acceptance or rational belief need not be postponed until the time when such a theory is available, any more than reflection on rational preference must wait upon the formulation of an adequate psychological theory of preference.

3] *Deductive Cogency*

Let L be the applied lower predicate logic with identity used by an investigator. Let Γ be any (finite or infinite) set of sentences in L.

D.1: Γ is consistent in L if and only if no sentence of the form P&−P in L is deducible from a finite subset of Γ.

D.2: Γ is deductively closed in L if and only if whenever H and G are members of Γ, H&G and the deductive consequences of H&G in L are also members of Γ.

Given these two notions, the following principle of deductive methodology may be laid down:

Principle of Deductive Cogency: The set of sentences in L accepted as true by an investigator ought to include all logical truths in L and exclude all logical falsehoods. In addition, the set ought, everything else being equal, to be a deductively consistent and closed set in L.

An investigator, even one ideally situated to the extent that he could use the language L, would not ordinarily fulfill or be capable of fulfilling this requirement, if for no other reason than that he would not always be able to tell whether a given sentence was a logical truth or not. It would be reasonable, however, to take him to be committed to accepting such logical truths when he recognizes them as such. Nonetheless, although strictly speaking only such commitments to acceptance and rejection are involved, it will be simpler to formulate these requirements as conditions for rational acceptance and rejection.

The principle of deductive cogency is formulated in two parts: one governs the acceptance of logical truths and the rejection of logical falsehoods; the other extends the scope of the cogency requirement to cover the acceptance of sentences that belong in neither of these categories.

In the second part of the principle, a *ceteris paribus* clause was introduced. The scope of deductive cogency cannot be extended to cover all the sentences that are accepted by an individual in his lifetime or even in his adult lifetime. Shifts in available evidence may warrant accepting as true today a sentence that had previously been held to be false. Clearly, deductive cogency should be in some way restricted to sentences that are accepted relative to a given body of evidence. The *ceteris paribus* clause is intended to take cognizance of the necessity for restricting deductive cogency to sets of sentences that have been accepted under certain conditions.

To be sure, much remains to be done in the way of specifying these conditions. As has just been indicated, some sort of total evidence requirement is involved. However, it is doubtful that this requirement is the only one. In this chapter, the total evidence requirement will be supplemented by another restriction on the scope of deductive cogency; subsequently, some others will be introduced. No claim can be made that the list of restrictions introduced in this book is complete, nor are the proposals introduced subsequently to be taken as being thereby immune from revision. However, there does seem to be strong presystematic precedent for a deductive cogency requirement. The principle of deductive cogency as formulated with a *ceteris paribus* clause is intended to recognize this precedent while leaving open the resolution of potentially controversial details. Even when it is stated in this manner, the deductive cogency requirement does conflict with views put forward by some authors—most notably those of Henry Kyburg, who has advocated abandonment of the deductive closure requirement. Kyburg's position will be considered at somewhat greater length near the end of this chapter. In any event, the fact that rejection of the principle of deductive cogency can be taken seriously by responsible writers, even when it is formulated with a blank-check *ceteris paribus* clause, suggests that the principle is not entirely vacuous.

4] *Acceptance as Evidence*

If we attempt to justify accepting one sentence or set of sentences by an appeal to others already accepted, the set of sentences to which the appeal is made should be accepted not only as true but as evidence. Although acceptance as true is a necessary condition for acceptance as evidence, the converse does not hold. A medical research worker might believe in Enovid's freedom from deleterious side effects, yet he might with good reason continue to conduct tests of its safety. While he may believe that it is safe, he surely cannot take that hypothesis as evidence in the context of testing.

To attempt the formulation at this point of those conditions under which an investigator is warranted in accepting a sentence as evidence would complicate the already difficult problems to be faced in this discussion. Although some observations regarding rational acceptance as evidence will be made subsequently, for the most part the notion of acceptance of evidence will be taken as given and the discussion restricted to consideration of rational acceptance as true relative to evidence. However, some comments are in order with regard to the properties of the set of sentences E that are accepted as evidence at a given time and the statement of certain terminological decisions.

As the notion of evidence is to be understood here, the set of logical truths in L ought rationally to be accepted as evidence. Moreover, no self-contradiction in L ought rationally to be accepted as evidence. Evidence sentences may be observation reports, but they may also be theoretical. Which theoretical sentences and observation reports in L ought to be included in the set of evidence sentences will not be explored in any great detail here.

Since the main concern of this book is with nondeductive inference from evidence, it may be taken for granted that the deductive consequences of sentences accepted as evidence ought to be accepted as true and are, moreover, usable as evidence sentences for purposes of inductive inference. Given also that the set of sentences accepted as evidence ought to be consistent, that set may at a given time be required to be a consistent and deductively closed set. Perhaps the reference to a time might better be replaced by a specific set of conditions or, since such conditions cannot at present be itemized, by a *ceteris paribus* clause. For present purposes, however, the requirement can be relativized as to time.

5] *Strongest Sentences Accepted as Evidence*

The requirement that the set of sentences accepted as evidence be consistent and closed in L implies that the set will be infinite. However, for present purposes no restriction of great significance is involved in supposing that this set of sentences be axiomatizable, either by a finite list of sentences or by a finite number of axiom schemata.[2] This property of closed and consistent sets to be considered as total evidence suggests the following two definitions.

D.3: If the set of sentences Γ is deductively closed and consistent in L, a strongest sentence in Γ is a sentence in Γ which entails all elements of Γ in L.

If Γ is axiomatizable with the aid of a finite number of axioms, there is at least one strongest sentence in Γ—to wit, the conjunction of these axioms.

D.4: If Γ is deductively closed and consistent in L and is axiomatizable by means of axiom schemata (and axioms),

[2] If L contains ordinary arithmetic, the set of sentences that consists of a set of axioms for arithmetic, Gödel sentences for these, sentences undecidable when the Gödel sentences are added to the axioms, etc., as well as all deductive consequences of these, will be a closed and consistent set (if arithmetic is consistent). But it will not be axiomatizable. For present purposes, there is no need to regard Gödel sentences as evidence sentences or even as having been accepted as true.

any sentence that is a conjunction of finite substitution instances of schemata and axioms is a "virtually strongest" sentence.

In the subsequent discussion, the set of sentences accepted as evidence at any given time will be characterized either in terms of a strongest sentence accepted as evidence at that time, or by the set of virtually strongest sentences accepted as evidence at that time. In most contexts, the difference between sets of evidence sentences for which there is a strongest sentence and those for which there is none will play no role of any importance. For this reason, total evidence will be represented by expressions that may be taken either as strongest evidence sentences or as schemata from which virtually strongest sentences can be generated.

6] *Background Information and New Evidence*

The strongest sentence (set of virtually strongest sentences) accepted as evidence at a given time will be represented by a conjunction b&e. This device serves to accommodate situations in which opinions vary with changes in evidence. At the outset of inquiry, certain "background information" b is accepted as evidence; "new evidence" e is obtained subsequently. On the assumption that b and e are consistent, the "total evidence" will be b&e.

7] *Acceptance as True*

The total evidence b&e is one of the factors that delimit the scope of the principle of deductive cogency. This restriction on cogency has strong presystematic precedent and for present purposes should occasion no further comment. According to the proposals to be made, however, it is not the only factor that limits the scope of deductive cogency. An additional factor will be introduced shortly, and still others in later chapters. Nonetheless, for the present, it will prove sufficient to make cogency relative to total evidence.

Given that the set of sentences accepted as evidence must be closed and consistent and must, moreover, be accepted as true relative to the total evidence, the principle of deductive cogency requires, in effect, that two consistent and closed sets of sentences be considered:

(a) the set of sentences that are the deductive consequences of b&e;

(b) the set of sentences accepted as true relative to b&e.

Set (a) is a subset of set (b). In cases in which investigators do not feel that the total evidence warrants conclusions other than those entailed by the evidence, sets (a) and (b) are identical. Otherwise, set (a) is a proper subset of (b).

As in the case of set (a), set (b) can be characterized by a strongest sentence accepted as true, or by a set of virtually strongest sentences accepted as true. If set (a) has no strongest sentence, then set (b) will not have one either. However, even in such cases, it is sometimes possible to single out a specific sentence in order to characterize the set of sentences accepted as true relative to b&e; for in many cases (for example, in prediction, estimation, and universal generalization), set (b) can be generated by considering a sentence H, the set of evidence sentences and the deductive consequences of H and the evidence sentences. H will be neither an evidence sentence nor the strongest sentence accepted as true relative to the evidence. (H will be a deductive consequence of b&e&H.) It will be called a "strongest sentence accepted as true *via induction* from the evidence."

It is important to keep in mind the implication of deductive cogency which is to require that "conclusions" of inductive inferences involve commitments to accept as true *sets* of sentences and not single sentences. Disagreements between investigators are not necessarily of the sort in which incompatible sentences are accepted as true relative to given evidence; they may reflect the acceptance of different consistent and closed sets of sentences *whose union may also be consistent and closed*. Such differences can often be registered by indicating the sentences accepted as strongest via induction from the evidence.

Consider two political forecasters Smith and Jones, who are engaged in predicting the outcome of an election contest between X, Y, and Z. Smith predicts that X will win, whereas Jones predicts that X or Y will win. They do not accept incompatible sentences as true. However, if their predictions are taken as indicating which sentences they accept as strongest via induction from their evidence, the closed and consistent sets of sentences to whose acceptance as true they are committed relative to the evidence at their disposal are different. This may be put in a relatively commonplace way by saying that, whereas Smith believes X will win, Jones remains agnostic on that question.

There may be situations in which the set of sentences accepted as true relative to given evidence cannot be characterized by a strongest sentence accepted as true via induction, except with the aid of a set of virtually strongest sentences to be accepted as true via induction. This means that the expansion of the set of evidence sentences to the set of accepted sentences is the result of adding axiom schemata and forming the deductive closure. Such a situation could conceivably arise in cases where new theories are accepted on the basis of given evidence.

8] *Relevant Answers and Ultimate Partitions*

The evidence available to the forecaster Smith at the time he is considering the future outcome of the election could conceivably allow him to reach a conclusion not only with regard to the winner but also about the order in which the candidates will finish. It might also justify conclusions concerning earthquakes in Yugoslavia on election eve or the feelings of Hobbes' mother upon hearing of the advent of the Spanish Armada.

Indeed, a situation can be envisaged in which Smith might not be warranted in reaching any conclusion about the election that is not entailed by his evidence and yet be justified in reaching conclusions on various other matters. Such a condition would hardly be satisfactory to Smith, interested as he is in the outcome of the election. In point of fact, therefore, he will make no reference to these other matters, but simply indicate that the available evidence requires of him suspension of judgment.

Considerations such as these suggest that justifications of conclusions reached from given evidence ought to be made relative not only to that evidence but to a characterization of what is to count as a "relevant answer" to the problem raised. The supposition that, when an investigator is seeking a conclusion via induction, he will take into consideration all those sentences in L whose truth value is not decided via deduction from his evidence, is simply and rather obviously false—even in the case of idealized investigators of the sort that are being considered here. During the course of inquiry, what counts as a relevant answer is subject to change; but in defending a given conclusion as warranted by the evidence, it seems plausible to suppose that such defense should be made relative to a set of sentences that are taken to be relevant answers—i.e., eligible for acceptance as strongest or virtually strongest via induction from the evidence. Adoption of this approach necessitates the introduction of some way of representing the set of relevant answers to a given problem.

The proposals regarding inductive inference to be made in this book are designed to handle problems of prediction, estimation, and generalization from observed samples of confirming instances. Whether these proposals can be modified, without their being thereby mutilated beyond recognition, in order to render them applicable to choosing among theories, will remain an open question.

Given this restriction on the scope of the discussion, conclusions of inductive inference can be identified by specifying the strongest sentences accepted as true via induction from the total evidence. Virtually strongest sentences can be ignored. In effect, therefore, the set of relevant answers to a given question is determined by the set of sentences in L that are eligible for acceptance as strongest via induction from the given evidence.

Understood in this way, a relevant answer is, among other things, a sentence in L whose truth value is not decidable via deduction from the total evidence. As a rule, the deductive consequences of such a sentence taken by itself will be poorer than the deductive consequences of that sentence taken together with the total evidence.

One further restriction will be imposed upon sets of relevant answers. Even though it does restrict the scope of applicability of the proposals to be made, it does not render them useless, and methods for relaxing this restriction can and will be introduced in some special cases when the need arises.

It will be assumed that the members of the set of sentences eligible for acceptance as strongest via induction are logically equivalent to those sentences that are members of a *finite* set of sentences M in L. This restriction amounts, in a certain sense, to keeping the set of relevant answers finite, and thereby ruling out cases of point estimation in which a given magnitude can take infinitely many values, as well as problems of universal generalization, in which the population is either indefinitely or infinitely large. The latter case will receive separate discussion in later chapters.

Given this restriction, the set of relevant answers can be represented as follows:

Let U_e be a finite set of n sentences in L such that each element of U_e is consistent with the set of evidence sentences (sentences entailed by b&e), and such that b&e entails that at least and at most one element of U_e is true. (If the total evidence is b, a set of the sort described will be called U.) The elements of U_e are to be arranged in some definite alphabetical order. Relative to such an ordering, the set M_e can be defined as follows:

D.5: (a) Let S_e be the sentence in L that is the disjunction of all elements of U_e, where each disjunct appears once and only once and in alphabetical order.

S_e is in M_e

(b) Let C_e be the sentence in L that is the conjunction of all elements of U_e, where each conjunct appears once and only once in alphabetical order.

C_e is in M_e

(c) Let G be a sentence in L that is a disjunction of m elements of U_e ($1 \leqq m < n$), where each disjunct appears once and only once and in alphabetical order. There are $2^n - 2$ such sentences.

G is in M_e

(d) Only the 2^n sentences covered by (a), (b), and (c) are elements of the set M_e generated by the set U_e relative to total evidence b&e.

Note that the subscripts on U, M, S, and C refer to the new evidence and can be dropped when the total evidence consists of background information b. (See Chapter IV, Section 2 for further comments.)

An investigator can be understood to have fixed the set of relevant answers by selecting a partition U_e and restricting the relevant answers (i.e., sentences eligible for acceptance as strongest via induction) to those sentences that are logically equivalent to elements of the set M_e generated by U_e.

D.6: An ultimate partition U_e relative to total evidence b&e is a set of sentences in L exclusive and exhaustive relative to b&e, such that no element of U_e is entailed by b&e and such that each relevant answer considered by the investigator using U_e is logically equivalent to an element of the set M_e generated by U_e.

Clearly, D.6 cannot be used to define the notion of a relevant answer, since that notion is used to define an ultimate partition. However, ultimate partitions can be used to characterize commitments to specific lists of relevant answers under the conditions which have been mentioned.

Note that the sentences S_e and C_e are deductively decidable relative to b&e. The former is entailed by b&e, as is the contradictory of the latter. Strictly speaking, neither of these sentences is eligible for acceptance as strongest via induction from the evidence. It is convenient, however, to include them in the set M_e. Acceptance of S_e as strongest via induction from the evidence is to be understood, then, as tantamount to suspension of judgment—i.e., as refusal to accept any sentence as true relative to b&e save evidence sentences.

To accept C_e as strongest via induction is to contradict oneself; for deductive closure requires that all the deductive consequences of C_e and b&e be accepted as true. Since C_e is inconsistent with b&e, the result is contradiction. Although any adequate account of inference should preclude accepting C_e as strongest via induction, it is useful to have some method for representing self-contradiction, in order to discuss the consistency of proposed criteria for inductive inference.

The remaining members of M_e represent sentences which, if they are accepted as strongest via induction from b&e, furnish information when conjoined with b&e that is additional to the information afforded by sentences accepted as evidence. They do so, moreover, while preserving consistency.

The elements of the ultimate partition U_e are also elements of M_e. They represent the strongest sentences consistent with b&e

that are eligible for acceptance as strongest via induction from b&e. They are the strongest consistent relevant answers.

The way in which this apparatus operates can be illustrated by the problem that confronts the forecaster Smith. He is interested in ascertaining which of the three candidates, X, Y, or Z, will win the election. He is not attempting to find out who will place second or third, nor is he interested in the total votes for each candidate. Under these circumstances, his ultimate partition—i.e., the strongest relevant answers—can be represented by the three sentences "X will win," "Y will win," "Z will win." The set M generated by this ultimate partition consists of the eight sentences listed below:

- (i)　Either X or Y or Z will win　　(S)
- (ii)　Either X or Y will win
- (iii)　Either X or Z will win
- (iv)　Either Y or Z will win
- (v)　X will win
- (vi)　Y will win
- (vii)　Z will win
- (viii)　X and Y and Z will win　　(C)

Should Smith admit that, relative to his evidence, he can make no prediction as to who will win, this can be represented by saying that he accepts (i)—i.e., S—as strongest via induction and S&e as strongest via induction and deduction.

If he accepts (v) as strongest via induction, he also accepts (i), (ii), and (iii) as true relative to his evidence, as well as any sentences deductively entailed by (i) and his evidence e.

If, on the other hand, he accepts (ii) as strongest via induction, he remains agnostic about the truth of (v).

9] *Ultimate Partitions and Deductive Cogency*

Ultimate partitions have been introduced to take cognizance of the obvious fact that investigators do not entertain as relevant answers to their questions all those sentences whose truth values are undecided by the evidence available to them. Whether for any given context there is a system of criteria for determining the ultimate partition that ought to be used is a difficult question; it cannot be answered here. To attempt to answer this question would be like trying to decide whether there is some logic of questions that determines what is the right question to ask on any given occasion. Would Smith be functioning properly as a rational investigator, for example, if he chose as ultimate the sentences "X will win" and "Y or Z will win"? One might be tempted to suggest that he should have used as ultimate the threefold partition mentioned earlier, on the grounds that some elements of that partition are stronger than some elements of the twofold partition, whereas the converse does not hold. But this kind of argument would obligate Smith to regard as ultimate those partitions whose elements specify not only who will win but the total vote for each candidate, the times when losers conceded defeat, the violence of any earthquakes that occur in Yugoslavia on election eve, etc.

In the face of difficulties such as this, no attempt will be made to propose criteria for selecting ultimate partitions. Instead, the fact that investigators restrict the set of answers they regard as relevant to the questions they raise will be taken as given, and the implications of a commitment to an ultimate partition will be explored.

The introduction of ultimate partitions permits reopening the question of deductive cogency. Thus far, the requirements of deductive consistency and closure have been restricted to sentences that are accepted relative to a given body of sentences accepted as evidence. It should be clear, however, that when ultimate partitions are introduced—and something very much like ultimate partitions seem necessary, in order to accommodate restriction of relevant answers to those sentences that are to be eligible for acceptance as strongest—deductive closure must be made relative to ultimate partitions as well as to total evidence.

Suppose that political forecaster Jones uses as ultimate the twofold partition that consists of the sentences "X or Y will win" and "Z will win." Assume that Martin adopts as ultimate the partition that consists of "X will win" and "Y or Z will win." Both Jones and Martin agree that the available evidence warrants assigning a very high probability to "Y will win." (For the sake of the argument, it is assumed that both Jones and Martin can assign probabilities to any sentence in L.) Martin will then predict that Y or Z will win, whereas Jones will predict that X or Y will win.

Can Jones and Martin pool their conclusions to reach the prediction that Y will win? Not without betraying their commitments about what is to count as a relevant answer. The conjunction of "X or Y will win" and "Y or Z will win" (whose equivalence to "Y will win" can be deduced from the available evidence) is not logically equivalent to any element in the set M_e generated by Jones' ultimate partition or to any element in the corresponding set for Martin. Neither Jones nor Martin counts that sentence as a relevant answer to his question. To the extent that they do not alter their ultimate partitions, they cannot coherently accept the conjunction as true.

Thus, conclusions that are reached relative to different ultimate partitions, like conclusions reached relative to different bodies of evidence, cannot be pooled, and the resulting set of sentences then expected to be consistent and deductively closed. The scope of deductive cogency is limited not only by the total relevant evidence, but by the investigator's commitment concerning what is to count as a relevant answer to his question.

10] *The Lottery Paradox*

Henry Kyburg is notable among contemporary writers on inductive inference for his attempt to construct an account of rational belief according to which the principle of deductive cogency is no longer operative. In particular, Kyburg has urged abandonment of the rule of conjunction, which requires that, if sentences H and G are accepted as true, H&G must be accepted as true.

Care should be taken to distinguish Kyburg's position on this question from the view proposed here. According to the requirement of deductive closure incorporated in the principle of deductive cogency, an investigator is not required to accept H&G simply because he has accepted H and G, unless the conditions under which these three sentences are each accepted are the same in all relevant respects, including reference to total evidence and an ultimate partition. Kyburg, however, appears to hold that there is no set of conditions such that all sentences accepted relative to those conditions can be expected to constitute a deductively closed and consistent set. To handle deductive closure, Kyburg suggests that the totality of sentences accepted relative to given evidence (he does not recognize ultimate partitions) belong in different "rational corpora," such that all sentences that belong in a higher-level rational corpus are included in the set of sentences accepted in a lower-level rational corpus, but not conversely. The rule of conjunction and hence the deductive closure requirement are not in general applicable in a given rational corpus. They are, however, partially applicable in going from corpora on higher levels to those on lower levels.[3] But even if the union of all rational corpora relative to given evidence is considered, the result is not as a general rule a deductively closed set. Thus, Kyburg is frankly and openly committed to rejecting the deductive closure requirement, even when it is qualified by some *ceteris paribus* clause.[4] His reason will now be considered.

Kyburg thinks that the untenability of the rule of conjunction can be supported by an appeal to intuitions with regard to certain cases, of which lotteries are typical:

In a lottery of 1,000,000 tickets there is one winner. It is as rational to accept the hypothesis that ticket i will not win as it is to accept any statistical hypothesis that I can think of. But to accept the hypothesis that ticket i will not win, for every i, is (on most ordinary views) to accept the hypothesis that *no* ticket will win, which contradicts our knowledge that one ticket will win.[5]

Kyburg is clearly convinced that, in the lottery problem, accepting each of the million sentences of the form "ticket i will not win" has as much warrant as accepting any sentence can have that is not deductively entailed by the available evidence. (Note,

[3] See H. Kyburg, *Probability and the Logic of Rational Belief* (Middletown: Wesleyan University Press, 1961), especially pp. 196–197. For critical discussion, see F. Schick's excellent review, "Consistency and Rationality," *Journal of Philosophy*, 60 (1963), 5–19.

[4] This remains true in spite of Kyburg's admission of the seriousness of some of Schick's criticisms of his position. He takes the difficulties with the rule of conjunction pointed out by Schick to be difficulties in his notion of randomness rather than in any way suggesting that he might be wrong in abandoning the rule of conjunction. See H. Kyburg, "A Further Note on Rationality and Consistency," *Journal of Philosophy*, 60 (1963), 465, where in response to Schick's difficulties, Kyburg writes: "Clearly, the system must be changed—i.e., the definition of randomness must be changed; but whether this can be done in a plausible way remains open to question."

[5] *Ibid.*, p. 463.

by the way, that Kyburg assumes the lottery to be fair in order to reach this conclusion.) To form the conjunction of these million sentences and then to accept it as true is, he says, to accept as true the sentence "none of the tickets in the lottery will win," which is clearly inconsistent with the available evidence. Kyburg concludes that the rules of conjunction and deductive closure have to be abandoned.

Kyburg's example is unfortunate for his own purposes. Upon consulting my own intuitions on the matter (which, I suspect, agree with those of many others), it seems clear that one ought to suspend judgment regarding the outcome of a fair lottery. Indeed, one should do so *precisely because the lottery is fair*. In a less dogmatic vein, I would say that it seems at least as plausible to take this view as it does to take Kyburg's. If this is so, appealing to fair lotteries to support rejection of closure and with it cogency is unjustified. The strong presystematic backing for cogency suggests that preserving cogency and adopting my intuition is to be preferred.

But Kyburg can appeal to other examples. Consider an urn with 999,999 black balls and 1 white one. If a person were asked to predict the outcome of a single draw, he should, so it would seem, predict that a black ball will be drawn. Predictions of blacks would be justified on each of 1 billion draws (where the ball drawn is replaced and the contents of the urn thoroughly mixed). Cogency requires concluding that all billion draws show black. But in 1 billion draws it seems reasonable to expect that at least 1 draw will show white.

In this case, utilization of the rule of conjunction to support the conclusion that all billion draws will show black seems to have been the malefactor. But the example does not necessarily sustain abandoning the rule of conjunction; for it is possible to insist that the rule is sound, but that the conditions for its application are not present.

Thus, when a person is interested in predicting whether a black ball will be drawn on the nth trial, his ultimate partition consists of the hypotheses "a black will show on the nth trial" and "a white will show on the nth trial." This rules out conjoining the conclusion obtained regarding the nth trial with any regarding the mth.

On the other hand, the prediction that at least 1 trial (out of

1 billion trials) will show a white ball can be taken as a prediction relative to a problem in which the concern is to predict the relative frequency with which blacks are drawn in 1 billion draws.

Thus, even the best examples that are forthcoming in support of scrapping deductive cogency are far from decisive. To be sure, if deductive cogency is supposed to apply to all the beliefs held by a person over his entire career, without any restrictions, cogency clearly deserves to be abandoned. But it is highly doubtful whether anyone ever seriously took the principle to be understood in that sense. In any event, as it is understood here, the principle of deductive cogency has its scope of application restricted to beliefs that are held relative to a fixed body of evidence and a given set of relevant answers. Such a construction allows for the tenability of the rule of deductive cogency in the face of both the lottery and the urn problems just cited.

11] *Cogency and High Probability*

Appeals to intuitions regarding urns and lotteries may not warrant rejecting the cogency rule. But what about the requirement that is utilized more or less explicitly by Kyburg, to the effect that high probabilities are necessary and sufficient for acceptance? This requirement is inconsistent with the rule of deductive cogency, even when it is qualified in the manner suggested here. Let k be any probability greater than .5 and less than 1. Suppose that a necessary and sufficient condition for accepting H is that H have a probability greater than or equal to k. Now if H and G separately have probabilities greater than k, the multiplication theorem indicates that for many such H and G the probability of H&G will be less than k (indeed, less than .5). Accepting H and accepting G will each be justified, but accepting H&G will not.

Thus, either cogency or the requirement of high probability as necessary and sufficient for acceptance must be abandoned. Which shall it be?

I doubt that any argument used to defend the high-probability requirement will provide clear support for that view that is acceptable to any cognitivist who is serious about his commitment to the position. But no attempt will be made to review possible arguments of that sort here. Instead a presystematic counter-instance will be cited—one that comes from a surprising quarter.

The very lottery problem used by Kyburg to argue that cogency is untenable shows (to those who share my firm intuitions) that high probability cannot be sufficient for acceptance. If agnosticism is the appropriate response to a request for an opinion regarding the outcome of a million-ticket fair lottery, the high probability accorded the hypothesis "ticket 1 will not win" is insufficient to warrant its acceptance.

Citing this precedent cannot be taken as an ironclad refutation of Kyburg's (and others') assumption that high probabilities are necessary and sufficient for acceptance. But its introduction ought to pave the way for consideration of a view that rejects the high probability requirement in favor of the deductive cogency requirement, which (to put it mildly) has considerable intuitive plausibility in its own right.

Needless to say, final judgment on issues of this sort, where conflicting intuitions are involved, ought to await the construction of theories designed to accommodate them. It is in this tentative spirit that the insufficiency of high probabilities for acceptance will be taken as established, and conformity to the principle of deductive cogency, restricted in scope to sentences accepted relative to total evidence b&e and to ultimate partitions U_e, will be taken as a condition of adequacy for an account of rational inductive inference.

III

✳✳✳✳✳✳✳✳✳✳✳✳✳✳✳✳✳✳✳✳✳✳✳✳

Bayes' Rule

1] *Cognitive Options*

An investigator who is interested in reaching conclusions from
evidence b&e will, according to the account given in the last
chapter, restrict the set of relevant answers available to him. On
many occasions, the restrictions instituted can be represented as
a choice of a finite ultimate partition U_e and a set of sentences
M_e generated by U_e. The investigator is constrained, thereby, to
accept at least and at most one element of M_e as strongest sentence accepted as true via induction from b&e[1]; his choice of an
element of M_e is a commitment on his part to accept as true all
deductive consequences (in L) of the sentence chosen and the
sentences accepted as evidence.

In this sense, the investigator faces a decision problem. He
must decide which element of M_e to accept as strongest via induction. The assertion that the investigator actually "decides"
may be subject to doubt, because of the conceptual difficulties

---

[1] Observe that he cannot refuse to pick an element of M_e once he has
chosen U_e—not even if he wishes to be agnostic; for agnosticism is tantamount to accepting S_e as strongest via induction.

that are involved in the notion of a decision. However, men are held responsible for their beliefs to the extent that they can be called upon to justify them and to the extent that the rationality of those beliefs can be assessed. Such justification involves reference to alternative opinions. In these respects, deciding what to believe is analogous to deciding how to act.

This point suggests the possibility of exploiting analogies between practical and cognitive decision-making for the purpose of constructing criteria of rationality that will be applicable both to inductive inference and to inductive behavior. An approach of this sort is compatible with the critical cognitivist rejection of naive cognitivist and behavioralist assimilations of belief to action; yet it preserves one of the central insights of the pragmatist tradition—that scientific inquiry is controlled by considerations analogous to those that are relevant in practical decision-making.

2] *Bayes' Rule*

Consider a decision-maker so ideally situated that he has, as part of his evidence, the following items of information:

(i) A finite list of options $A_1, A_2, ..., A_m$, from which he can choose one and only one.[2]

(ii) A finite list of hypotheses ("states of nature") $H_1, H_2, ..., H_n$, such that the total evidence entails that at least and at most one of these H_j's is true and such that each of the H_j's is consistent with the total evidence b&e.

(iii) A set of $m \times n$ (not necessarily distinct) descriptions of possible outcomes of his actions that meet the following conditions:

(a) Given that a state of nature H_j is true, the decision-maker knows (as part of his evidence) that if he adopts A_i, outcome o_{ij} will ensue.

(b) The decision-maker is able to describe the o_{ij}'s in all respects relevant to his goals, ethical commitments, etc.

[2] Infinite cases will not be considered unless explicitly indicated.

(iv) A system of probability assignments $p(H_j,e)$ to each of the states of nature relative to the total evidence b&e. (Since the background evidence b is held constant, it is dropped in the notation.) It is assumed that the probability that H_j is true, given b&e, and that A_i is done is equal to $p(H_j,e)$. This assumption restricts somewhat the generality of the discussion, but it does not materially affect the specific applications of the approach that will be made in subsequent developments.

In addition, the ideally situated decision-maker is able to weigh his practical objectives, moral commitments, aesthetic attitudes, etc., and combine them into a numerical measure of the value (to him) of each of the outcomes. This measure of cardinal utility $u(o_{ij}) = u_{ij}$ is unique up to the choice of a 0 point and unit (i.e., utility is interval-measurable).

On the basis of the utility assignments and items (i)–(iv), the decision-maker is able to compute the "expected utility" of each of the options A_i relative to the total evidence b&e.

$$E(A_i,e) = \sum_{i=1}^{n} p(H_j,e)u(o_{ij})$$

The well-known Bayes' rule recommends that such a decision-maker proceed as follows:

Bayes' Rule: An ideally situated decision-maker in the sense just described ought rationally to pick that option (or one of those options) bearing maximum expected utility.

Bayes' rule will be used as a criterion for rational decision-making in the subsequent discussion.

3] *Ideally Situated Agents*

The all too brief sketch of Bayes' rule just given cannot mask the extreme demands imposed upon the information available to the decision-maker or to his critics with regard to his circumstances at the time of decision. Only rarely are they realized or realizable in real life. Even if qualms about the information required in (i)–(iii) are ignored on the grounds that they are somewhat like the demands for precision required in order to evaluate the validity of a deductive argument, the need to specify a numerical probability distribution over the states of nature and a cardinal utility function for the outcomes would appear to rule out the serious application of Bayes' rule in all real-life situations, except for certain games of chance. And a criterion for rational decision-making that is inapplicable is hardly a promising basis for the construction of an account of inductive inference.

Ignoring the arguments of those who maintain that the scope of Bayesian methods is not so limited as appearances may suggest,[3] it should be noted that, in a systematic account of conditions of rational behavior or rational belief, not all of the principles invoked need be directly applicable in real-life situations. A principle whose scope of applicability is limited to the point of vanishing might still prove to be of central importance for deriving and otherwise systematizing criteria that are more directly applicable. Thus, Bayes' rule together with the probability calculus recommends that one should not take the same risk on a coin's landing heads on two tosses that one would take on its landing heads on a single toss; there are some situations in which an agent who relies only on comparative judgments of probability and utility can utilize this qualitative prescription. To take another simple illustration, if all the possible consequences of one option are better than any of the possible consequences of another, that first option is to be preferred. Bayes' rule (among others) entails this as a consequence. Bayes' rule is not indispensable for the application of the principles cited in these two examples. Its use does, however, yield a systematization of these and other criteria that might prove more applicable in real life.

In addition, the exploration of a Bayesian model for rational decision-making might (as some advocates of Bayesian statistics maintain that it has done) yield results that allow for the extension of its scope of application beyond the few games of chance that have provided the best classical examples of its use.

In the subsequent discussion, Bayes' rule will be incorporated into a system of criteria for inductive inference that is applicable to investigators who, like the decision-makers of this chapter, are

[3] See L. J. Savage, *et. al.*, *The Foundations of Statistical Inference* (New York: Wiley, 1962), pp. 9–35.

"ideally situated." An attempt will be made to show that this strategy does shed some systematic light on various features of inductive inference and its relation to rational decision-making. Needless to say, the proof of the pudding is in the eating. However, judgment regarding the propriety of taking Bayes' rule as a criterion for rational decision-making ought at least to await the baking of the pudding.

4] *The Propriety of Bayes' Rule*

If we concede that the treatment of ideal cases can be useful in attempts to systematize criteria for inductive inference and behavior, why, it may nevertheless be asked, should Bayes' rule be adopted as a condition of rationality for the ideally situated investigator who is capable of using it?

Part of the answer is that one should wait for the pudding. If with the aid of Bayes' rule results can be obtained that are applicable in real life and at the same time conform in good measure with presystematic intuitions, some justification for the use of Bayes' rule as a condition of rationality is thereby established.

Other considerations suggest the propriety of beginning with Bayes' rule rather than with some alternative.

First, in some gambling situations, the conditions for applying Bayes' rule are realized to a good approximation. Coins, dice, and lotteries can often be judged fair; the outcomes of gambles based on these random devices can be described and evaluated (using monetary payoffs as a rough yardstick of value). Many writers who question the applicability of Bayes' rule in most real-life situations would nevertheless concede the propriety of adopting it in those cases in which its use is feasible.[4]

Second, alternatives to the Bayesian approach are often viewed as attempts to provide criteria for rational decision-making at times when the ideal circumstances required for using Bayes' rule are not realized. It has been shown that several important alternatives fail to meet certain intuitively plausible requirements for rational decision-making. In particular, when it is expressly indicated that the decision-maker cannot assign probabilities to

[4] A. Wald, *Statistical Decision Functions* (New York: Wiley, 1960), p. 16.

states of nature, it has been shown that he must violate at least one such intuitively plausible requirement.[5]

Finally, one of the aims of this book will be to examine critically certain accounts of induction that require idealizations no less stringent than those introduced here. In particular, many attempts have been made to make some notion of probability central to accounts of inductive inference and inductive behavior. The idealization that requires that agents be able to assign probabilities to sentences relative to their total evidence will allow for systematic comment on the relations between rational acceptance and belief, on the one hand, and rational assignments of degrees of probability (confirmation and the like), on the other.

The justification for adopting a Bayesian approach has been based upon expectations that this strategy will prove fruitful in providing a systematic account of the relations between inductive inference and inductive behavior. However, this decision has been made at some cost.

Recall that one of the reasons cited in the first chapter for embarking on this discussion was the need for a rational alternative to the behavioralist justification frequently provided for those statistical procedures that are actually employed in scientific research. The fondest wishes of the most ardent Bayesians notwithstanding, Bayesian procedures are rarely employed in real-life inquiry. If one concentrates on a theory based on Bayes' rule, methods that are actually or allegedly used will not receive the attention they deserve.

In order to keep the discussion within reasonable limits, no effort will be made to consider here minimax, significance tests, confidence intervals, etc. Bayes' rule has been chosen for its systematic virtues rather than for its prevalence in real-life statistical inference. These other methods do deserve attention but hopefully they can be examined elsewhere.[6] Nevertheless, if it can be shown that, at least in the case of ideally situated investigators, plausible models for cognitive decision problems can be constructed, some grounds can be provided for supposing that both

[5] A useful survey of these matters is found in R. D. Luce and H. Raiffa, *Games and Decisions* (New York: Wiley, 1957), Ch. 13.

[6] I have already considered some aspects of significance testing in "On the Seriousness of Mistakes," *Philosophy of Science*, 29 (1962), 558–563.

the virtues and the defects of Bayes' rule have little to do with the cognitive or practical character of the decision problem under consideration. This, in itself, would afford grounds for assuming that the desirable and undesirable features of alternatives to Bayes' rule do not depend upon their application to cognitive decision problems any more than they depend upon features peculiar to practical decision problems in military logistics or quality control. In short, successful reconstruction of cognitive decision problems after the fashion of Bayesian decision theory does provide grounds for supposing that critical cognitivist rationales can be furnished for using other decision rules, including those actually used in research, and that these rationales will be no better and no worse than the rationales that support their application to practical problems.

These considerations do not constitute an ironclad case for the adoption of Bayes' rule as a condition for rational inductive behavior and inductive inference, but they should at least warrant its being tentatively considered.

5] *Utility*

Bayes' rule requires for its application that the decision-maker assign numerical weights to the outcomes such as will reflect the values he attaches to them. These "utilities" are supposed to reflect moral, prudential, aesthetic, etc. evaluations on the part of the agent, and need not consist merely of assessments of anticipated pleasures and pains. The classical problem about adjudication of the claims of prudence and morals is bypassed as a question to be settled prior to the assignment of utilities. Bayes' rule (as well as alternative criteria proposed for rational decision-making) is designed to make recommendations about what ought to be done, given (among other things) a system of utility assignments. It provides no instruction as to what factors ought to determine utility assignments in the first place.

Much recent discussion of utility has centered around the problem of measuring the utilities in a manner that reflects the personal commitments of agents. The by now classical approach of Von Neumann and Morgenstern in effect proceeds on the assumption that were an agent ideally situated to the extent that he could employ Bayes' rule he should do so. This assumption is articulated as a system of conditions for rational preference for an agent who is able to discriminate preferences among a given set of prizes and arbitrary gambles with these prizes as payoffs.[7] They are able to show that an agent who meets these conditions can assign numerical utilities to the prizes that are unique up to the choice of a 0 point and unit.

Serious problems confront the use of Von Neumann-Morgenstern utility theory or variants thereof to determine empirically the utility assignments made by agents in real life. In some contexts, however, these problems can be bypassed. If the question is not what value commitments an agent does have in a given situation but what value commitments he should have, standardized utility assignments might sometimes be possible. Thus, if an agent should, as Kant insists, always keep his promises, the standardized utility assigned to the outcomes of promise-keeping would always be higher than that assigned to the outcomes of promise-breaking.

Utility functions that reflect imposed moral considerations are unlikely to prove promising for purposes of treating moral decision problems. However, in the subsequent discussion, an attempt will be made to show how standardized utility assignments can represent commitments imposed upon a scientific investigator who declares himself engaged in the disinterested pursuit of the truth. To the extent that this effort is successful, the problem of attempting to measure the personal values of the agent or investigator can, for the purposes of this discussion, be neglected.

6] *Probability*

As was indicated earlier, no attempt will be made here to provide a reconstruction of the notion of belief. Instead, some account of rational belief—or rather rational acceptance—is to be offered. In a similar vein, the notion of a probability assignment to a sentence—which is, like the notion of belief, a psychological concept—will not be analyzed. Instead, some conditions are to be imposed for rational probability assignments. Thus far, the following conditions have been introduced:

(a) Given a set of sentences $H_1, H_2, ..., H_n$ which are compatible with the total evidence b&e such that b&e entails the truth of one and only one of these sentences, numerical probability assignments to these sentences and to all Boolean combinations of these ought rationally to constitute a regular probability measure in the following sense:

   (1) $p(H_i, e)$ is positive for each of the H_i's.

   (2) $\sum_{i=1}^{n} p(H_i, e) = 1$

   (3) If G is incompatible with b&e, $p(G, e) = 0$.

   (4) Let F be equivalent to a disjunction of m distinct H_i's or to the conjunction of such a disjunction with b&e. $p(F, e) =$ the sum of the probabilities assigned to the m H_i's.

(b) Let A be an option open to a decision-maker and let $o_1, o_2, ..., o_n$ be the outcomes of A for the various states of nature $H_1, H_2, ..., H_n$. If the decision-maker assigns utilities $u_1, u_2, ..., u_n$ to the outcomes and the expected value $E(A, e)$ to A, he is rationally committed to assigning probabilities to the H_i's in a manner conforming to the following condition:

$$E(A, e) = \sum_{i=1}^{n} p(H_i, e) u_i$$

The first condition imposes familiar formal properties on probability assignments on sentences. Condition (b) is another statement of Bayes' rule. It asserts, in effect, that the probability assignments made by an ideally situated, rational decision-maker reflect the risks he is prepared to take in acting as if sentences to which probabilities are assigned are true. Thus, if an agent is offered a bet on the truth of H, according to which he receives $1.00 if H is true and $0.00 if H is false, and is prepared to pay no more than 60¢ for the privilege of taking this bet, then (if money can be taken, in the present example, as a measure of utility) he is rationally committed to assigning a probability of .6 to H. To assign a greater probability would mean that the expected value is greater than 60¢ and he should be prepared to pay more for the gamble. To assign a probability less than .6 would mean that the expected value should be less than 60¢ and he is overpaying.

Conditions (a) and (b) provide an informal sketch of the constraints on rational probability assignments that are imposed by advocates of subjective or "personal" probability. They allow considerable room for differences among rational agents with regard to the subjective probabilities they assign to sentences relative to given evidence. Nonetheless, they do impose restrictions on how probability assignments are to be made to different sentences that bear definite logical relations to one another, and how probability assignments are related to rational choice.

It may prove possible, however, to supply further conditions of rationality that narrow the scope of arbitrariness in probability assignments. For the present, no further restrictions will be imposed. Subsequent to the development of the theory of inductive inference to be proposed here, however, the properties of this theory will be explored under circumstances in which additional constraints on probability assignments are introduced.

7] *Probability, Belief, and Certainty*

I believe and (in July, 1964) in that sense am certain that Lyndon Johnson will win the presidential election in 1964. However, I am not prepared to risk my life on this. My reluctance to do so indicates, according to Bayesian theory, that I accord a probability less than 1 to the prospect of his winning. It also indicates that I do not think that the evidence available to me entails that he will win; when regular probability measures are employed, this is equivalent to saying that the probability I assign is less than 1.

It might be objected that I have no warrant for being certain that Johnson will win unless I can deduce my prediction from my evidence. This reproach is predicated upon a confusion between two senses of certainty.

(i) "A is certain that P" means that A believes that P.
(ii) "A is certain that P" means that A takes −P to be inconsistent with his evidence.

Confusion of these two notions of certainty seems to be one
source of the view that a person can justifiably believe that P if
and only if he assigns to P a probability of 1, and is prepared to
act as if P were true, no matter what the cost of error. In order
to render this conclusion more palatable to people of empiricist
persuasion, resort might be made to the claim that most belief-
attributions imply not that A believes that P but only that A
believes that P to a degree, or that A is certain that P to a degree.
Such degrees of belief are then construed as subjective probabilities.

As it stands, the force of this apology is entirely verbal. Taken
literally, the behavioralist view either holds that there is no
warrant for accepting a sentence as true or else concedes such a
warrant only when the degree of acceptance (the degree of
belief, the degree of subjective probability) warranted is the
maximum. But this is precisely the sort of position that is rejected by one contemporary version of empiricism to which lip
service is frequently paid.

To this observation, behavioralists could offer the following
reply: We grant that in presystematic discussions a notion of
belief or acceptance is used that is qualitative. However, presystematically, there is much precedent for the idea that belief
admits of degrees. The situation is analogous to the one that obtains with respect to a predicate like "tall." The information conveyed by asserting that a man is tall can be conveyed with much
greater precision by introducing a measure of degrees of tallness.
Similarly, when someone is alleged to be warranted in believing
that P, all that is meant is that he is justified in assigning a high
degree of belief to P (without that degree of belief necessarily
equaling 1). A more precise statement would indicate the degree
of belief actually assigned to P.

If the deductive cogency requirement discussed in the previous
chapter is taken as legislative for rational acceptance as true (or
for rational belief), then this account is untenable. The multiplication theorem for probabilities precludes holding that a high
degree of probability is a necessary and sufficient condition for

acceptance. And the lottery problem gives substantial intuitive support to the view that a high probability cannot be sufficient. Once it is granted that a person may be justified in accepting sentences as true that are not entailed by his evidence, the proposed analysis of a belief-attribution as merely an allegation that the person is assigning a high probability to a sentence loses whatever plausibility it might appear to have.

Yet there is a grain of truth in the behavioralist position—actually two grains. First, there is a presystematic notion of degrees of belief, which is of some importance to inductive inference. However, it is not related to the notion of belief in the way that height is related to tallness. Nor would measures of degrees of belief be regular probability measures. These points will be expanded upon later. Second, if Bayes' rule is adopted as the condition for rational decision-making (in ideal situations), then subjective probabilities are surrogates for beliefs in the role they play in the naive cognitivist model for decision-making. In that sense and in that sense alone it is appropriate to call subjective probabilities "degrees of belief." In order to avoid confusion with the notion of degree of belief mentioned above, subjective probabilities will be called "subjective probabilities" and not "degrees of belief." Later on, new terminology will be introduced to cover the other notion of degrees of belief.

8] *Cognitive Decision Problems*

The reason for introducing this admittedly sketchy outline of Bayes' rule is to provide a basis for constructing an analogy between inductive inference and inductive behavior. An investigator who is interested in making predictions or estimates, or in deriving generalizations from confirming instances and other evidence, will be construed as deciding what conclusions to reach via induction from given evidence. His decision will be taken to be a "cognitive option" analogous to "practical options," although no cognitive option will be understood to be a decision to act relative to a practical objective. A system of "states of nature" will be constructed and outcomes of the cognitive options for the various states of nature will be specified. An attempt will be made to construct an "epistemic utility function" for these outcomes. Finally, the results of applying Bayes' rule to cognitive decision problems of the sort described will be explored.

This program will not only attempt to construct an analogy between inductive inference and inductive behavior but will (hopefully) be useful in providing a coherent scheme for relating various factors that are of importance in inductive inference. The chapters that follow are devoted to this program.

IV

✳✳✳✳✳✳✳✳✳✳✳✳✳✳✳✳✳✳✳✳✳✳

Replacing Agnosticism by True Belief

1] *A Cognitive Decision Problem*

Consider the political forecaster Smith who sets out to predict which of three candidates—X, Y, or Z—will win an election. It is, of course, conceivable that in some contexts Smith's problem can be reduced to a practical decision problem; but there are situations in which such a prediction could be undertaken simply in order to determine in advance what will happen. For such situations, in which predictions, estimates, or universal generalizations are requested, the proposals made thus far suggest that an investigator such as Smith can be characterized as choosing to accept one sentence from a set M_e generated by an ultimate partition U_e, as strongest sentence accepted as true via induction from his total evidence b&e.

In order to construct a decision-theoretic model for such a "cognitive decision problem," states of nature, "cognitive" outcomes, and epistemic utility assignments to these outcomes will have to be introduced. Once this has been done, it will be possible to explore the consequences of applying Bayes' rule.

The characterization provided thus far for a cognitive decision problem is too weak to provide a useful basis upon which to build a decision-theoretic model of the sort required. An investigator might accept a given sentence as strongest via induction in order to realize many different kinds of goals, none of which is readily reducible to "practical" goals; the goals of a decision problem, whether it be practical or cognitive, are relevant to specifying states of nature, outcomes, and utilities.

Thus, when a scientist is engaged in selecting a theory for purposes of explanation, it is an open question whether the objectives of his inquiry are the same as those that are of concern to someone who attempts to make predictions or estimations on the basis of given data and theories.

In the subsequent discussion, attention will be restricted by and large to cognitive decision problems that represent efforts at prediction, estimation, and universal generalization from confirming instances. An attempt will be made to specify the desiderata for such decision problems and to utilize them in the construction of the decision-theoretic model to be proposed. The extent to which these proposals would then need modification, in order to be able to handle the problem of choosing among theories, will remain an open question.

Insofar as the forecaster Smith is not making policy recommendations to decision-makers, it seems reasonable to suppose that one of the desiderata of his inquiry is to obtain true answers—i.e., to accept as true via induction only such sentences as are true. However, were this the only desideratum involved, he would obtain a satisfactory result with no risk whatsoever, by suspending judgment—i.e., by accepting only those sentences that he accepts as evidence.[1] He would never accept any conclusion via induction from his evidence, except the sentence S_e, which is the disjunction of all elements in his ultimate partition U_e. On the assumption that investigators are sometimes rationally war-

[1] As in the case of inductive behavior, so in inductive inference the risk of error is assessed on the assumption that the sentences accepted as evidence are true. This does not imply that sentences accepted as evidence are forever immune to revision, but it does imply that, as long as they are accepted as evidence, they are assigned a probability of 1.

ranted in risking error, it follows that some other desideratum (or many) is involved.

Relief from agnostic doubt[2] is the second desideratum that appears to be involved in estimation, prediction, and universal generalization. The forecaster Smith would plainly be dissatisfied with the prediction that either X or Y or Z will win. He would much rather predict that X will win (provided the prediction is true), and would even prefer predicting that either X or Y will win. Smith may be taken to be motivated not only by a desire for truth but also by a "will to believe." This way of putting the matter is admittedly too picturesque to be accurate. Investigators engage in scientific inquiry for a variety of personal motives. However, in certain kinds of inquiry, an investigator commits himself to certain standards in the light of which his conclusions are to be judged. The proposal to be made here is that, when efforts at prediction and estimation are not reducible to practical decision-making, the conclusions are to be judged in the light of two desiderata: truth and relief from agnosticism, and that the conclusions are to be judged this way regardless of the scientist's private motives and values.

Cognitive decision problems of this sort will be called "efforts to replace agnosticism by true belief" and subsequent discussion will be devoted almost entirely to such problems. Although questions of choosing among theories are fairly construed as cognitive decision problems, it is widely held that desiderata other than truth and relief from agnosticism are also involved (for example, simplicity and explanatory power). Of course, these other desiderata might prove reducible to the two cited here. This matter will not, however, be considered.

[2] "Doubt" is, of course, ambiguous. "A doubts that S" may mean that A believes that S is false. Alternatively, it can mean that A believes neither that S nor that −S. Furthermore, doubt can be any condition that motivates a person to further inquiry. Thus, a person could accept a sentence as true and yet remain in a state of lingering doubt, in the sense that he feels that the matter deserves further investigation. At the outset of the inquiry, Smith was agnostic regarding which of the candidates would win. He was also in doubt, in the sense that he was motivated to reflect on the matter, collect new evidence, etc. Subsequent to inquiry, he might still remain agnostic but cease further inquiry, because the matter is not of sufficient importance to carry on or because he judges further inquiry to be fruitless. In this discussion, the sort of doubt under consideration is agnostic doubt or suspension of judgment.

2] *Background Information and New Evidence*

No investigator begins an inquiry without some body of sentences that he accepts as evidential. It is usually relative to such "background information" that his problem receives its initial formulation. In particular, the ultimate partitions that determine the set of sentences eligible for acceptance as strongest will at the outset consist of a set of sentences that are consistent with the background information but not deducible from it, such that at least and at most one of the sentences is true if the background information is true.

As the investigator acquires new evidence, it will sometimes happen that he has to revise some of the assumptions in the background information. And even if this should not be the case, the new evidence together with the old might deductively entail the falsity of some element of the erstwhile ultimate partition. Either eventuality could thus lead to a revision of the ultimate partition.

In the subsequent discussion, situations in which new evidence conflicts with old will not be considered. However, machinery will be constructed for tracing the alterations in conclusions that are reached as new evidence is added to background information (on the assumption that the background information and new evidence are consistent). For this purpose, it will prove convenient to distinguish initially ultimate partitions U, which are exclusive and exhaustive relative to background knowledge b, and in which the elements of U are consistent with but not deducible from b, from ultimate partitions that are truncated with respect to new evidence e—U_e. Given an initially ultimate partition U with n elements, and new evidence e, the ultimate partition truncated with respect to e will consist of all those elements of U that are consistent with b and e.

In determining the appropriate conclusions to reach relative to "total evidence" b&e, an investigator who uses U as initially ultimate should adopt U_e as his ultimate partition, and consider as sentences eligible for acceptance as strongest via induction from b&e those sentences that are logically equivalent to elements of M_e generated from U_e.

The fact that at the outset an investigator has chosen U as initially ultimate need not obligate him to continue using it as initially ultimate. He may decide to revise his problem during the course of inquiry. The initially ultimate partition to be considered is one that is used to assess the legitimacy of conclusions reached at the termination of inquiry. It is "initial" only in the sense that it is exclusive and exhaustive relative to the background information and that its elements are consistent with and not deducible from the background information.

3] *The Cognitive Outcomes*

For purposes of illustration, consider once again the forecaster Smith, whose ultimate partition consists of the three sentences "X will win," "Y will win," and "Z will win." Assume that the new evidence e (obtained from opinion polls, etc.) does not alter the ultimate partition—i.e., $U_e = U$. The set M_e of sentences eligible for acceptance as strongest via induction will consist of the following:

  (i) X or Y or Z will win   (S)
  (ii) X or Y will win
  (iii) X or Z will win
  (iv) Y or Z will win
  (v) X will win
  (vi) Y will win
  (vii) Z will win
  (viii) X and Y and Z will win   (C)

On the assumption that Smith is attempting to replace agnosticism with true belief, the outcomes of the eight distinct cognitive options open to him are adequately described in terms of the relief from agnosticism afforded, and whether, in choosing a cognitive option, an error is or is not committed.

4] *The States of Nature*

The states of nature involved in a decision problem are required to be such that, given a state of nature, the outcome of a given option is uniquely determined. In efforts to replace agnosticism by true belief, this means that, if the true state of nature is specified, the relief from agnosticism afforded by a cognitive option and the question of the avoidance or commission of error should be uniquely determined.

Observe, however, that the relief from agnosticism afforded by accepting an element of M_e as strongest via induction is uniquely determined by the cognitive option itself. If Smith suspends judgment—accepts S_e as strongest—he is totally agnostic. If he accepts (ii) as strongest, then whether or not he does so correctly, he has rejected the hypothesis that Z will win, while remaining in doubt as to whether X or Y will win.

Thus, the states of nature can be factors only in determining whether Smith commits an error—i.e., accepts a false sentence as true. But, on the assumption that his total evidence is correct, the necessary and sufficient condition for his committing an error by accepting an element H in M_e as strongest is that H be false; for if H is true, then all the sentences accepted on his evidence must be true, since they are deductive consequences of H and his evidence. And if H is false, then he has accepted as true at least one false sentence.

Observe further that truth values of all elements of M_e are uniquely determined by the truth values of the elements of U_e. The upshot is that the truth values of U_e determine whether Smith will obtain correct answers or errors in accepting any given element of M_e as strongest via induction. They may therefore function as the "states of nature" for the cognitive decision problem.

If $R(H)$ is the relief from agnosticism afforded by accepting H as strongest via induction from the total evidence, Smith's problem can be represented by the matrix in Table 1.

Table 1

Element in M_e Accepted as Strongest	The States of Nature					
	X will win		Y will win		Z will win	
(i)	Correct	R(i)	Correct	R(i)	Correct	R(i)
(ii)	Correct	R(ii)	Correct	R(ii)	Error	R(ii)
(iii)	Correct	R(iii)	Error	R(iii)	Correct	R(iii)
(iv)	Error	R(iv)	Correct	R(iv)	Correct	R(iv)
(v)	Correct	R(v)	Error	R(v)	Error	R(v)
(vi)	Error	R(vi)	Correct	R(vi)	Error	R(vi)
(vii)	Error	R(vii)	Error	R(vii)	Correct	R(vii)
(viii)	Error	R(viii)	Error	R(viii)	Error	R(viii)

5] *Relief from Agnosticism*

Thus far little has been said about the relief from agnosticism afforded by a cognitive option. The cognitive options available to Smith seem susceptible to a partial ordering in this respect. Suspension of judgment (accepting (i) as strongest) yields minimum—0—relief from agnosticism. Accepting (ii) as strongest yields greater relief from agnosticism, but not so much as accepting (v) as strongest: accepting (v) as strongest settles the matter of which candidate will win; accepting (ii) as strongest only partially does so.[3]

This line of reasoning suggests that the elements of M_e can be partially ordered, with respect to the relief from agnosticism afforded by accepting them as strongest, as follows:

(I) If H and G are distinct elements of M_e and H deductively entails G,

$$R(G) < R(H)$$

This principle implies that contradicting oneself relieves agnosticism to a greater degree than does any other option—a result that appears to be counterintuitive. Care should be taken, however, to distinguish between the relief from agnosticism afforded by accepting a sentence as strongest and the truth or falsity of the sentence so accepted. The counterintuitive flavor stems, it would seem, from the assumption that one cannot truly relieve doubt

---

[3] Relief from agnosticism could be understood as the effect of accepting a given sentence as strongest. As such, it would depend upon idiosyncrasies of individual agents. As the notion is understood here, however, relief from agnosticism has a normative component and, perhaps, a more accurate if pedantic terminology would have used the epithet "rational relief from agnosticism." The point is that, if an investigator commits himself to a given list of answers being relevant to his question, as represented by an ultimate partition, the conditions laid down in the following discussion determine the degrees of relief from agnosticism that ought to be accorded to accepting elements of M_e as strongest via induction. The first two conditions (or variants thereof) are independent of the choice of an ultimate partition, but condition (III) is not. Insofar as the choice of U_e is not dictated by conditions of rationality (and unique determination does remain an open question here), an element of subjectivity does remain in the ordering of hypotheses with respect to degrees of relief from agnosticism.

by accepting a falsehood as true. One may not be able to do so truly, but one can do so erroneously.

The point is that every rational investigator may be presumed to know that contradicting oneself inevitably leads to error and would on these grounds never accept a self-contradiction. Hence, the relief from agnosticism afforded by this option is not considered seriously. There is, as a consequence, no presystematic precedent for deciding how contradicting oneself is to be ordered with respect to relief from agnosticism. Where intuition does not decide, it is perfectly legitimate to allow an otherwise adequate principle to be legislative.

The partial ordering of cognitive options just proposed can be taken either as definitive of the notion of relief from agnosticism or as a condition of rationality imposed upon degrees of relief from agnosticism. For our present purposes, it does not matter which view is taken. The latter approach presupposes a notion of relief from agnosticism of the sort that implies that an irrational person would violate (I). Presumably some independent account of relief from agnosticism in terms of a psychological theory would be needed to characterize this notion. Observe, however, that such a characterization is unnecessary for the purpose of a systematic account of rational degrees of relief from agnosticism just as a psychological theory of preference need not have been developed, in order for us to construct a theory of rational preference.

Thus, it is irrelevant whether Smith would feel greater relief from agnosticism (whatever such an emotion might be) as a result of predicting that X will win than he would by predicting that either X or Y will win. If he declares himself to be interested in replacing agnosticism by true belief, he is obliged rationally to rate degrees of relief from agnosticism according to (I), whether this will reflect his "true feelings" or not.

The partial ordering of Smith's options can be represented according to the diagram given in Figure 1 (where the Roman numerals represent the elements of M accepted as strongest).

Figure 1

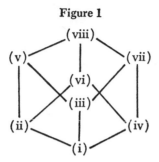

6] *Measuring Relief from Agnosticism*

If accepting (v) as strongest via induction should relieve agnosticism to a greater degree than so accepting (ii), by how much more should it do so? Sentence (ii) is the disjunction of (v) and (vi) which are elements of U_e and hence are exclusive. Consequently, if we accept (v) as strongest, (vi) is thereby rejected.[4]

Thus, the increment in relief from agnosticism would seem to be due to the rejection of (vi). This suggests the following condition.

(II) Let H and G be elements in M_e that are exclusive relative to e.

$$R(HvG) = R(H) - R(-G)$$

Condition (II) entails the partial ordering generated by (I) and consequently can replace (I). From (II), the following theorems can be derived:

[4] Strictly speaking, the rejection of (vi) is tantamount to the acceptance its contradictory as deduced from (v) together with the total evidence. (v) and (vi) are assumed to be contraries relative to the total evidence. They may not be logically exclusive.

In the subsequent discussion, $-H$ (where H is in M_e) will be understood to be either the contradictory of H, or the disjunction of those elements of U_e that are not disjuncts in H. Which interpretation is adopted makes no essential difference to the results obtained, since the contradictory of H can be deduced from the disjunction of the elements of U_e not in H, together with the total evidence b&e.

In a similar vein, the various Boolean combinations of elements of M_e, such as H&G, H&−G, etc. can be taken literally or as abbreviatory representations of the elements of M_e to which such combinations (taken literally) are equivalent, given the total evidence.

T.1: $R(S_e) = R(Hv-H)$
$= R(H)-R(H)$
$= 0$

S_e is the disjunction of all elements of U_e

T.2: $R(H) = R(C_evH)$
$= R(C_e)-R(-H)$

Convention: $R(C_e) = 1$

C_e is the contradictory element in M_e and, hence, H and C_e are exclusive (given b&e)

T.3: $R(-H) = 1-R(H)$

T.4: Let H and G be exclusive (relative to b&e)
$R(-H\&-G) = R(-(HvG))$
$= 1-R(HvG)$
$= 1-R(H)+R(-G)$
$= R(-H)+R(-G)$

T.5: Let H in M_e be a disjunction of $a_1, a_2,...,a_m$, which are elements in U_e.
Let $b_1, b_2,...,b_k$ be the remaining elements of U_e.
$R(H) = R(a_1va_2v...,va_m)$
$= R(-b_1\&-b_2\&...\&-b_k)$
$$= \sum_{i=1}^{k} R(-b_j)$$

T.6: Let $a_1, a_2,...,a_n$ be the elements of U_e
$$\sum_{i=1}^{n} R(-a_i) = R(-a_1\&-a_2\&...\&-a_n)$$
$= R(C_e)$
$= 1$

Since every element H of M_e can be characterized as a conjunction of contradictories of elements of U_e that are not disjuncts in H, once the contradictories of all the elements of U_e are assigned definite R-values, T.5 determines the value of $R(H)$. Hence, the problem of measuring relief from agnosticism reduces to the problem of assigning R-values to the options that involve acceptance of elements of U_e as strongest via induction.

Recall that the elements of U_e are the strongest sentences consistent with the total evidence b&e that the investigator is prepared to consider as relevant answers to his question. Although he may very well understand sentences stronger than sentences in U_e, such sentences are not of interest to him as answers to his question.

Thus, Smith the forecaster surely understands the sentence "X will win, Y will be second and Z third," which is stronger than (v). But within the context of his problem, he does not consider the accepting of that sentence as strongest to be a cognitive option open to him. Given the constraints of the problem, there is no basis on which Smith can distinguish between the elements of his ultimate partition with respect to the relief from agnosticism that is afforded by accepting them as strongest. It seems plausible to expect him to accord to each element of his ultimate partition an equal R-value.

This line of reasoning leads to the following requirement:

(III) Accord equal R-values to the cognitive options involving acceptance of elements of U_e as strongest sentences accepted via induction from total evidence b&e. That is, if a_i and a_j are elements of U_e,

$$R(a_j) = R(a_i)$$

T.7: If a_i and a_j are elements of U_e,

$$R(-a_i) = R(-a_j)$$

T.8: If U_e has n elements and a_i is an element of U_e,

$$R(-a_i) = \frac{1}{n}$$
$$R(a_i) = \frac{n-1}{n}$$

Two comments are in order with regard to (III) and the considerations that motivate it.

Suppose that the sentences (v), (vi), and (vii) are Smith's initially ultimate partition U. Subsequently, he acquires information leading him to accept as new evidence the sentence "It is not the case that X will come first, Y second, and Z third." His ultimate partition relative to e—U_e—will remain identical with his initial partition U. In other words, the relief from agnosticism afforded by accepting (v) as strongest is in no wise altered by Smith's acquisition of information that rules out one possible way in which (v) can be true. The new evidence might alter Smith's assignments of probability to the elements of the ultimate partition. But as far as he is concerned, the new evidence has not relieved agnosticism in the manner in which he wishes it to be relieved.

Suppose that another political forecaster, Jones, chooses as his initially ultimate partition U the sentences "X will win" and "Y or Z will win." He may be fully aware that three candidates are running, but he is interested only in whether X will win or not. He does not recognize the sentences "Y will win" and "Z will win" as relevant answers to his question. "Y or Z will win" is a strongest relevant answer on a par with "X will win." Given such a commitment, (III) requires that Jones assign equal R-values to these two sentences.

This result does seem counterintuitive: most people, confronted with such a forecasting problem, would choose the ultimate partition used by Smith rather than the one chosen by Jones. In a large number of inquiries, it is quite likely that agreement can be reached with regard to the ultimate partition to be used. However, it would be very difficult to provide criteria for selecting certain partitions as legitimate and rejecting others. As has already been indicated in Chapter II, no attempt will be made to provide such criteria in this book. However, in the subsequent discussion, some observations will be made about ultimate partitions that are generally held to be legitimate in certain kinds of problems.

Thus, the proposals being made here do lead to counterintuitive results when certain partitions are chosen as ultimate. This should not count as a decisive objection against these proposals but should be recognized as due to the fact that supplementary judgments are needed to decide the propriety of using certain kinds of partitions rather than others.

Similar difficulties arise with regard to other accounts of inductive inference. A notable example is Nelson Goodman's paradox of "grue" and "green."[5] Goodman does not use these

[5] N. Goodman, *Fact, Fiction and Forecast* (Cambridge: Harvard University Press, 1955), pp. 73–80.

difficulties to condemn the theories that this paradox infects. Rather, he looks for some supplementary grounds for distinguishing predicates such as "grue" from predicates such as "green."[6]

The reason for introducing ultimate partitions in the first place was to accommodate the seemingly incontestable fact that, within the context of any given problem, not all intelligible sentences are to be considered relevant answers. The proposals made here attempt to exploit this fact without trying to explain why investigators choose the ultimate partitions they do, or providing criteria that justify the use of certain kinds of ultimate partitions rather than others.

One final point ought to be made in this connection. It might be suggested that the choice of an ultimate partition depends upon the practical objectives of the investigator and, hence, that so-called "cognitive decision problems" are reducible to practical decision problems, after all. But if this should prove true, all that will have been established is that the choice of a cognitive decision problem is itself some sort of practical decision problem; it would not show that the cognitive decision problem is reducible to a practical decision problem.

7] *Content and Relief from Agnosticism*

The R-values are, strictly speaking, measures assigned to the cognitive options that are open to an investigator, or to the outcomes of such options. But these R-values are functions of the sentences in M_e that have been accepted as strongest, according to the options. This suggests that R-values assigned to cognitive options can be associated with measures assigned to the sentences accepted as strongest. And it would seem that these measures of sentences should indicate in some sense the amount of information or content that these sentences contain. Considerations of that sort motivate the following definitions and theorems:

[6] *Ibid.*, pp. 80–83. Note that the "grue-green" problem is analogous in some respects to the problem of choosing an ultimate partition. However, Goodman's difficulty raises problems for probability measures as well as for acceptance procedures. There does not seem to be any compelling reason, however, for making probability assignments relative to ultimate partitions, in the sense understood here.

D.1: Let U be an initially ultimate partition. A regular measure function on M is a function from elements of M to (real) numbers that satisfy the following conditions:

(1) If a is an element of U, $0 < m(a)$.

(2) Let $a_1, a_2, ..., a_n$ be the elements of U.

$$\sum_{i=1}^{n} m(a_i) = 1$$

(3) $m(C) = 0$

(4) If H is in M and $a_1, a_2, ..., a_k$ are the elements of U which are disjuncts in H,

$$m(H) = \sum_{i=1}^{k} m(a_i)$$

D.2: cont(H) is a regular content measure on M if and only if there is a regular measure function on M such that for each H in M,

$$\text{cont}(H) = m(-H) = 1 - m(H)$$

D.3: m(H) is a uniform regular measure function on M if and only if m(H) is regular on M and for each a_i and a_j in U,

$$m(a_i) = m(a_j)$$

D.4: cont(H) is a uniform regular content measure on M if and only if there is a uniform regular measure function m(H) on M such that

$$\text{cont}(H) = m(-H) = 1 - m(H)$$

D.5: Let U_e be the initially ultimate partition U truncated with respect to e. Let m(H) be a regular measure function on M.

$$m(H,e) = \frac{m(H \& S_e)}{m(S_e)}$$

D.6: Let U_e be as in D.5 and let cont(H) be a regular content measure defined on M.

$$\text{cont}(H,e) = \frac{\text{cont}(Hv - S_e)}{\text{cont}(-S_e)}$$

T.9: Let G be an element of M which is not an element of M_e.
Case (i), all disjuncts in G are incompatible with b&e.

$$m(G,e) = 0$$
$$cont(G,e) = 1$$

Case (ii), $a_1, a_2, ..., a_k$ are the elements of U_e that are
disjuncts in G. Let G′ be the disjunction of these k
sentences in M_e.

$$m(G,e) = m(G',e)$$

$$cont(G,e) = cont(G',e)$$

T.10: $m(H,e)$ is a regular measure function on elements of
M_e and $cont(H,e)$ is a regular content function on
elements of M_e.

T.11: If $m(H)$ is a uniform regular measure function on M,
$m(H,e)$ is a uniform regular measure function on M_e.

If $cont(H)$ is a uniform regular content measure on M,
$cont(H,e)$ is a uniform regular content measure on M_e.

T.12: Let U_e contain n elements, a be an element of U_e,
$m(H,e)$ be a uniform regular measure function on M_e
and $cont(H,e)$ be a uniform regular content measure
on M_e.

$$cont(H,e) = 1-m(H,e) \text{ for each H in } M_e$$
$$m(a,e) = cont(-a,e) = \frac{1}{n}$$
$$cont(a,e) = m(-a,e) = \frac{n-1}{n}$$

If H in M_e is a disjunction of m elements of U_e,

$$cont(H,e) = \frac{n-m}{n} = m(-H,e)$$
$$cont(-H,e) = \frac{m}{n} = m(H,e)$$

Instead of characterizing outcomes of cognitive options in terms
of R-values, cont-values will be used. This procedure is legitimized
by the following principle:

(IV) Let $cont(H)$ be a uniform content measure defined over elements of a set M generated by an initially ultimate partition U. Let e be new evidence acquired in addition to background information b. Let G be an element of M_e.

$$R(G) = \text{cont}(G,e)$$

Measures of content have been discussed by several authors and much importance has been attached to their role in scientific inference—most notably by Karl Popper.[7] Popper's views, as well as those of Bar Hillel, Carnap, Hempel, and Kemeny, will be considered after the theory proposed here has been completely presented. For the present, a few brief comments are in order concerning differences between content measures introduced here and those customarily found in the literature.

First, content measures have been relativized to ultimate partitions rather than to languages. This deviation from the usual approach is justified by the use of content measures as indices of rational relief from agnosticism, which (according to arguments previously offered) is a function of ultimate partitions.

Second, given an initially ultimate partition, unique content measures are determined for it and for its truncations relative to new evidence. These measures are the uniform regular content measures. The requirement of uniformity is not universally adopted. The reason for introducing it here has already been indicated. The elements of an ultimate partition are the strongest relevant answers open to an investigator. In that context, there is no feature of these sentences that can be used to distinguish the relief from doubt afforded by accepting one element of an ultimate partition rather than another as strongest. To do so by referring to sentences that entail elements of the ultimate partition but are not entailed by them would be to consider these sentences relevant answers—counter to the investigator's commitments. Since content is, according to (IV), supposed to equal relief from agnosticism, the same argument applies to the content of elements of the ultimate partition as well.

Finally, note should be taken of the fact that regular measure functions in the sense introduced here satisfy the conditions mentioned previously for probability measures. However, the regular measure functions used to generate content measures can and in general will differ from the regular measure functions

that are used for probability assignments, in the following respects:

(a) Probability assignments to elements of U relative to b
and to U_e relative to b&e need not be uniform. The regular
m-functions introduced here for purposes of measuring
content are.

(b) Probability assignments are not restricted to elements of M
(and to sentences logically equivalent with these, or
equivalent with these given the total evidence).

(c) If p(H)—the probability of H given b—and p(e)—the
probability of new evidence e given b—are given,

$$p(H,e)\text{—the probability of H, given b\&e—} = \frac{p(H\&e)}{p(e)}$$

Observe, however, that the regular measure functions used for
generating content measures are not, in general, defined for new
evidence sentences (unless e is equivalent to an element of M).
Instead

$$m(H,e) = \frac{m(H\&S_e)}{m(S_e)}$$

where S_e is the disjunction of all elements of M_e. The justification
for this definition stems from the fact that the new evidence e
alters the relief from agnosticism afforded by accepting H as
strongest only insofar as it rules out elements of U that are disjuncts of H. The relief from agnosticism afforded by accepting H
relative to b&e is equal to that afforded by ruling out those disjuncts of —H that are not already ruled out by e. But these are
precisely the disjuncts of the element of M equivalent to $-H\&S_e$.
Hence, $m(-H\&S_e)$ could be used as a measure of cont(H,e).
For purposes of normalization, however, it is divided by $m(S_e)$.

When U consists of the sentences (v), (vi), and (vii) of
Smith's ultimate partition, and e is the sentence "It is not the
case that X will win, Y will place second and Z third,"
then $U_e = U$ and $S_e = S$. Since accepting e as evidence does not
lead to the rejection via deduction of any element of U, the R-
values assigned to elements of M should not be changed. Hence,
cont(H,e) should equal cont(H) even though it is possible that
p(H,e) differs from p(H).

With the aid of the content measure proposed, Smith's cognitive decision problem can be represented as in Table 2.

Table 2

Elements of M Accepted as Strongest	*The States of Nature*		
	X will win	Y will win	Z will win
(i)	Correct 0	Correct 0	Correct 0
(ii)	Correct $\frac{1}{3}$	Correct $\frac{1}{3}$	Error $\frac{1}{3}$
(iii)	Correct $\frac{1}{3}$	Error $\frac{1}{3}$	Correct $\frac{1}{3}$
(iv)	Error $\frac{1}{3}$	Correct $\frac{1}{3}$	Correct $\frac{1}{3}$
(v)	Correct $\frac{2}{3}$	Error $\frac{2}{3}$	Error $\frac{2}{3}$
(vi)	Error $\frac{2}{3}$	Correct $\frac{2}{3}$	Error $\frac{2}{3}$
(vii)	Error $\frac{2}{3}$	Error $\frac{2}{3}$	Correct $\frac{2}{3}$
(viii)	Error 1	Error 1	Error 1

Had Smith acquired new evidence that entailed the conclusion that Z will not win, U_e would consist of sentences (v) and (vi), and M_e would consist of (ii)—i.e., S_e, (v), (vi) and the sentence C_e, which is the conjunction of (v) and (vi). Table 3 describes the situation then.

Table 3

Elements of M_e Accepted as Strongest	*The States of Nature*	
	X will win	Y will win
(ii)	Correct 0	Correct 0
(v)	Correct $\frac{1}{2}$	Error $\frac{1}{2}$
(vi)	Error $\frac{1}{2}$	Correct $\frac{1}{2}$
C_e	Error 1	Error 1

Recall Jones, who adopted (iv) and (v) as his ultimate partition. In his case, the cognitive decision problem is presented in Table 4.

Table 4

Elements of M Accepted as Strongest	*The States of Nature*	
	X will win	Y or Z will win
(i)	Correct 0	Correct 0
(iv)	Error $\frac{1}{2}$	Correct $\frac{1}{2}$
(v)	Correct $\frac{1}{2}$	Error $\frac{1}{2}$
(viii)	Error 1	Error 1

If Jones acquires the information that Z will not win, then unless he alters his initially ultimate partition, his cognitive options and their outcomes will continue to be described as in Table 4. The new information will not in any way settle the question in which he was interested.

8] *Conclusion*

Given an initially ultimate partition U, relative to background information b, and new information e, it is possible to specify the following items of information regarding cognitive decision problems of the sort described previously as cases of replacing agnosticism by true belief.

(a) The states of nature are the elements of U_e.

(b) The cognitive options are all instances of accepting H as strongest via induction from b&e, where H is an element of M_e.

(c) Accepting H as strongest eventuates in a correct answer if and only if the element of U_e, which is true, is a disjunct in H.

(d) Accepting H as strongest eventuates in a degree of relief from agnosticism equal to cont(H,e), which equals m/n where n is the number of elements in U_e and m is the number of elements in U_e that are inconsistent with H.

The next step in the development of the model for replacing agnosticism by true belief is the construction of an epistemic utility function on the outcomes of cognitive options. This matter will be taken up in the next chapter.

V

****

Epistemic Utility

1] *Epistemic Preference*

Theories of utility that are currently applied in decision theory generally presuppose the intelligibility of some notion of preference that is taken to be an order relation, ranging over the "outcomes" of acts and the acts themselves. Difficulties arise when an attempt is made to interpret "A prefers a to b" in terms of choice behavior or some other overt behavior of the agent A. Nonetheless, the intelligibility of the notion of preference itself is rarely seriously questioned.

The problems of providing a behavioristic interpretation of preference are increased when this notion is applied to the outcomes of cognitive options. Nevertheless, to say that Smith would rather be right in his predictions than wrong, or that he would rather make a highly informative prediction than one that is virtually vacuous, is not utter nonsense. To be sure, it would be extremely difficult to ascertain in many cases whether or not Smith did feel this way. It is also difficult, at least on many occasions, to determine Smith's preference for blondes as compared to brunettes.

In any event, when an investigator declares himself to be engaged in an effort to replace agnosticism by true belief, or when the conclusions he reaches via induction may fairly be judged on the assumption that he is so engaged, there is no need to ascertain his "true feelings" concerning the outcomes of his options. The "epistemic worth" of the outcomes of his cognitive options is determined according to the standards that are imposed upon anyone who is engaged in a disinterested inquiry that can be satisfactorily described as an attempt to replace agnosticism by true belief. Whether Smith's preferences for the outcomes of his cognitive options conform to these standards of "epistemic preference" is not crucial; what does matter is whether the conclusions he reaches are those that are justified when epistemic worth does conform to these standards.

In efforts to replace agnosticism by true belief, the following two conditions for ordering outcomes with respect to epistemic preference seem to be almost definitive:

(1) Correct answers ought to be epistemically preferred to errors.

(2) Correct answers (errors) that afford a high degree of relief from agnosticism ought to be preferred to correct answers (errors) that afford a low degree of relief from agnosticism.

Conditions (1) and (2), together with the methods for measuring relief from agnosticism proposed in the last chapter, yield a complete ordering of outcomes of cognitive options with respect to epistemic preference. They also suffice to rule out the contradictory option—accepting C_e as strongest via induction—as an optimal cognitive option. Although the outcome of self-contradiction is to be preferred to any other error, it is nonetheless an error, no matter what the true state of nature might be. As a consequence, it is strongly dominated by at least one other cognitive option—suspension of judgment that inevitably leads to a correct answer. As long as utility assignments conform to the ordering with respect to epistemic preference, self-contradiction cannot be optimal, no matter what the probability distribution over the states of nature might be.

2] *Cardinal Epistemic Utility*

Let $U(H)$ be the epistemic utility of correctly accepting H as strongest via induction, where H is in M; let $u(H)$ be the epistemic utility of erroneously accepting H as strongest. Similarly, $U(H,e)$ and $u(H,e)$ are the utilities of accepting H as strongest—correctly and erroneously, respectively—when H is in M_e. Given that cardinal epistemic utility assignments must satisfy the ordering requirements imposed by condition (1) and (2) of Section 1, these two requirements can be restated as follows:

(3) For every H and G in M, $u(H) < U(G)$
     For every H and G in M_e, $u(H,e) < U(G,e)$

(4) For every H and G in M,

$U(H) \lesseqqgtr U(G)$ if and only if $\text{cont}(H) \lesseqqgtr \text{cont}(G)$

$u(H) \lesseqqgtr u(G)$ if and only if $\text{cont}(H) \lesseqqgtr \text{cont}(G)$

For every H and G in M_e,

$U(H,e) \lesseqqgtr U(G,e)$ if and only if $\text{cont}(H,e) \lesseqqgtr \text{cont}(G,e)$

$u(H,e) \lesseqqgtr u(G,e)$ if and only if $\text{cont}(H,e) \lesseqqgtr \text{cont}(G,e)$

These two conditions do not uniquely determine cardinal epistemic utility assignments. However, such unique determination is unnecessary; for, as was noted in Chapter III, all that is required is an interval-measure—i.e., a measure that is unique up to the choice of a 0 point and a unit of measurement.

Two cardinal epistemic utility functions[1] $V(H)$ $(V(H,e))$ and $V'(H)$ $(V'(H,e))$ will be called essentially identical if and only if there is a positive number a, and another number b, such that

$$V'(H) = aV(H)+b \qquad \text{for each H in M}$$
$$V'(H,e) = aV(H,e)+b \qquad \text{for each H in } M_e$$

[1] A cardinal epistemic utility function defined over the elements of $M(M_e)$ is a pair of functions, $U(H)$ $(U(H,e))$, defined over correct answers, and $u(H)$ $(u(H,e))$, defined over errors.

Two epistemic utility functions are essentially distinct when and only when this condition does not obtain. The problem is to construct a system of conditions sufficient to determine a unique family of essentially identical utility functions for efforts to replace agnosticism by true belief. Conditions (3) and (4) remain insufficient even for this purpose.

In order to simplify the following discussion of ways to strengthen (3) and (4), a 0 point will be fixed at the outset. This will have the effect of restricting consideration to epistemic utility functions V and V′, which are essentially identical if and only if V′ = aV for some positive a.

The 0 point to be chosen will be $u(C)$ or $u(C_e,e)$ as the case may be.

Let $f(x)$ and $g(x)$ be two functions such that $f(0) = g(0) = 0$ and both functions increase as x increases.

Given that utilities are interval-measurable, differences in utility are additively measurable—i.e., they are arbitrary only to the choice of unit. This means that condition (4) can be restated as follows:

(4)　For every H and G in M,
$$U(H)-U(G) = f(\text{cont}(H)-\text{cont}(G))$$
$$u(H)-u(G) = g(\text{cont}(H)-\text{cont}(G))$$

For every H and G in M_e,
$$U(H,e)-U(G,e) = f(\text{cont}(H,e)-\text{cont}(G,e))$$
$$u(H,e)-u(G,e) = g(\text{cont}(H,e)-\text{cont}(G,e))$$

What additional restrictions can be imposed on the functions f and g? The first proposal to be made in this connection runs as follows:

(5)　$U(H)-U(G) = u(H)-u(G)$
　　　$U(H,e)-U(G,e) = u(H,e)-u(G,e)$

Condition (5) taken together with condition (4) implies that f = g. The motivation for (5) depends on the observation that differences in the epistemic utilities of correct answers (errors) depend only on the content of the sentences accepted as strongest and not on the fact that they are correct answers (errors). The differences between the epistemic utilities of correct answers and errors are taken care of by condition (3). No other basis for discrimination between correct answers and errors seems to be implied in efforts to replace agnosticism by true belief.

Given condition (5), the characterization of functions f and g reduces to the determination of a single function f. For present purposes, it is sufficient to consider two possibilities:

(a) Functions f such that $\dfrac{f(x)-f(y)}{x-y} = q$ where q is a positive constant and x and y are values for which f is defined.

(b) Functions f such that $\dfrac{f(x)-f(y)}{x-y}$ is a nonconstant function of x and y.

Case (b) would obtain if a principle of increasing or diminishing returns in content were operative. But the introduction of such a principle would introduce factors that are extraneous to efforts to replace agnosticism by true belief. In any case, in the subsequent discussion, it will be assumed that condition (a) obtains. Hence $f(x) = qx+D$, where q is positive. Since $f(0) = 0$, $D = 0$. This leads to the following requirement:

(6) $f(\text{cont}(H)-\text{cont}(G)) = q(\text{cont}(H)-\text{cont}(G))$, where q is positive.

$f(\text{cont}(H,e)-\text{cont}(G,e)) = q(\text{cont}(H,e)-\text{cont}(G,e))$, where q is positive.

Conditions (5) and (6) can be combined in the following simple requirement:

T.1: $U(H)-U(G)$ $= u(H)-u(G)$
$= q(\text{cont}(H)-\text{cont}(G))$, where q is positive.

$U(H,e)-U(G,e) = u(H,e)-u(G,e)$
$= q(\text{cont}(H,e)-\text{cont}(G,e))$, where q is positive.

From condition (3) and T.1, the following series of theorems can be proved. They will be stated only for elements of M_e. The corresponding theorems for elements of M can be viewed as special cases.

T.2: If H is in M_e, $u(H,e) = -q\text{cont}(-H,e)$

    Proof: $u(C_e,e) - u(H,e) = q(\text{cont}(C_e,e) - \text{cont}(H,e))$

$$= q(1 - \text{cont}(H,e))$$
$$= q(\text{cont}(-H,e))$$
$$u(C_e,e) = 0 \text{ by convention.}$$
$$u(H,e) = -q\text{cont}(-H,e)$$

T.3: $U(S_e,e) - u(C_e,e) = s$ where s is positive.
    By condition (3),

T.4: $U(S_e,e) = s$ where s is positive.
    By T.3 and convention that $u(C_e,e) = 0$,

T.5: Let s be as in T.3 and T.4 and H be in M_e.
    $U(H,e) = (q+s) - q\text{cont}(-H,e)$

    Proof: $U(H,e) - U(S_e,e) = q(\text{cont}(H,e) - \text{cont}(S_e,e))$

$$= q\text{cont}(H,e)$$
$$U(H,e) - s = q\text{cont}(H,e)$$
$$U(H,e) = q\text{cont}(H,e) + s$$
$$= q - q\text{cont}(-H,e) + s$$
$$= (q+s) - q\text{cont}(-H,e)$$

T.6: If $u(C_e,e) = 0$, the class of epistemic utility functions permitted by condition (3) and T.1 are represented by pairs of equations of the following form, where q and s are any pair of positive numbers:

$$U(H,e) = (q+s) - q\text{cont}(-H,e)$$
$$u(H,e) = -q\text{cont}(-H,e)$$

The conditions (3)–(6), which delimit the utility functions given in T.6, clearly fail to determine a unique set of essentially identical epistemic utility functions. What is more, the set of epistemic utility functions that satisfy the conditions of T.6 is overabundant, in the sense that it includes functions that are not essentially distinct. This is to be expected; for although a 0 point has been fixed, a unit has not thus far been selected.

At this stage, it will prove convenient first to select a unit for measuring epistemic utility. Once this is done, all the essentially distinct classes of epistemic utility functions that satisfy T.6 can be represented by single members of these classes.

A standard unit for measuring epistemic utility can be chosen indirectly by requiring that all pairs (q,s) be such that their sums equal a fixed value c. When pairs of positive integers are restricted in this way, the utility functions characterized by these functions that also satisfy T.6 will be essentially distinct. If $q \neq q'$ and $s \neq s'$ but $q+s = q'+s'$, there is no positive a, such that $aq' = q$ and $as' = s$. In the following discussion, the constant value of c will be unity. Hence, $s = 1-q$. T.7 specifies the set of essentially distinct epistemic utility functions generated thereby.

T.7: The set of epistemic utility functions that satisfy conditions (1)–(4) are linear transformations of epistemic utility functions satisfying the following conditions where $0 < q < 1$.

$$U(H,e) = 1-qcont(-H,e)$$
$$u(H,e) = -qcont(-H,e)$$

Thus, the choice of a unique epistemic utility function for an effort to replace agnosticism by true belief depends upon the selection of a value for q. No attempt will be made to introduce a value for q. Instead, some indication of the significance of a commitment to a q value will be given. It should then become

Table 1

Sentences Accepted as Strongest	The States of Nature		
	X will win	Y will win	Z will win
(i)	$U(i) = 1-q$	$U(i) = 1-q$	$U(i) = 1-q$
(ii)	$U(ii) = 1-\dfrac{2q}{3}$	$U(ii) = 1-\dfrac{2q}{3}$	$u(ii) = -\dfrac{2q}{3}$
(iii)	$U(iii) = 1-\dfrac{2q}{3}$	$u(iii) = -\dfrac{2q}{3}$	$U(iii) = 1-\dfrac{2q}{3}$
(iv)	$u(iv) = -\dfrac{2q}{3}$	$U(iv) = 1-\dfrac{2q}{3}$	$U(iv) = 1-\dfrac{2q}{3}$
(v)	$U(v) = 1-\dfrac{q}{3}$	$u(v) = -\dfrac{q}{3}$	$u(v) = -\dfrac{q}{3}$
(vi)	$u(vi) = -\dfrac{q}{3}$	$U(vi) = 1-\dfrac{q}{3}$	$u(vi) = -\dfrac{q}{3}$
(vii)	$u(vii) = -\dfrac{q}{3}$	$u(vii) = -\dfrac{q}{3}$	$U(vii) = 1-\dfrac{q}{3}$
(viii)	0	0	0

clear that the intuitive ideas motivating the construction of a model for replacing agnosticism by true belief fail to provide a standard way of selecting a q-index, just as they fail to indicate how ultimate partitions are to be chosen.

Further discussion of the q-index will be delayed, however, until the application of Bayes' rule has been considered. The information regarding Smith's problem given in Table 2 of the previous chapter is used in Table 1 to illustrate the results obtained thus far.

3] *Expected Epistemic Utility*

As in the case of practical decision problems, so in cognitive decision problems the application of Bayes' rule requires an ability on the part of the investigator to assign to the states of nature probabilities relative to his total evidence. In this discussion, the investigator will be assumed to be ideally situated, in the sense that he has this talent. Observe that the ideally situated investigator need not be as ideally situated as the comparable decision-maker, for he is not expected to be able to assign numerical values to his epistemic preferences. The cardinal epistemic utility assignments are determined by a standard system of criteria, provided that the investigator can specify his ultimate partition and the q-value that he is using and declare that he is replacing agnosticism by true belief. The fact that these requirements need not be so troublesome as those required of a Bayesian decision-maker should become clear when one considers applications to real-life situations of the proposals made here. In any event, the idealizations are different. What remains the same for both Bayesian decision-makers and Bayesian investigators is the need to be able to assign probabilities to the states of nature.

In this discussion, $E(H)$ will be the expected epistemic utility of accepting H as strongest, relative to the background information, where H is in M; $E(H,e)$ will be the epistemic utility of accepting H as strongest relative to total evidence b&e, where H is an element of M_e. $p(H)$ is the probability of H given b, $p(H,e)$ the probability of H given b&e.

$$E(H) = p(H)U(H)+p(-H)u(H)$$
$$E(H,e) = p(H,e)U(H,e)+p(-H,e)u(H,e)$$

While the following theorems will be stated for $E(H,e)$, their analogues for $E(H)$ are obvious corollaries.

T.8: $E(H,e) = p(H,e)-qcont(-H,e)$

> *Proof:* $E(H,e) = p(H,e)(1-qcont(-H,e))$
> $\qquad\qquad\quad -(1-p(H,e))qcont(-H,e)$
> $\qquad\quad = p(H,e)-qcont(-H,e)$

T.9: $E(HvG,e) = E(H,e)+E(G,e)-E(H\&G,e)$

> *Proof:* $E(HvG,e) = p(HvG,e)-qcont(-H\&-G,e)$
> $\qquad\qquad\quad = p(H,e)+p(G,e)-p(H\&G,e)$
> $\qquad\qquad\qquad -qcont(-H,e)-qcont(-G,e)+$
> $\qquad\qquad\qquad qcont(-Hv-G,e)$
> $\qquad\qquad\quad = p(H,e)-qcont(-H,e)+p(G,e)-$
> $\qquad\qquad\qquad qcont(-G,e)+p(H\&G,e)-$
> $\qquad\qquad\qquad qcont(-(H\&G),e)$
> $\qquad\qquad\quad = E(H,e)+E(G,e)-E(H\&G,e)$

D.1: $E(H,e)$ is maximal in M_e if and only if, for every G in M_e, $E(G,e) \leqq E(H,e)$

T.10: If $E(H,e)$ and $E(G,e)$ are both maximal in M_e, $E(HvG,e)$ is also maximal in M_e.

> *Proof:* Let $E(H,e)$ and $E(G,e)$ be maximal
> $\qquad E(H,e) = E(G,e)$
> $\qquad E(HvG,e) = 2E(H,e)-E(H\&G,e)$
> $\qquad$ If $E(HvG,e) < E(H,e)$, $E(H,e) < E(H\&G,e)$,
> $\qquad$ which is inconsistent with the maximality of
> $\qquad E(H,e)$.
> $\qquad$ Hence, $E(HvG,e) = E(H,e)$.

D.2: $E(H,e)$ is strongly maximal in M_e if and only if $E(H,e)$ is maximal, and for every G other than H, such that $E(G,e)$ is maximal in M_e, $cont(H,e) < cont(G,e)$.

T.11: There is one and only one H in M_e such that $E(H,e)$ is strongly maximal in M_e.

> *Proof:* There is at least one element H in M_e, such that $E(H,e)$ is maximal in M_e. If it is the only one, $E(H,e)$ is strongly maximal.

Let there be k elements in M_e, $H_1, H_2, ..., H_k$, such that $E(H_i, e)$ is maximal in M_e for each i from 1 to k. $H_1 v H_2 v, ..., H_k$ is equivalent to one and only one of the H_i's—say H^*—by T.10 and the fact that no two elements of M_e are logically equivalent.

$cont(H^*, e) < cont(H_i, e)$ for each H_i distinct from H^*. $E(H^*, e)$ is strongly maximal.

4] *Bayes' Rule and the Rule for Ties*

Bayes' rule requires choosing any cognitive option whose expected epistemic utility is maximal. However, it is possible for two or more cognitive options to have maximal epistemic utility.

When ties arise in practical decision problems, either the options that tie for optimality are considered equally good and the agent is allowed free choice, or else some other features of the decision problem are used to decide between them.

In the case of cognitive decision problems of the sort under consideration here, free choice does not seem legitimate. If Smith is in a position to consider as optimal accepting "X will win" as strongest and "Y will win" as strongest, the appropriate prescription seems to be that he should suspend judgment as to which of these two candidates will win—i.e., that he should accept "X or Y will win" as strongest.

Now, according to T.10, accepting "X or Y will win" as strongest will yield maximal expected epistemic utility if the expected epistemic utilities of accepting "X will win" as strongest and accepting "Y will win" as strongest are maximal. If these are the only three optimal options according to Bayes' rule, the expected epistemic utility of accepting "X or Y will win" as strongest will be strongly maximal.

These considerations suggest that Bayes' rule be supplemented by the following "rule for ties" which, by virtue of T.11, ensures that a unique cognitive option will be selected as optimal:

Rule for Ties: Accept that element of M_e as strongest via induction from b&e whose expected epistemic utility is strongly maximal in M_e relative to the probability distribution.

The rule for ties allows a slight modification of the method for assigning epistemic utilities. Condition (1) of Section 1, which requires that correct answers be preferred to errors, can be weakened to read as follows:

(1′) No error should be epistemically preferred to any correct answer.

The only effect of this modification is to allow the same epistemic utility to correctly suspending judgment (accepting S_e as strongest) as it does to erroneously contradicting oneself. It does this by allowing q to take the value 1. All the theorems that have been proven regarding epistemic utility go through without modification, except for this one.

If $q = 1$, self-contradiction is no longer a dominated option. Observe, however, that its expected epistemic utility could be maximal only if $E(S_e,e)$ is maximal. (Both expected epistemic utilities would be 0 for all probability distributions.) Under these circumstances, $E(S_e,e)$ would be strongly maximal. The rule for ties ensures that suspension of judgment would be recommended.

It is convenient to allow q to take a maximum value of 1. Since the rule for ties ensures that this modification will be harmless, it will be adopted.

5] *More Theorems*

T.12: $E(H,e)$ is maximal only if it is non-negative.

Proof: $E(S_e,e) = 1-q$, which is non-negative.

T.13: Let $a_1, a_2, ..., a_k$ be all and only elements of U_e, such that $p(a_i,e) \geqq q\text{cont}(-a_i,e)$. Let H be the element in M_e that is the disjunction of these k sentences.

$E(H,e)$ is strongly maximal in M_e.

Proof: $E(a_i,e) = p(a_i,e) - q\text{cont}(-a_i,e) \geqq 0$

$E(H,e) = \sum_{i=1}^{k} E(a_i,e)$. T.9 where the disjuncts are exclusive.

$E(H,e)$ is maximal; for any G in M_e, such that $E(G,e)$ is maximal, must be a disjunction of some subset of the a_i's; and no such G can be such that $E(G,e)$ is greater than $E(H,e)$.

If G is a disjunction of some but not all of the a_i's,

$E(G,e) \leqq E(H,e)$
$\text{cont}(H,e) < \text{cont}(G,e)$

Hence, $E(H,e)$ must be strongly maximal.

6] *An Inductive Acceptance Rule*

T.13 of Section 5 provides the basis of a simple criterion for recommending which element in M_e ought to be accepted as strongest via induction from b&e, given a probability distribution over the elements of U_e relative to b&e.

Rule (A):   (a) Accept b&e and all its deductive consequences.

                (b) Reject all elements a_i of U_e, such that $p(a_i,e) < \text{qcont}(-a_i,e)$ — i.e., accept the disjunction of all unrejected elements of U_e as the strongest element in M_e accepted via induction from b&e.

                (c) Conjoin the sentence accepted as strongest via induction according to (b) with the total evidence b&e and accept all deductive consequences.

                (d) Do not accept (relative to b, e, U_e, the probability distribution, and q) any sentences other than these in your language.

Rule (A) incorporates in clause (b) the result of applying Bayes' rule and the rule for ties to the model for replacing agnosticism by true belief, in order to decide which sentence ought to be accepted as strongest via induction. It provides a convenient summary of the results obtained thus far. Any inadequacies in rule (A) must be inadequacies in the proposals that have been made; its virtues, if any, lend some support to these proposals.

7] *Degree of Caution*

Rule (A) was derived via Bayes' rule and the rule for ties, on the assumption that epistemic utility assignments satisfy conditions (3)–(6) of Section 2. These four conditions were intended to articulate the commitments of an investigator whose two desiderata are relief from agnosticism and truth.

In deriving epistemic utility assignments for the outcomes of cognitive options, the conditions (3)–(6) proved insufficient to determine a unique utility function $V(x)$, such that every legitimate utility function is essentially identical to V. Even when the 0 point and unit were fixed, uniqueness could be ensured only when a specific value was assigned to the parameter q.

The reason for this is that efforts to replace agnosticism by true belief involve two desiderata, not one. This means that investigators engaged in such efforts can differ with respect to the relative importance they attach to one desideratum as compared to another. In some cases, the "will to believe" may be relatively strong—implying that, relatively speaking, small weight is attached to truth or, alternatively, that truth may be deemed to be of greater worth than relief from agnosticism.

Given this variation in the relative weight that is accorded truth and relief from agnosticism, it is to be expected that a unique epistemic utility function will not be generated from the conditions laid down. Consideration of Smith's decision problem, as represented by Table 1 of this chapter, illustrates how variation in q within the permitted interval determines the relative importance attached to truth and relief from agnosticism.

When $q = 1$, the epistemic utility accorded accepting (i) as strongest via induction—i.e., suspension of judgment—is equal to 0, which is the same as the epistemic utility of self-contradiction. This case reflects situations in which the premium placed on relief from agnosticism is the maximum permitted, if contradictions are to be barred. If q were greater than 1, then conditions could arise where the desire for relief from agnosticism would be so great as to warrant one's contradicting oneself, even at the cost of committing an inevitable error.

As q decreases and approaches 0, the difference increases between the utility of suspending judgment and self-contradiction. What is more, the utilities of all correct answers tend to become equal, approaching 1 as q approaches 0. Similarly, the utilities of all errors approach 0 as q approaches 0. Thus, for very small values of q, the role of content in epistemic utility assignments is diminished.

The choice of a value for q does seem to reflect, therefore, the relative importance attached to the two desiderata: truth and relief from agnosticism.

Note, however, that the choice of q can be viewed in a slightly different way. If q were allowed, contrary to fact, to take the value 0, all correct answers would receive the value 1 and all errors the value 0. No premium would be placed on relief from agnosticism. The use of Bayes' rule and the rule for ties (or, alternatively, the use of rule (A)) results in the recommendation that the investigator suspend judgment, no matter what the probability distribution might be. In other words, the investigator who chooses the value $q = 0$ would be committed to accepting only those sentences that are deductive consequences of his total evidence. He would be a skeptic, in the sense of at least one among the many different interpretations of skepticism.

As q is allowed to increase, the investigator would tend to be less skeptical or cautious in the conclusions he reaches via induction. According to rule (A), he rejects all elements of U_e whose probabilities relative to the total evidence are less than q/n, where n is the number of elements in U_e. As q increases, more elements of U_e will, in general, be rejected, thereby leading to the acceptance of stronger elements of M_e as strongest via induction. In some cases, of course, an increase in q will not lead to this result, because of the features of the probability distribution. Thus, in Smith's problem, if there is an equal chance that any one of the candidates will win, suspension of judgment will be recommended, no matter what value of q is chosen. However, it is impossible for elements of U_e to be rejected for a value of q and not to be rejected for higher values; sometimes, however, an increase in q will lead to an increase in the number of elements of U_e that are rejected.

Thus, the q-index reflects the degree of skepticism, degree of credulity, or degree of caution exercised by the investigator. In the subsequent discussion, q will in fact be called "the q-index of the degree of caution exercised by an investigator." As q increases, the degree of caution that is exercised decreases. It is more convenient to use q rather than $s = 1-q$ as the index of caution, because the "rejection level," at which elements of U_e are rejected according to rule (A), is then represented as q/n, rather than as the more complicated $(1-s)/n$.

The degree of caution is the third parameter, along with the total evidence and the ultimate partition relative to which the requirements of deductive closure and consistency discussed in Chapter II will be relativized. No effort will be made to obtain a standard value for q. However, the q-index of caution will be exploited in the introduction of certain important concepts in subsequent chapters.

One final point should be mentioned. The epistemic utility function for efforts to replace agnosticism by true belief need not reflect the feelings of investigators who declare themselves to be committed to such efforts. This function is imposed upon them when they attempt to justify the conclusions they reach by their declared commitments.

Observe, however, that the choice of q-index is a subjective factor, which does in some sense reflect the investigator's attitudes. Is it plausible to expect that investigators will be able to ascertain their "true feelings" about the degrees of caution that they exercise? Surely it would be difficult to elicit from them a commitment to numbers representing the degrees of caution that they were exercising.

In the case of ideally situated investigators, the problem is made somewhat easier by the fact that such investigators can compare the conclusions warranted relative to different values for q on the probability distributions to which they are committed. They can then adjust the value of q to allow those conclusions that they wish to reach—provided these conclusions are warranted by some value of q within the permitted interval.

A more general line of reply would be to reject the implausibility of supposing investigators to be capable of committing themselves to definite values of q. Perhaps these values of q will not reflect their true feelings in some sense. But the choice of a value of q will be a commitment on the part of an investigator to have his conclusions evaluated according to certain standards. Once he understands what these standards are, he may very well so commit himself.

There is some precedent for this in statistical theory. The levels of significance used in the Neyman-Pearson theory for testing statistical hypotheses seem to reflect commitments to something like degrees of caution, when they are interpreted in a nonbehavioralistic manner. In any event, investigators who use such methods appear to be quite capable of selecting a significance level in many situations. To be sure, the ability to do so requires some understanding of the theory. The tolerance accorded in many textbooks on statistics to the problem of selecting a significance level can be accorded to the choice of a q-level. Whether such a choice reflects the outcome of deep and profound reflection on "inner states" is really unimportant. The choice of a q-index is a commitment to having one's inferences publicly evaluated in a certain way.

8] *Conclusion*

Rule (A) summarizes the results of applying Bayes' rule to the model that has been proposed for replacing agnosticism by true belief. As such, it may be taken to be applicable to evaluating inferences of ideally situated investigators, who are attempting to make predictions, estimates, or universal generalizations. Whether rule (A) can be applied to choices among theories remains an open question, not to be considered in this essay.

Nonetheless, in spite of its limitation to ideally situated investigators who are engaged in prediction, estimation, or universal generalization, rule (A) was obtained with the aid of decision-theoretic ideas. This was done without reducing these problems to questions of inductive behavior.

In the subsequent discussion, several properties of rule (A) will be examined and exploited, in considering some familiar topics in induction and confirmation theory as well as in examining the views of other writers on these subjects.

VI

Probability and Belief

1] *Introduction*

Rule (A) *is a probability-based* acceptance rule, in the sense that probabilities must be assigned to sentences relative to given evidence in order that it may be applied.

Now probabilities—in the sense under consideration—are intended to be indices of the risks that a person is prepared to take (or ought rationally be prepared to take) in acting as if certain sentences were true.

Since one of the main purposes of this book is to consider the relations between belief and action, a consideration of how probabilities are related to beliefs in efforts to replace agnosticism by true belief is of some importance.

2] *Deductive Cogency*

Rule (A) is not only probability-based; it is deductively cogent. An inductive acceptance rule is considered to be deductively cogent if there is a system of conditions K such that all sentences accepted under K are required to form a consistent and deductively closed set.

In the case of rule (A), the conditions K are the available evidence b&e, the ultimate partition U (which, together with b&e, determines the truncated partition U_e), and the degree of caution as indexed by q.

Consistency is ensured by the requirement that q be less than or equal to 1 and, as a consequence, that the level at which elements of U_e are rejected must be less than $1/n$ where n is the number of elements of U_e. Deductive closure is guaranteed by the requirement that, if an element H in M_e is accepted as strongest via induction, all the deductive consequences of H and b&e must be accepted as true.

In Section 7 of Chapter II, the principle of deductive cogency was shown to be incompatible with the requirement that a high probability be a necessary and sufficient condition for accepting a sentence as true. Consideration of fair lotteries provided some intuitive support for the view that high probabilities are not sufficient (unless they are equal to 1).

Application of rule (A) to the fair million-ticket lottery illustrates these points. When q = 1, the rejection level for elements of the millionfold ultimate partition that consists of sentences of the form "ticket i will win" is .000001. Since no element of the ultimate partition U has a probability less than that figure, suspension of judgment is recommended. This same recommendation obviously obtains when q is less than 1.

Thus, application of rule (A) to this problem yields a result in conformity with presystematic ideas—provided that the millionfold partition just mentioned is used as ultimate. Observe, however, that rule (A) does concede some truth to Kyburg's intuitions on the matter.

Let H be any sentence whose truth is not decided by the total evidence b&e. There is one ultimate partition U_e^* such that H is accepted relative to U_e^* and a q-value equal to 1, if and only if $p(H,e)$ is greater than .5. U_e^* consists of the sentences H and $-H$.

Thus, in the lottery problem, it is possible to predict that ticket 1 will not win if the ultimate partition U_1, which consists of the sentences "ticket 1 will win" and "ticket 1 will not win," is used. Similarly, the corresponding partition U_2 can be used to warrant predicting that ticket 2 will not win; and, more generally,

U_i can be used to predict that ticket i will not win. But the conclusions that are reached relative to these distinct partitions cannot legitimately be pooled in order to reach the contradictory conclusion that is feared by Kyburg. This is not due to any rejection of the principle of deductive cogency, but to restriction of the scope of deductive cogency to those sentences that are accepted relative to a given ultimate partition. Just as no one requires closure over sentences accepted relative to different bodies of evidence, so too closure ought not to be required over sentences accepted relative to different ultimate partitions.

Here someone may object that what was promised has not been fulfilled. The declared aim of this discussion was to provide criteria for rational acceptance or rational belief. What has been offered instead is a criterion for rational conditional belief.

Someone who is interested in the outcome of the lottery might say that, if he were to use U_1 as ultimate, he would predict that ticket 1 will not win, but that if he were to use U (the millionfold partition), he would suspend judgment. But he could still be asked what, after all, he did believe.

This objection—if well founded—would apply just as well to theories of inductive inference that relativize rational belief to total available evidence. Such criteria indicate what a man ought to believe if he has available to him such and such evidence. In this case, however, it might be conceded that these criteria, together with the information that the man in question has certain evidence at his disposal, indicate that he is obliged to accept the appropriate conclusion in an unconditional sense. Of course, if the available evidence is not clearly specified, perhaps only a conditional judgment is warranted. But "detachment" is in principle always possible.

A similar reply is appropriate in the case of ultimate partitions. Most men, upon being faced with the lottery, would pick the millionfold partition as ultimate, but rule (A) recommends suspension of judgment if this partition is ultimate. When it is detached, rule (A) recommends suspension of judgment in an unconditional sense.

To this reply it might be countered that relativization to total evidence precludes reaching conclusions relative to two distinct bodies of evidence at the same time. One cannot both believe that P and not believe that P simultaneously, and continue to do so rationally when total evidence is taken into account. On the other hand, it might prove to be the case that two ultimate partitions are simultaneously detached—i.e., U and U_1—and, as a consequence, rule (A) sanctions believing that 1 will not win and at the same time not believing that 1 will not win.

Now it must be admitted that no criteria have been offered that preclude simultaneous detachment of two or more ultimate partitions; later on, some evidence will be adduced to suggest that in certain special kinds of situations two or more ultimate partitions are indeed simultaneously detached (not necessarily consciously detached at the same time, yet both ultimate partitions are at the same time in the condition of having been detached). But such situations do not often arise. If this is so, the proposals made here will only rarely lead to the allegedly counterintuitive result described above.

Furthermore, it is far from clear that a rule that allows simultaneously belief that P and agnosticism regarding P (and even belief that not P) is counterintuitive. Who is prepared to say that the reason why a person who believes that P and believes that not P can do so rationally is that he holds these beliefs at different times? Is time the factor that determines rationality here? Or is it the different conditions that prevail at these times?

If time is not a factor in rational belief (and it seems plausible to suppose that it is not), then why is it impossible for conditions K and K' to prevail at the same time, such that a man believes a deductively consistent and closed system of sentences Γ based on K and simultaneously a deductively consistent and closed system of sentences Γ' based on K'? To be sure he will believe, and believe rationally, all sentences in the set Γ ∪ Γ', and this set may very well be neither consistent nor closed. But unless time is supposed to be a factor that determines the scope of deductive cogency, why should this be objectionable? It may still remain true that the set of sentences accepted because of K is consistent and closed and at the same time the set of sentences accepted because of K' is also consistent and closed.

To repeat, situations do not occur very often in which two ultimate partitions that yield "conflicting" conclusions are detached at the same time. To the extent that this is so, the allegedly counterintuitive results of rule (A) rarely appear.

In any event, rule (A) succeeds in preserving deductive cogency and accommodating common sense with regard to the lottery problem by recommending suspension of judgment when the lottery is fair, on the grounds that in this problem most men would consider each sentence of the form "ticket i will win" to be a relevant answer in the same respect. As a sop to Kyburg's Cerberus, rule (A) accommodates the idea that a high probability is a sufficient condition for acceptance, by holding that for any sentence H that has high probability there is an ultimate partition such that if that ultimate partition is detached (and it may or may not be detached) rule (A) recommends accepting H. Rule (A) also admits the *possibility* that at certain times a person may rationally accept as true a set of sentences that is not consistent and closed. However, the rule requires that this set must be divisible into subsets which are consistent and closed relative to the total evidence and the ultimate partitions detached at that time.

3] *Elimination*

In relativizing inductive acceptance to ultimate partitions, it was assumed that the investigator had available to him as cognitive options all cases of accepting H as strongest where H is an element of M_e generated by the ultimate partition U_e. This imposes both an upper and a lower limit on the cognitive options available (these are, of course, identical). That no other distinct options are open is simply a reflection of the fact that no answers are considered relevant other than those sentences that are logically equivalent to elements of M_e. Might there not, however, be fewer options? Some authors have thought this to be the case. Thus, Carl Hempel, who attempted to construct a decision-theoretic model for inductive inference using Bayes' rule, in effect restricted the cognitive options to acceptance of elements of U_e as strongest and suspension of judgment.[1] I adopted the same procedure in another publication.[2] But such restriction does in-

[1] C. G. Hempel, "Inductive Inconsistencies," *Synthese,* 12 (1960), 462–469.
[2] I. Levi, "On the Seriousness of Mistakes," *Philosophy of Science,* 29 (1962), 52–57. In spite of important similarities to Hempel's discussion, this article was written in ignorance of his views.

deed lead to strongly counterintuitive results. If Bob wishes to guess the color of Mary's eyes, knowing that they can be only blue or brown, he will not be able to conclude that they will either both be blue or both be brown. For he will not be able to rule out the possibility that the left eye may be a different color from the right.

Note that rule (A), which allows all 2^n cognitive options (where n is the number of elements of U_e), is in effect an eliminative rule. Each cognitive option can be characterized as a case of rejecting 0 or more elements of U_e via induction. Except for the case of the contradictory option of rejecting all n elements of U_e, what considerations would lead to prohibiting a priori any of these options? The approach previously adopted by Hempel and me is an "all-or-nothing-at-all" approach. Either no elements of U_e are rejected, or all but one are rejected. This prevents Bob from rejecting the hypothesis that Mary's left eye is blue and her right is brown, even though its probability may be very low (though it is still positive). To see this in detail, let H_1 be "Mary's right and left eyes are blue," H_2 be "Mary's right and left eyes are brown," H_3 be "Mary's right eye is brown and her left eye blue," and H_4 be "Mary's right eye is blue and left eye brown." Now, unless H_3 and H_4 are incompatible with Bob's evidence, they will bear positive probability. Moreover, it may be the case that H_1 and H_2 bear equal probability. Thus, the probability distribution could run: $p(H_1) = .49$, $p(H_2) = .49$, $p(H_3) = .01$, and $p(H_4) = .01$. When cognitive options are restricted in the manner mentioned above, inconsistency can be avoided only by requiring a probability greater than .5 for acceptance. But this means that Bob must suspend judgment!

4] *High Probability*

With the aid of the lottery problem and the assumption of deductive cogency, it has been argued that a high probability is not sufficient for acceptance as true. Is it necessary?

If the original Hempel–Levi approach is adopted, it surely must be. At any rate, a probability greater than .5 must be required for acceptance, in order to avoid inconsistency.

Observe, however, that when all 2^n cognitive options generated by an ultimate partition are considered, consistency does not require high probability.

What consistency does require is that no element of U_e be rejected, unless its probability is less than its content, where content is measured via some regular measure function over M_e. On the assumption that the appropriate measure function is uniform—i.e., results in equal content assignments to all elements of U_e—consistency demands that no element of U_e be rejected unless its probability is less than $1/n$. Note that the "rejection level" $1/n$ is a necessary but not a sufficient condition for rejection relative to an n-fold U_e. The rejection level might be set lower by taking a value of q less than 1. What is important here, however, is that considerations of consistency do not demand a probability greater than .5 as a necessary condition for acceptance, except when the ultimate partition contains only two elements.

Thus, in a threefold ultimate partition, rule (A) would warrant accepting H_1 if its probability were .4 and the remaining elements of U_e had probabilities of .3 each—provided that $q = 1$. No inconsistency can arise. What happens is that H_2 and H_3 are rejected because their probabilities are lower than a given rejection level of $1/3$. The surviving element of U_e is accepted as true.

Hence, if a high probability is to be required as a necessary condition for acceptance, considerations other than consistency must be introduced. It would be difficult to anticipate all the considerations to which an appeal might be made. There is, however, one that does deserve special attention.

It might be argued that, if a man believes that P, he ought to be prepared to act as if P were true, and that he would be justified in doing so only if P bore a very high probability. But, according to arguments introduced in the first chapter, if he must act as if P were true no matter what the "stakes" might be, the probability would have to be 1—in other words, he could only believe that P if P were entailed by his evidence. On the other hand, if belief that P is permitted when the probability that P is less than 1, there will be some stakes relative to which an agent who believes that P ought not to act as if P were true. This will be true no matter whether the probability that P is very high or very low.

Thus, an appeal to some conception of the relation between belief and action as a basis for requiring high probability for rational acceptance breaks down for essentially those reasons that led to the (tentative) rejection of naive cognitivism and behavioralism.

In the subsequent discussion, rejection levels that permit acceptance when probabilities are less than .5 will be considered legitimate. In other words, no further restrictions will be imposed on the upper limit for the q-index. In any event, the role of probability in a probabilistic rejection rule such as (A), though important, does not determine acceptance by requiring a minimum acceptance level. Whether or not a given sentence is accepted depends not so much on its total probability taken in isolation, but on that probability as compared to the probabilities of the alternative hypotheses being considered. A hypothesis that bears very low probability might be accepted as true, not because its probability is "high enough," but because its competitors bear probabilities "low enough" to warrant their "elimination." A high probability is neither necessary nor sufficient for acceptance as true.

5] *Low Probability*

According to rule (A) the "rejection level" for "eliminating" elements of U_e is q/n where n is the number of elements in U_e. Thus, the rejection level used depends not only on the degree of caution exercised but on the number of elements in the ultimate partition.

This result conforms with intuitions about fair lotteries. If suspension of judgment is plausible in a fair lottery, it is plausible no matter how many tickets there are in the lottery. Thus, if a positive rejection level r is fixed for making predictions about a lottery of 100 tickets, there will be some number n such that $1/n$ is less than r. A lottery in which there are more than n tickets will require a rejection level less than r. Hence, the only way in which a rejection level could be set as independent of the number of elements of the ultimate partition would be to make it 0. But this is the skeptic's rejection level—i.e., the one used by an investigator who refuses to reach conclusions unless they are deductively entailed by the evidence. Hence, it seems clear that deductive cogency—in particular, deductive consistency—requires that rejection levels depend upon the number of elements in U_e.

In sum, a fixed low probability is neither necessary nor sufficient for rejection. However, once an ultimate partition is chosen, a necessary condition for rejecting elements of that partition can be determined—namely, bearing a probability less than $1/n$, where the number of elements in the partition is n.

VII

****

Cognitive Objectives

1] Corroboration and Rules of Acceptance

According to Karl Popper, ". . . the doctrine that *degree of corroboration or acceptability cannot be a probability* is one of the most interesting findings in the philosophy of knowledge."[1] Unfortunately the debate that raged a few years ago between Popper and the apologists for Carnap made the significance of Popper's thesis depend upon a determination of who had explicated what presystematic concept adequately.[2] Taking Popper's "finding" to be a gambit in a game of "button, button, who has the button" hardly makes it "interesting." The philosophical importance of Popper's thesis should be assessed in terms of the success with which Popper can apply his measure of corroboration to the problems he designed this measure to handle and in terms of the philosophical significance of those problems.

Popper's writings offer ample evidence of his intention to for-

[1] K. R. Popper, *The Logic of Scientific Discovery* (London: Hutchinson, 1959), p. 394.

[2] See notes in the *British Journal for the Philosophy of Science* by K. R. Popper, 6 (1955), 157–163, 7 (1956), 244–245, 249–256; R. Carnap, 7 (1956), 243–244; and Y. Bar Hillel, 6 (1955), 155–157, 7 (1956), 245–248.

mulate rules for accepting and rejecting scientific hypotheses with the aid of his corroboration measures.

Furthermore, the degree of confirmation is supposed to have an influence upon the question whether we should *accept* or choose a certain hypothesis x, if only tentatively; a high degree of confirmation is supposed to characterize a hypothesis as 'good' (or 'acceptable') while a disconfirmed hypothesis is supposed to be 'bad'.[3]

This passage not only indicates that Popper considers degrees of corroboration to be relevant to formulating acceptance rules but also suggests, by its use of locutions such as "choose," that acceptance involves singling out certain sentences or sets of sentences for acceptance rather than others. Finally, the prescription he offers for acceptance seems to be to accept as strongest the sentence that bears maximum corroboration (in his sense).

Understood in this way, Popper's assertion that corroboration is not a probability has genuine significance. He is rejecting the scientific propriety of any rule that recommends maximizing probability. Moreover, he does this without denying all relevance to probabilities in formulating rules of acceptance; for degree of corroboration is a function of probability.

Obviously the dispute between the Carnapians and Popperites has been over the wrong issue. Carnap nowhere claims that scientists maximize probabilities when they accept hypotheses; as a good behavioralist, he denies that scientists accept hypotheses at all.

Nonetheless, the prescription that recommends the maximizing of probability deserves consideration as an acceptance rule, if only to be discarded; and the position taken here is in full agreement with Popper about the propriety of abandoning this prescription. In efforts to replace agnosticism by true belief, the function whose value is to be maximized is $E(H,e) = p(H,e) - qcont(-H,e)$. This is clearly not a probability.

Moreover, the arguments deemed to be relevant in attacking the prescription that probability be maximized come from roughly the same sources. Acceptance procedures are to be evaluated in the light of their conformity with presystematic precedent, on the one hand, and with reference to the ends of scientific inquiry on the other.

[3] Popper, *The Logic of Scientific Discovery*, p. 399.

The difficulty with Popper's view, which marks it off from the approach taken here, is that he provides no theory of rational procedures for attaining objectives that can be used to show that maximizing corroboration is the best way to realize the goals of scientific inquiry (as understood by him). In the absence of such a theory, no clear grounds are available for ascertaining the relations between the ends of science as understood by Popper and the prescription that corroboration be maximized.

To appreciate the thrust of the point being made here, consider the rule that recommends maximization of probability. If the prescription is to be applied to a cognitive decision problem, involving the selection of some element of M_e generated by an ultimate partition U_e for acceptance as strongest via induction from b&e, the rule is clearly objectionable on presystematic grounds. For such a rule recommends accepting as strongest the sentence S_e—i.e., accepting only deductive consequences of the total evidence b&e.

Other counterintuitive results could doubtless be obtained from the recommendation to maximize probability. But without some theory by which to relate inductive acceptance rules to objectives, no comment can be made about the ramifications for scientific objectives of the prescription under consideration.

On the other hand, suppose it is assumed (as has been done here) that acceptance procedures are consequences of the use of Bayes' rule in cognitive decision problems. The derivation requires representation of the cognitive objective by an epistemic utility function. Some understanding of the ramifications of the prescription to maximize probability can be gained by determining the sorts of utility functions that (together with Bayes' rule) support that prescription; for $p(H,e)$ will have to be equal to the expected epistemic utility of accepting H as strongest, no matter what the probability distribution over the elements of the ultimate partition happens to be. It can be shown that only one system of utility values satisfies this requirement—to wit, one in which correct answers receive utility 1 and errors utility 0. (Of course, any linear transformation of this utility function will do equally well. What is strictly true of all permitted numerical assignments is that correct answers bear equal utility [as do errors], and correct answers are preferred to errors.)

Thus, on the assumption that Bayes' rule is legitimate, the prescription that probability be maximized involves a conception of science as having as its objective "seeking the truth and nothing but the truth." The objections leveled on presystematic grounds, therefore, constitute a basis for concluding that the aims of scientific inquiry involve desiderata other than truth.

The charge being brought against Popper is not that he refuses to use Bayes' rule. Some other criterion for rational decision-making could conceivably be better (although, since Popper makes free use of logical probabilities, he would seem to have no strong reason against adopting Bayes' rule). The trouble is that he has no decision theory. As a consequence, his observations about the relations between ends of inquiry and corroboration remain disconnected. And, in particular, he is not able to show in any illuminating way what conception of the ends of inquiry is ruled out when probability maximization is abandoned.

These remarks apply *mutatis mutandis* to Popper's own prescription that corroboration be maximized, where corroboration is measured by one of a family of functions on sentences considered by him.[4] Popper has some well-known views regarding the ends of inquiry. And he apparently thinks that maximizing corroboration is the best way to attain these ends. But again Popper fails to provide any sort of decision theory that is capable of showing why maximizing corroboration is the best procedure for reaching conclusions when one is attempting to gain scientific objectives. His case for the measures of corroboration he proposes is based on the consideration of certain conditions of adequacy which—so he maintains—capture certain presystematic precedents.[5]

Now even if Popper were right in his conception of the ends of scientific inquiry (this conception will be considered later) and even if he had succeeded (contrary, I think, to fact) in showing that reaching conclusions via the policy of maximizing corroboration conformed to presystematic precedent, he would still have failed to show that his conception of the ends of inquiry was consonant with the alleged adequacy of the acceptance rule that recommends maximizing corroboration.

In the subsequent discussion, "corroboration" will refer to a function on relevant answers such that an inductive acceptance

[4] *Ibid.*, pp. 395–419.
[5] *Ibid.*, pp. 400–401.

procedure requires that a relevant answer be accepted as strongest, only if its corroboration relative to the evidence is no less than that for any other relevant answer. Given the commitment to a Bayesian decision theory made in this book, corroboration is to be equated with expected epistemic utility.

Corroboration, therefore, is a function of two factors: probability and epistemic utility. The latter characterizes the cognitive objective and in that way provides the basis for relating an acceptance procedure with a cognitive objective. Since there may well be several distinct kinds of cognitive objectives that are appropriate to different kinds of scientific inquiry, it is possible that (even on the level of idealization employed) no single measure of corroboration will do justice to the acceptance procedures that are found in various kinds of scientific inquiry. In any event, when corroboration is understood in this way, proposed measures of corroboration and the acceptance procedures associated with them are related in a fairly definite way to conceptions of the aims of science.

On this interpretation, Popper's thesis that corroboration is not a probability does acquire philosophical significance. The prescription to maximize probability in fixing beliefs precludes accepting any conclusion unless it is entailed by the evidence. And this policy, as has already been indicated, reflects a commitment to seek the truth and nothing but the truth. Skeptics may care for truth alone; scientists qua scientists have other interests as well.

2] *Objectives and Desiderata*

If it is not only the truth that scientists seek, what is the objective of their inquiries? The question is, strictly speaking, complex in that it presupposes that scientific inquiry has a single institutional objective. But even if it is conceded that different kinds of inquiries that are important in science have different kinds of objectives, one can still ask for some characterization of each of the important kinds of cognitive objectives and the kinds of inquiries that they control.

In this discussion, only one objective has been considered: replacing agnosticism by true belief. But brief reflection on this objective indicates that, even though "the truth and nothing but the truth" is not a suitable description for the goal of any important scientific inquiry, truth plays an important role in some kinds of investigations. Truth may not be an objective of inquiry, but it is a desideratum ingredient in some scientific objectives. For example, just as a president of the United States might form policy with the aim of accommodating several often sharply conflicting interests, so efforts to replace agnosticism by true belief are attempts to satisfy two different sorts of demands—one of which is the demand for truth.

Insofar as cognitive objectives that are important in inquiry do have this characteristic—namely, that of accommodating several cognitive interests—representation of such objectives via utility functions will mask philosophically important features of these objectives. What is wanted is some indication of how the utility function is determined by the separate contributions of the various desiderata ingredient in the objective. Thus, in constructing the utility function for replacing agnosticism by true belief, the most interesting and important features of the analysis dealt with the way in which relief from agnosticism (as measured by content) and truth contributed to determination of that utility function.

3] *A Principle of Combination*

The Bayesian decision theory that has been tentatively adopted in this discussion has allowed for interpretation of corroboration measures as measures of expected epistemic utility. In this way, it becomes possible to isolate the probability and utility components in measures of corroboration.

In the case of complex objectives—in particular, complex cognitive objectives—it is equally desirable to have some principle of combination that indicates how the utilities that represent different desiderata are combined to determine a utility function that represents the objective. Such a principle of combination will now be introduced. No strong argument can be offered in its favor except that it is mathematically tractable and that the utility function for replacing agnosticism by true belief, derived from two desiderata of truth and relief from agnosticism, conforms to it. The only reason for commitment to a specific rule here, however, is to permit certain general comments about cognitive objectives that are important in science, should there be others besides replacing agnosticism by true belief. If commitment to the rule vitiates these comments, it will at least have served as a starting point for further exploration of these matters.

Consider some objective to be represented by a utility function $U(H,x)$. H is taken to be some relevant answer in the set M_e generated by U_e, and the values of x are elements of U_e. $U(H,x)$ is the epistemic utility of accepting H as strongest when x is true. In cases where that utility is constant for all "states of nature" in which H bears the same truth value, the values t (for true) and f (for false) will be substituted for x.

Let the objective be broken down into n desiderata. Each of these will be taken to be represented by an epistemic utility function $D_i(H,x)$, which represents the epistemic utility of accepting H as strongest when x is true relative to desideratum D_i. It will be assumed that each of these functions has a maximum and a minimum value for the outcomes of any specific cognitive decision problem. Hence, in any such problem, the numerical values assigned to $D_i(H,x)$ can be defined so that the maximum value that $[D_i(H,x) - D_i(G,y)]$ can have will be 1.

Let $a_1, a_2, ..., a_n$ be numbers between 0 and 1, such that $\sum_{i=1}^{n} a_i = 1$. The principle of combination that is being proposed requires that $U(H,x)$ satisfy the following condition:

$$U(H,x) - U(G,y) = \sum_{i=1}^{n} a_i (D_i(H,x) - D_i(G,y))$$

Thus, differences in epistemic utilities that represent a given objective become weighted sums of differences in utilities, relative to ingredient desiderata.

The indices a_i can easily be interpreted as indicating the relative importance accorded to each of the desiderata that are ingredient in the given objective. And one can contemplate imposing constraints on the a_i's, which will limit the extent to which one desideratum can dominate or be subordinated to others.

Let $T(H,t) = 1$ and $T(H,f) = 0$. $T(H,x)$ is suitable as a utility function for the objective of seeking the truth and nothing but the truth. It also represents the utility function for truth taken as a desideratum that is ingredient in other objectives—for example, in efforts to replace agnosticism by true belief.

The other desideratum that is ingredient in that complex objective is relief from agnosticism. The utility of accepting H as strongest with respect to the desideratum of relief from agnosticism can be conveniently represented by $\text{cont}(H,e)$.

According to the rule laid down, the epistemic utility function for replacing agnosticism by true belief $V(H,x)$ can be represented as follows:

$$V(H,x) - V(G,y) = (1-a)(T(H,x) - T(G,y) + a(\text{cont}(H,e) - \text{cont}(G,e))$$

where a takes values between 0 and 1.

Actually, this characterization is somewhat too permissive, for it allows the relative importance of the two desiderata to be adjusted in ways that would seem to be objectionable. If a were to take the value 1, for example, the epistemic utility function could be suitably represented by $\text{cont}(H,e)$. This would also become the corroboration measure, which has its maximum for the sentence C_e that is inconsistent with the evidence.

This case is the extreme one in which relief from agnosticism becomes the only desideratum. It represents the agent who wants answers to his questions, no matter whether they are true or false. He is the companion to the skeptic, who is interested in the truth and nothing but the truth (for whom a is therefore 0).

But not only are these two extreme cases ruled out. So too are all values of a greater than $1/2$. For all these allow some errors to be preferred to some correct answers—which intuitively runs counter to the objective of replacing agnosticism by true belief taken as an aim of serious inquiry.

As in the previous discussion, let $V(C_e,f)$—the utility of erroneously contradicting oneself—bear utility 0. It can be shown by elementary calculation that the following condition holds:

$$V(H,t) = 1 - a - a\text{cont}(H,e)$$
$$V(H,f) = \quad\quad -a\text{cont}(-H,e)$$

Consider some definite pair of values a and a' within the range between 0 and $1/2$. The utility functions obtained with their aid are essentially distinct—i.e., they are not linear transformations of one another. Now let $q = a/(1-a)$ and $q' = a'/(1-a')$. The utility function obtained by dividing V(H,x) (determined by a) by $(1-a)$ can be represented as follows:

$$Z(H,t) = 1-qcont(-H,e)$$
$$Z(H,f) = -qcont(-H,e)$$

where q bears some value between 0 and 1.

Similarly the utility function obtained by dividing V'(H,x) (determined by a') by $(1-a')$ can be represented by

$$Z'(H,t) = 1-q'cont(-H,e)$$
$$Z'(H,f) = -q'cont(-H,e)$$

where q' bears some value other than q between 0 and 1.

Z(H,x) and Z'(H,x) are essentially distinct, but Z(H,x) is essentially similar to V(H,x), and Z'(H,x) is essentially similar to V'(H,x). Thus, the family of epistemic utility functions that was obtained by a somewhat different route in the earlier discussion proves to be essentially similar to the one just obtained, in terms of the principle of combination here proposed.

4] *Testability or Falsifiability*

Throughout this discussion it has been taken for granted that cognitive objectives other than replacing agnosticism by true belief may prove of importance in scientific inquiry. This possibility is warranted by the oft-cited importance of explanatory power, simplicity and other factors in choosing between theories.

However, one desideratum would appear to be ingredient in all objectives that are central to scientific inquiry—to wit, truth. And in addition the weight given to truth as compared to other desiderata would appear to be such that false answers are never preferred (epistemically) to true ones—i.e., if the linear principle of combination described in the last section is employed, the weight accorded to T(H,x) should not be less than 1/2.

The *prima facie* plausibility of this view notwithstanding, many authors have adopted positions that seem to run counter to it. Most notable among these writers is Karl Popper. As has been said, Popper is committed to denying that truth is the only desideratum in scientific inquiry. But, at least on some occasions, he seems to deny that truth is a desideratum at all. The "seems" is important here; for often he explicitly states that inquiry is engaged in a "quest" for truth.

Consider the closing paragraphs of *The Logic of Scientific Discovery*:

> With the idol of certainty (including that of degrees of imperfect certainty or probability) there falls one of the defences of obscurantism which bars the way of scientific advance, checking the boldness of our questions, and endangering the rigour and integrity of our tests. The wrong view of science betrays itself in the craving to be right; for it is not his *possession* of knowledge, of irrefutable truth, that makes the man of science, but his persistent and recklessly critical *quest* for truth.
>
> Has our attitude, then, to be one of resignation? Have we to say that science can fulfil only its biological task; that it can, at best merely prove its mettle in practical applications which may corroborate it? Are its intellectual problems insoluble? I do not think so. Science never pursues the illusory aim of making its answers final, or even probable. Its advance is, rather, towards the infinite yet attainable aim of ever discovering new, deeper, and more general problems, and of subjecting its ever tentative answers to ever renewed and ever more rigourous tests.[6]

Popper is, of course, quite right in tearing down the idol of infallible knowledge, and he is in agreement with the view taken here when he says that the scientist is marked by his quest for truth. But in the second of the two paragraphs quoted, the quest for truth somehow drops out of sight and the aim of science is declared to be that "of ever discovering new, deeper, and more general problems, and of subjecting its ever tentative answers to ever renewed and ever more rigourous tests." It is this description of the objectives of inquiry that is associated with his well-known ideas about falsifiability and content.

According to Popper, the content of a hypothesis increases with its falsifiability;[7] it is falsifiability that is the mark of scientific value. Why? Because highly falsifiable hypotheses are susceptible to critical scrutiny with the aid of empirical tests, and, to repeat, the aim of science is to discover "deeper, and more general problems," and to subject "its ever tentative answers to ever renewed and more rigourous tests."

[6] *Ibid.*, pp. 280–281.
[7] *Ibid.*, p. 113.

Although it is far from obvious that the two desiderata cited here (fecundity in problem-raising and testing) are to be conflated, as Popper seems to do, they do have one feature in common —namely, that accepting false answers will often serve as well as accepting true ones for attaining these ends. Hypotheses that are false but are highly amenable to rigorous testing are abundantly available. What is more, hypotheses that are false but survive rigorous testing are also far from lacking.

To suggest, therefore, that hypotheses are selected in science *in order to* raise problems or to subject them to rigorous testing seems to be quite different from maintaining that scientists accept hypotheses in a "quest for truth."

Popper's claim that fecundity in problem-raising is a desideratum in scientific inquiry is difficult to take seriously. Inquiry begins in wonder; is that wonder how to end in wonder? Of course, the resolution of one problem often occasions another. But if the purpose of inquiry, in terms of which the success of its results is to be evaluated, is what Popper says it is, it might be better not to begin inquiring at all.

In any event, the number, variety, generality, and depth of problems engendered at the termination of any one inquiry would seem to depend largely on the idiosyncrasies of the investigator. No clear reason can be offered why the conclusions of one inquiry ought to raise new problems, except for those cases in which these conclusions conflict with previous views or new data. If they conflict with previous opinions, that fact is surely not in itself a mark in favor of the new conclusions. Nor can the discovery of new data that conflict with these conclusions count as a virtue at the termination of inquiry. And, above all, conflict of the sort under consideration presents problems precisely because it is clear from the context that some view that is being maintained must be false. Unless truth were a desideratum, there would be no problem; if it is a desideratum, then conflict that is due to inconsistency cannot be one.

Perhaps, however, it is unfair to take Popper's words too literally. He does, after all, provide another account of the aim of inquiry—to wit, to subject "its ever tentative answers to ever renewed and ever more rigourous tests." Highly falsifiable hypotheses (which, therefore, bear high content) are allegedly susceptible to more rigorous testing than those that verge on vacuity.

But this reading of Popper is no better than the previous one. In effect, he is saying that the purpose of inquiry is to nurse its doubt to keep it warm. Why should one want to subject to new tests conclusions that have already been reached, unless one continues to harbor doubts as to the truth of these conclusions? Fallibilism concedes that the conclusions of inquiry are always open to further tests. But it does not follow from this that they are reached in order to be subjected to further tests.[8]

Nonetheless, there is an important truth to be found in Popper's remarks about testing as an aim of scientific inquiry.[9] Throughout this essay, the investigator under consideration has been taken to be an ideally situated one who, among other things, is capable of specifying what are to count as relevant answers to his question, and is able to ascertain their probabilities relative to his evidence.

Leaving aside the problem of assigning precise numerical probabilities to hypotheses, in many cases of prediction, estimation, and generalization it is not excessively difficult to spell out a suitable ultimate partition that will determine relevant answers, and at least to make qualitative judgments about the probabilities provided these hypotheses by the evidence.

But when it comes to choosing among theories, the situation is quite different. One of the most difficult problems facing scientific inquiry is the specification of those theories that are to count as relevant answers to the questions raised, and the articulation of these theories in sufficient detail, so as to render them susceptible to confrontation by the evidence. Rarely, if ever, is a set of theories presented that can be viewed as exclusive and exhaustive relative to the evidence. Many hypotheses that could legitimately count as relevant answers are left out of consideration because of failure to think of them, or because the development of these hypotheses, in detail that is sufficiently rich to allow them to be subjected to empirical scrutiny, would require considerable intellectual labor. For these and, perhaps, other reasons, when issues are raised

---

[8] Although it is true that any empirical judgment is, in principle, open to revision, it is also true that on some occasions there is no point in carrying on inquiry further, in order to ascertain whether revision is needed. Some extremely sketchy and tentative comments regarding the occasions when it is and is not appropriate to continue the search for new evidence will be made in Chapter IX.

[9] These observations were suggested in remarks made to me by Sidney Morgenbesser.

over which theory to adopt, the alternatives amount to two or three fairly well-articulated hypotheses, which are far from exhaustive and are made exhaustive only by adding a residual hypothesis that asserts some other unspecified alternative to be true.

A plausible way in which to assimilate this type of situation into the scheme proposed here for representing relevant answers is to view the scientist as incorporating into his total evidence the assumption that the residual hypothesis is false, thereby converting into an ultimate partition the alternative hypotheses that have been articulated. No matter how a theory of rational acceptance as evidence turns out, it is doubtful that rejection of the residual hypothesis could be legitimately viewed as evidential. The strategy of taking it as such might be excused, for reasons just indicated; but it is fair to say that such an excuse imposes an obligation on a scientific investigator to be alert to ways of creating viable new alternatives to them in his ultimate partitions, and thus rendering them susceptible to empirical test.

Thus, in a certain sense, testability is a major desideratum of scientific inquiry; for, if a hypothesis is testable, then it will be included in the set of relevant answers. Popper's account of the aims of scientific inquiry gains in plausibility when such inquiry is concerned with increasing the supply of well-articulated relevant answers. What Popper fails to note is that providing relevant answers is quite a different enterprise from choosing among relevant answers.

Now it is clear that, when one provides a list of relevant answers and renders them susceptible to empirical criticism, truth is not an immediate desideratum, except insofar as hypotheses inconsistent with the evidence are ruled out automatically. In a broad sense, therefore, the assertion that all cognitive objectives of scientific inquiry involve truth as a desideratum has to be qualified.

What does remain true, however, is that those cognitive objectives in which relevant answers are specified and the options are cases of accepting relevant answers and their deductive consequences as true have truth as one of their desiderata. Moreover, since there would be no point in providing lists of relevant answers if, upon there being a supply, no effort was to be made to choose between them, in at least one sense the cognitive objectives described by Popper are subsidiary to those that have truth as an ingredient desideratum.

5] *Other Desiderata*

Returning once more to consideration of cognitive objectives in situations where the options are accepting sentences (sets of sentences) as true, agreement with Popper has already been registered regarding the fact that truth is not the only desideratum of scientific objectives. And in the kind of objective characterized here as replacing agnosticism by true belief, content plays, as it does for Popper, an important role.

But in contrast with Popper, who associates the importance of content with a concern to raise further problems and to conduct ever more rigorous tests, in this discussion content is an index of the relief from agnosticism that is afforded by accepting a sentence as strongest via induction. Highly informative conclusions are desirable because they settle questions, not because they introduce new ones. To be sure, they are more vulnerable to error than more vacuous conclusions. But they are not prized for that reason. Indeed, were the aim of science to reach conclusions utterly vulnerable to error, the best policy would be conscious self-contradiction.

Highly informative conclusions are indeed highly vulnerable to error, but that fact is of importance only because truth is a desideratum of inquiry. Given this interest in truth, vulnerability to error is a defect, not a virtue, of highly informative answers; it is compensated for only by the fact that such answers are highly informative.

Note should be taken of an important difference between truth as a desideratum and relief from agnosticism. In accepting H as strongest via induction, the investigator cannot deduce from his evidence whether his conclusion is true or false. Whether he obtains a correct answer or commits an error depends on which element of his ultimate partition is true. In the case of relief from agnosticism, however, the degree of agnosticism that is afforded by accepting H as strongest is independent of the state of nature.

If there are any central objectives of inquiry other than re-placing agnosticism by true belief, truth, as has already been maintained, is one of the desiderata. But, as has also been con-tended, truth is not the only one. It does not seem far-fetched to suppose that the additional desiderata resemble relief from agnosticism in at least one respect: the epistemic utility function determined by any such desideratum assigns the same utility to accepting H as strongest, no matter what the state of nature happens to be.

6] *Simplicity*

Support for the conjecture just made should come from a closer examination of objectives of scientific inquiry (if there are any) other than replacing agnosticism by true belief. However, brief reflection on factors that could plausibly be held to be desiderata in inquiry suggests that the claim is correct.

For example, simplicity in the various interpretations of this notion is obtained by accepting a theory or law, no matter what the truth value of the hypothesis happens to be. On the assump-tion that simplicity is distinct from content, it is not far-fetched to suppose that simplicity is a desideratum in cases where the problem is to choose among theories or laws or in questions that pertain to curve-fitting.

Actually, in the case of simplicity, the interesting feature is not the independence of the simplicity of a hypothesis from its truth value, but the assumption that simplicity is a desideratum of certain kinds of scientific inquiry (where "desideratum" is under-stood in the special sense introduced here). To appreciate this, consider the following remarks by Quine:

The deliberate scientist goes on in essentially the same way, if more adroitly; and a law of least action remains prominent among his guid-ing principles. Working standards of simplicity, however difficult still of formulation, figure ever more explicitly. It is part of the scientist's busi-ness to generalize or extrapolate from sample data, and so to arrive at laws covering more phenomena than have been checked; and simplicity, by his lights, is just what guides his extrapolation. Simplicity is of the essence of statistical inference. If his data are represented by points on a graph, and his law is to be represented by a curve through the points, he draws the smoothest, simplest such curve he can. He even forces the points a little bit to make it simpler, pleading inaccuracy of measurement. If he can get a still simpler curve by omitting a few of the plotted points altogether, he tries to account for them separately.

Simplicity is not a desideratum on a par with conformity to observation. Observation serves to test hypotheses after adoption; simplicity prompts their adoption for testing. Still, decisive observation is commonly long delayed or impossible; and, insofar at least, simplicity is final arbiter.[1]

Quine, at one point, suggests that simplicity "prompts" the adoption of hypotheses "for testing." Were this the role of simplicity in scientific inquiry, then, as was noted in connection with Popper, simplicity would be a desideratum in selecting hypotheses for further articulation, in order to incorporate them in the list of relevant answers; but this would not account for the contribution of these same hypotheses to choices among relevant answers.

Quine does, however, also assign simplicity a place in the latter context when he says that if "decisive observation" is lacking, "simplicity becomes the final arbiter."

Recall that for Quine there cannot be, in the final analysis, any decisive observation, except insofar as a choice between entire theories cum conceptual schemes is contemplated. On the other hand, as Quine himself recognizes, no scientific inquiry is confronted with such global choices. Large areas of the conceptual and theoretical scene are held fixed (in the language of this book "accepted as evidence"), and only relatively local regions are subject to critical scrutiny. Presumably, by "decisive observation" in this context, Quine means observation that, together with the fixed portion of the conceptual and theoretical scheme, is inconsistent with some of the relevant answers under consideration. And it is in those frequent cases in which the evidence is not decisive in this sense that he holds simplicity to be "final arbiter."

Such situations are, of course, precisely those in which some sort of inductive inference is wanted; in these cases, Quine is suggesting that the appropriate policy is to maximize simplicity. In other words, simplicity is the measure of corroboration, in the broad sense used here.

Keep in mind, however, that the simplicity of a hypothesis is

[1] W. V. Quine, *Word and Object* (New York: Wiley, 1960), pp. 19–20.

independent of its truth value. What is more, it is independent of its probability. At any rate, this is true of the notions of simplicity that seem to be involved in the curve-fitting illustrations cited by Quine. Hence, if the acceptance procedure followed is maximization of simplicity, the epistemic utility function used must assign a constant epistemic utility to all outcomes of accepting a relevant answer H as strongest—namely, a utility equal to the simplicity of H. For only via such a procedure could the expected epistemic utility of accepting H as strongest equal the simplicity of H.

In other words, Quine's prescription reflects a point of view according to which the choice of a hypothesis, from a list of alternatives all of which are consistent with the evidence (including those portions of the conceptual scheme and theoretical framework that are not under critical scrutiny), does not take into consideration the truth values of the alternatives. It does not matter whether a hypothesis is true or false, as long as it is consistent with the evidence—and simple.

This point has been clothed in Bayesian dress; even when stripped, however, it does not disappear. Preference for simplicity in choice among conclusions consistent with the evidence does exhibit an indifference to truth value, as long as simplicity is not made to depend in some way on truth or probability. This point has been more or less explicitly recognized by several authors, who have introduced some postulate about the simplicity of nature to accompany its uniformity. "Simplicity," writes Hermann Weyl, "is considered *sigillum veri*."[2]

But the classical problem of induction has already been loaded down with more freight than it can bear. If possible, it would be desirable to relieve it of the burden of defending a postulate of simplicity. And this can be readily done. What is required is rejection of the view that simplicity is the only desideratum in inquiries in which simplicity is a relevant consideration. If truth is also recognized as a desideratum ingredient in the appropriate objective, there is no need to suppose that simple hypotheses are true or are most likely to be true. In curve-fitting, for example, the objective could be viewed as specifying a functional lawlike hypothesis that is both true and simple. Simplicity would play the same role in this situation as content does in efforts to replace

[2] H. Weyl, *Philosophy of Mathematics and Natural Science* (Princeton: Princeton University Press, 1949), p. 155.

agnosticism by true belief—namely, that of providing the inducement to run the risk of error.

One consequence of this approach is that the resulting acceptance rule would no longer recommend maximizing simplicity. The expected epistemic utility would be a function of the utility of truth, the utility of simplicity and the probability distribution over the states of nature.

To be sure, there would be one kind of situation in which simplicity could still be taken to be, as Quine says, "final arbiter"—namely, when the probabilities of the hypotheses involved were equal but their simplicity values were not. In real life, where probability judgments are, like comparisons about simplicity, much less precise than the discussion here supposes, cases in which simplicity does appear to be decisive can be construed without any great wrench in presystematic intuitions as situations in which the probabilities are roughly equal. Consequently, the approach adopted here cannot be held to run afoul in any obvious way of presystematic precedent, and it does provide a method for recognizing the relevance of both truth and simplicity to the assessment of inferences.

Needless to say, the relevance of simplicity to inference deserves more attention than has been devoted to it here. Not only should something be said about the various interpretations of this notion that are extant, but some consideration should be given to differences in the sorts of problems that are appropriately characterized as efforts to replace agnosticism by true belief and those in which truth and simplicity are desiderata. (Note that it remains an open question as to whether simplicity is reducible to relief from agnosticism or is some sort of generalization of that notion.) The point of this discussion was to illustrate some of the ramifications of the assumption made in the previous section, to the effect that, no matter what the cognitive objectives are that happen to be central in scientific inquiry, the desiderata other than truth that are ingredient in these objectives determine utilities whose values do not depend upon the truth values of the relevant answers.

7] *Causal vs. Noncausal Consequences*

The cognitive options in all the decision problems under consideration have been represented as cases of accepting a relevant answer H as strongest via induction from the total evidence. And with regard to efforts to replace agnosticism by true belief, outcomes have been described as cases of accepting H as strongest correctly (or incorrectly) if they relieve agnosticism to a certain degree.

The first point to note about the descriptions of the outcomes is that they are redescriptions of the cognitive options. Accepting H as strongest and accepting it as strongest correctly are not distinct conditions or processes, but the same conditions, described in different ways. Similarly, accepting H as strongest, and so accepting it while being relieved from agnosticism to a given degree, are identical conditions.

This point leads immediately to a second. Since the outcome of a cognitive option is the exercise of that option, the outcome is not related to the exercise of the option as cause to effect—unless one is willing to take seriously the notion of self-causation.

This circumstance is not peculiar to cognitive acts. To use an illustration of Donald Davidson's,[3] flipping a light switch and turning on a light may be the same act described in different ways; clearly, however, the one is not an effect of the other.

Observe, however, that the description of an act of flipping a light switch as turning on a light is a description that does make reference to the effects of the act. This does not hold true of cognitive options and outcomes. When accepting H as strongest is redescribed as accepting H correctly as strongest, no reference is made to effects of the cognitive act. And in spite of the fact that the locution "relief from agnosticism," when it is used to describe the outcome of a cognitive option, seems to make reference to the effects of accepting H as strongest, the way this expression has been interpreted in this discussion should make plain that the causal implication is entirely rhetorical. The relief from agnosti-

---

[3] D. Davidson, "Actions, Reasons and Causes," *Journal of Philosophy,* 60 (1963), 686.

cism that is afforded by accepting H as strongest is not some psychological effect of such acceptance, but an evaluation of what that effect ought rationally to be.

If these remarks can be generalized for all cognitive decision problems in which the task is to select a sentence from a set of relevant answers, then the claim can be made that the causal consequences of belief (presumably beliefs do have such consequences) are irrelevant to the attainment of cognitive objectives. Although a similar observation might also be true of some noncognitive decision problems, it is not typical in such cases. Hence, this feature of cognitive decision problems is one mark that separates these problems from those to which some behavioralists attempt to reduce them.

8] *Risk*

The fact that the relevant outcomes of cognitive decisions are not effects of these decisions does not imply that such decisions involve no risk. Although obtaining a false answer is not a causal consequence of obtaining an answer, one canot deduce from the fact that a given answer is accepted plus the total evidence that it is false.

If the account of cognitive objectives offered here is at all plausible, the risky character of cognitive decision problems is due to the fact that all cognitive objectives that are central to inquiry have truth as an ingredient desideratum. If content, simplicity, and so on were the only desiderata, the relevant outcomes of the several options could be deduced from adopting these options, together with the evidence.

It is of some interest to note, however, that if truth were the only desideratum, the risky character of cognitive decision problems would also disappear; for one can always be ensured of a correct answer relative to the total evidence by accepting only the deductive consequences of the evidence.

Thus, for any philosopher who is committed to the view that in scientific inquiry there is warrant for risking error, the view adopted here—that, no matter what the objectives of inquiry might be, truth is one but not the only desideratum—does seem to provide some backing for this empiricist assumption. Without

truth as a desideratum, the risk of error is unimportant. Without
other desiderata, however, no one would be justified in risking
error.

9] *Conclusion*

The observations made in this chapter are intended as specula-
tions about those features of the model for replacing agnosticism
by true beliefs that might prove typical of other cognitive objectives of importance in scientific inquiry. Allowing for the extreme
idealization that infects the entire discussion, it is to be hoped
that enough has been said to suggest the value, for purposes of
analysis, of adopting a decision-theoretic approach to scientific
inference. If we provide a framework in terms of which criteria
for valid inference can be related to the goals of inquiry, possibilities are opened up for interrelating notions of probability, simplicity, content, explanation, and other concepts whose analysis
has been of concern to philosophers of science, in a way whose
adequacy is controlled not only by presystematic judgments but
also by the manner in which these notions contribute to the understanding of the aims of scientific inquiry and function as canons
for evaluating scientific inferences.

In the subsequent discussion, no further remarks will be
directed to the analysis of cognitive objectives in general. Instead,
some ramifications of the model for replacing agnosticism by true
belief will be studied, when this model is taken as characterizing
problems of inductive prediction, estimation and generalization.
The larger program envisaged in the previous comments will be
left for a more appropriate occasion.

VIII

Probabilities and Degrees of Belief

1] *Subjective Probabilities as Degrees of Rational Belief*

According to the critical cognitivist view adopted in this book, men are often interested in resolving doubts in the sense that they wish to accept or reject hypotheses when they are warranted in doing so. The notion of belief or acceptance involved here is taken to be a qualitative one. Relative to conditions K (which according to Rule (A) involve total evidence, an ultimate partition and a degree of caution), a rational investigator either believes that P, believes that not P, or is agnostic regarding P. Belief is not a matter of degree any more than striking a match is.

Yet it must be admitted that, in presystematic discourse, different degrees of belief are recognized. Two political forecasters may agree that candidate X will win but one of them will be less confident than the other. One may be strongly convinced that there will not be a violent revolution in the United States in the next ten years, but only inclined to believe that there will be no such revolution in France.

Given that the notion of degree of belief does make sense, why, it may be asked, should much importance be attached to the notion of belief taken in a qualitative sense? Greater precision is obtained by replacing locutions such as "tall" and "short" by "taller than," and still greater precision as the result of the numerical measurement of height. Why not replace "A believes that P" by "A believes that P to degree k" if it is possible to provide some account of degrees of belief?

Considerations such as this provide an opening wedge for attempts to replace the qualitative notion of belief by a notion of degree of belief explicated as degree of subjective probability. Such an approach has, or seems to have, several advantages. Not only is there a formal theory of probability available for use in such explication, but subjective probabilities are supposed to be indices of the risks that rational agents are prepared to take in decision-making. Replacement of "belief" in the qualitative sense by "degree of belief" understood as interchangeable with "degree of subjective probability" provides a means for relating rational belief with rational action in a fairly straightforward manner. Given a certain system of values, goals, etc., an agent's beliefs may not determine what he ought to do but his degrees of belief— i.e., his subjective probabilities—will (at least ideally) do so.

Reasoning very much like this seems to underlie the widespread tendency among advocates of subjective or logical probability to take probability as a measure of degrees of belief. On this view, "belief" in the qualitative sense is regarded as a vague notion, better replaced by some variant of subjective probability that can be used to provide a more precise description of opinions.

If we ignore, for the moment, the problems involved in applying theories of subjective probability in real life, it remains far from clear that even perfected measures of subjective probability provide an adequate surrogate for the notion of belief.

Note, first, that in presystematic discourse, the notion of degree of belief is usually not regarded as being a more precise surrogate of the notion of belief; instead, it is related to belief in much the same way that "has length" is related to "is k units long." To have a positive length requires as a necessary precondition having a length. Similarly to believe that P to a positive degree (to believe positively that P) requires as a necessary and sufficient condition the belief that P. A man who declared that he believed to a positive degree that Lyndon Johnson would be elected President in 1964 but said that he was agnostic as to Johnson's prospects in 1964 would have to be accused either of a misuse of language or of an irrational system of opinions. If Jones is highly confident that Johnson will be elected, and Smith is inclined to that same belief but with less confidence, they nevertheless both believe that Johnson will be elected; one is simply less certain of that than the other is.

These considerations suggest the following conditions of adequacy for analyses of degrees of belief:

(i) A believes that P to a positive degree only if A believes that P.

(ii) A disbelieves that P to a positive degree only if A disbelieves that P (believes that −P).

(iii) A is agnostic regarding P if and only if he believes that P to a 0 degree and believes that −P to a 0 degree.

The only way in which subjective probability can replace degree of belief in a manner that satisfies these conditions is to partition the probability range from 0 to 1 into three intervals: one consists of values greater than k, the second consists of values less than m (m ≦ k), and there is an intermediate interval. But no matter how k and m are selected, they will still run afoul of the deductive cogency requirements. If a probability greater than k is necessary and sufficient for a positive degree of belief, then it is necessary and sufficient for belief. In effect, a specification of values for k and m (presumably m = 1−k) would amount to an inductive acceptance rule that required a high probability for acceptance as a necessary and sufficient condition. However, as has already been noted, if deductive cogency is to be preserved, acceptance rules of this sort will not prove satisfactory.

Appeal can be made to other intuitions in order to support rejection of attempted reductions of degree of belief to subjective probability. Consider once more the forecaster Smith, who is interested in finding out whether candidate X, Y or Z will win. He may believe that X will not win, to a positive degree and that Y will not win, to a positive degree. If degrees of belief were probabilities, he would be obliged to believe that neither X nor Y will win to a lower degree than he believes either of the conjuncts. Indeed, he might not believe it at all. Yet surely he should believe that neither X nor Y will win to no lower a degree than the degree of belief he accords to the conjunct that bears minimum belief. In other words, degrees of belief seem to obey the following rule of conjunction:

   (iv) degree of belief that H&G = min(degree of belief that H, degree of belief that G).

These considerations suggest, if they do not prove, the following two assertions:

   (a) "Belief that P" cannot be defined as a subjective probability assignment greater than some value k.
   (b) There is at least one notion of "degree of belief" in presystematic discourse according to which degrees of belief are not subjective probabilities.

The second point might be taken to be a terminological matter of slight importance—which would be true if degrees of belief in the non-probabilistic sense were of no significance to scientific inference. In the remainder of this chapter, an attempt will be made to construct a systematic account of degrees of belief. This reconstruction will be used in subsequent developments to show that, by assimilating degrees of belief to subjective probabilities, writers on inductive inference have neglected a concept that does have at least some importance for their concerns.

In order, however, to bypass idle disputes about ordinary usage regarding "degree of belief" (by now probability theorists have made their usage the ordinary one in many contexts), positive degrees of belief will be called "degrees of confidence with which sentences are accepted" and positive degrees of disbelief "degrees of confidence with which sentences are rejected."

2] *Confidence and Acceptance*

As was observed in the previous section, accepting H as true is a necessary and sufficient condition for positively believing H, or for accepting H with a positive degree of confidence. Similarly, rejecting H is a necessary and sufficient condition for disbelieving H with a positive degree of confidence. When an investigator is agnostic regarding H, the degree of confidence of both acceptance and rejection is equal to 0. This implies that rational confidence assignments must conform with requirements for rational acceptance. Hence, an explication of the notion of rational degrees of confidence must be relativized to criteria for rational acceptance and rejection.

In subsequent developments, rule (A) will be used for this purpose. However, at the outset, degrees of confidence will be relativized to some rule (X), which possesses features of rule (A) that rule (A) shares in common with a variety of other rules that might be proposed. In this way, we will make clear the extent to which the theory of degrees of confidence can be divorced from the model for replacing agnosticism by true belief and the extent to which it depends on that model.

3] *Confidence and Caution*

As of May, 1966, I believe that Barry Goldwater will not receive the Republican nomination for President in 1968. I also believe that Richard Nixon will fail to receive that nomination. Yet, I believe the former much more confidently than I believe the latter.

In addition, I believe that neither Goldwater nor Nixon will receive the nomination; I believe (or should rationally believe) that hypothesis to the same degree that I believe that Nixon will not receive the nomination.

These three beliefs and the degrees of confidence accorded to them seem quite sensible to me, given the evidence at my disposal. How are the degrees of confidence to be understood?

Note first that the differences in the degrees of confidence cannot reflect the risks I would be willing to take in acting as if these beliefs were true. If this account were plausible, then I could not reasonably accord equal confidence to "Neither Goldwater nor Nixon will receive the nomination" and "Nixon will not receive the nomination."

How, then, are differences in degrees of confidence to be characterized? Let us say that I believe much more strongly (in May, 1966) that Goldwater will not be nominated than that Nixon will not, even though I believe that neither of these candidates will be the Republican nominee. The difference between my two beliefs is that I recognize that, were I more cautious than I actually am, I could continue to believe that Goldwater will not be nominated but would no longer be able to believe the same thing about Nixon.

Different positive degrees of confidence of acceptance reflect differences in the increase in caution required to turn an accepted sentence into a nonaccepted one (assuming that we hold the ultimate partition and the available evidence constant).

Observe that, under this interpretation of degrees of confidence, the increase in degree of caution that is required to stop disbelieving in Nixon's nomination would at the same time be sufficient to lead to cessation of belief that neither Goldwater nor Nixon will be nominated. Thus, interpreting confidence with the aid of caution, together with the assumption of deductive cogency, does seem to conform to the "rule of conjunction" for confidence of acceptance stated in Section 1.

4] *Deductive Cogency and Ultimate Partitions*

Let rule (X) be some acceptance rule to be used to generate degrees of confidence of acceptance and rejection. From the discussion of the previous section, it is clear that rule (X) must share features in common with rule (A):

(i) Rule (X) must be deductively cogent.
(ii) Rule (X) must be caution-dependent.

The notion of caution-dependence will be discussed in Section 5. Before we consider it, however, some comments on deductive cogency are in order.

As has been repeatedly observed, requirements of deductive cogency are applicable only to sentences that are accepted under given conditions. And, in this book, only rules that include among these conditions total evidence and a system of restrictions on what is to count as a relevant answer have been considered. Furthermore, discussion has been restricted thus far (and will continue to be restricted, except in connection with a few topics) to cases in which relevant answers can be delimited by means of the choice of a finite initially ultimate partition (relative to background information b) U and its truncations relative to new evidence U_e.

In the subsequent discussion, rule (X) will be relativized in application to ultimate partitions. As a consequence, the measures of degrees of confidence to be considered will be defined relative to background information b, new evidence e, and an initially ultimate partition U or its truncation U_e with respect to e.

Let b(H,U,b&e) be the degree of confidence of acceptance accorded to H relative to U and total evidence b&e; let d(H,U,b&e) be the degree of confidence of rejection of H relative to U and total evidence b&e. There will be no point, for most purposes, in making all the arguments explicit. In the subsequent discussion, only "b(H,e)" and "d(H,e)" will be used.

The fact that these measures are relativized in application to an ultimate partition indicates that there is no point in assigning b-values and d-values to sentences that are ineligible for acceptance or rejection relative to the ultimate partition chosen. However, since the investigator will (relative to the ultimate partition) be agnostic regarding their truth values, 0 d-values and b-values can be accorded to these.

The sentences that are eligible for acceptance or rejection relative to an ultimate partition and total evidence can be conveniently considered under three categories:

(a) evidence sentences—i.e., deductive consequences of b&e;
(b) elements of M_e and sentences whose equivalence with elements of M_e is deducible from b&e;
(c) sentences that are deducible from b&e, together with consistent elements of M_e, but not of type (a) or (b).

Case (a): Relative to the total evidence, all evidence must be accepted; for these are deductive consequences of b&e. Hence, they must be accepted as true if and only if S_e in M_e is accepted as true (under the assumption that b&e is accepted as evidence).

Case (b): Let G be any sentence such that there is an element H in M_e, and b&e entails that G is equivalent with H. There will be at most one such H in M_e, by virtue of the manner in which M_e is generated. Furthermore, deductive cogency requires that G be accepted if and only if H is accepted. Note that case (b) includes all sentences that are incompatible with the evidence and, hence, are equivalent with C_e, given b&e.

Case (c): Let G be deducible from each of the sentences $H_1, H_2, H_3, ..., H_n$ in M_e, together with b&e but not equivalent to any one of them, given b&e. Form the disjunction of all of these H_i's. There will be an element F in M_e whose equivalence to that disjunction is deducible from b&e. Moreover, G will be deducible from F (but not conversely). In spite of the fact that the equivalence of G and F is not deducible from b&e, given b&e as total evidence, G will be accepted relative to b&e and U_e if and only if F is so accepted. The "if" part of the assertion follows from deductive cogency. The "only if" is the result of the limitations on relevant answers imposed by the choice of an ultimate partition. Suppose that F is not accepted. Then none of the H_i's will be accepted as the consequence of deductive cogency. (Remember that each of H_i's entails G, given b&e.) But the only sentences eligible for acceptance as strongest via induction from b&e are the elements of M_e. Hence, G cannot be accepted.

These considerations suffice to show that, for each G eligible for acceptance relative to b&e and U, there is one and only one element H of M_e such that it can be shown that accepting H is a necessary and sufficient condition for accepting G, from deductive cogency requirements and relativization to an ultimate partition alone. The element of M_e that corresponds in this way to a given G eligible for acceptance will be called $M_e(G)$.

The point of introducing $M_e(G)$ at this stage is to show that b-values assigned to sentences eligible for acceptance can be defined in terms of b-values assigned to elements of M_e. For if $b(G,e)$ reflects the extent that the degree of caution would have to be lowered for fixed U_e and b&e in order for G to be no longer believed, that extent will be the same as that associated with $M_e(G)$. Deductive cogency considerations, together with relativization to an ultimate partition, have alone sufficed to show that $M_e(G)$ will be accepted if and only if G is accepted. This means that this will hold true, no matter what degree of caution is exercised.

For this reason, it seems plausible to hold that

(1) $b(G,e) = b(M_e(G),e)$

Now deductive cogency alone requires that $-H$ be rejected if and only if H is accepted. By reasoning like that above,

(2) $d(-H,e) = b(H,e)$
$\qquad\quad = b(M_e(H),e)$

Observe that the range of d-values determined in terms of b-values of elements of M_e is not the same as those for b-values. In the case of sentences of type (a) and (b), it is easy to show that their contradictories are either of type (a) or type (b) and hence that, for any such sentence H, there is not only an $M_e(H)$ but also an $M_e(-H)$. The upshot is that for sentences of types (a) and (b), the following holds true:

(3) $d(H,e) = d(M_e(H),e)$.

Proof: $d(H,e) = b(-H,e)$
$= b(M_e(-H),e)$
$= b(-M_e(H),e) = d(M_e(H),e)$

(3) does not hold true for sentences of type (c). If a sentence H is of type (c) and if it were the case (contrary to fact) that $M_e(-H)$ was defined, then from b&e one could deduce H from $M_e(H)$ and $-H$ from $M_e(-H)$. Hence, from b&e and $Hv-H$ one could deduce the equivalence of $M_e(H)$ and $-M_e(-H)$. As a consequence, one could deduce the equivalence of H and $M_e(H)$ from b&e. This would make H a type (b) sentence, counter to the assumption made here.

The upshot is that a type (c) sentence is eligible for acceptance but not rejection. On the other hand, its contradictory is eligible for rejection but not acceptance. Thus, type (c) sentences will be assigned 0 d-values and their contradictories 0 b-values relative to b&e and U_e.

The net effect of these considerations is that the d-values accorded to all sentences eligible for acceptance and the d-values assigned to all sentences eligible for rejection, as well as the contradictories of all these, are determined once b-values are assigned to elements of M_e. As was the case when we were constructing rule (A), it is possible to restrict the discussion to elements of M_e and Boolean combinations of these elements.

5] *Caution Dependence*

The features of rule (X) used to delimit the scope of the b-function and the d-function were cogency and relativization to ultimate partitions.

Let H and G be elements of M_e. The degree of confidence with which H is rejected will be greater than the degree of confidence with which G is rejected if and only if:

(I)   (i) H is rejected relative to b&e, U_e, and the degree of caution used.

(ii) If G is rejected as well, then if b&e and U_e were held fixed and the degree of caution increased, G would cease being rejected while H remains rejected.

The notion of a degree of caution introduced in connection with rule (A) was characterized as an index of the relative importance to be placed on relief from agnosticism as compared to that placed on truth. This characterization acquires significance only in connection with efforts to replace agnosticism by true belief. Observe, however, that even rules quite different from rule (A)—indeed, rules that are not probability-based—might require for their application the choice of a value for some "caution-like" parameter. This parameter might not be susceptible to interpretation in quite the same way as the q-index of rule (A) is. But the behavior of rule (X) might resemble that of rule (A), relative to the choice of the value of the cautionlike parameter. Given a deductively cogent acceptance rule (X) relativized to an ultimate partition, it is caution-dependent if it requires for its application the choice of one from a set of values of a parameter k that satisfy the following conditions:

(II)   (i) The values of k are linearly ordered.

(ii) There is a "least" value of k, $\underline{k}$ such that when $\underline{k}$ is used, rule (X) recommends accepting all and only sentences deductively entailed by b&e.

(iii) Let $k' < k$. Given b&e and U_e, the set of elements of U_e that are rejected when k' is used is a subset (proper or improper) of the set of elements of U_e rejected when k is used. That is, an increase in the k-index tends to allow stronger conclusions to be rejected.

(iv) For every *consistent* H in M_e, there is a value k' of k, $\underline{k} < k'$ such that H is unrejected when k' is used relative to b&e and U_e.

Note that the linear ordering could have been reversed, so that condition (ii) would assert the existence of a greatest value of k. Then caution would increase with values of k. The procedure followed here preserves the similarity with the q-index, which decreases with an increase in caution. $\underline{k}$ is the "skeptic's index." The q-index of rule (A) does satisfy these four conditions. In addition, it meets the following requirements.

(v) For every *consistent* H in M_e there is a maximum value k' of k, $\underline{k} < k'$ such that H is unrejected when k' is used relative to b&e and U_e.

(vi) Values of k are interval-measurable.

Condition (v) will be used in place of condition (iv). It prevents the following kind of situation from arising. From condition (iv), together with (iii) and cogency, it can be shown that there is a least upper bound to the values of k relative to which a consistent element of M_e goes unrejected. However, that least upper bound could not be, according to some rules, the maximum value of k relative to which the sentence goes unrejected. (There may be no maximum.)

Consideration of this possibility only complicates the definitions and proofs of results without adding insight. Condition (v) guarantees the existence of the maximum.

Condition (vi) is needed only when the problem of numerical measurement of confidence is introduced. The major theorems regarding confidence do not depend upon numerical measurability but only on the linear orderability of degrees of confidence. Hence, for the present, condition (vi) will be dropped, to be introduced at a later stage in the discussion.

Thus, a caution-dependent deductively cogent rule (X) will require for its application a cautionlike parameter k that satisfies conditions (i)–(v) but not (vi).

6] *Degrees of Confidence Defined*

The definitions introduced in the subsequent discussion will be restricted to elements of M_e generated by the truncation U_e of U with respect to new evidence e. Extrapolation to all sentences of types (a), (b), and (c) in Section 4 proceeds according to instructions given there.

D.1: D(H,e) = the maximum value of k such that H is unrejected when that value of k is used, provided that H is consistent with b&e.

$$D(C_e,e) = \underline{k}$$

T.1: If H is an element of M_e (or Boolean combination of such elements),

$$D(H,e) \leqq D(S_e,e)$$

Proof: Deductive cogency requires that S_e go unrejected, no matter what value of k is employed. Since S_e is consistent with b&e, $D(S_e,e)$ is defined. It must be the maximum value of k.

T.2: $D(HvG,e) = \max(D(H,e), D(G,e))$

Proof: Let $D(H,e) = k''$ and $D(G,e) = k'$ where $k'' \leqq k'$.

HvG is rejected if and only if both H and G are rejected.

By condition (iii) of (II) in Section 5, G is unrejected for all values of k less than or equal to k' and H is unrejected for all values of k less than or equal to k''.

Since $k'' \leqq k'$, if G is rejected, then H is rejected. Hence, if G is rejected, both H and G are rejected. Hence, if G is rejected, HvG is rejected.

On the other hand, if HvG is rejected, then G is rejected.

Hence, k' is the maximum value at which HvG is unrejected.

$$D(HvG,e) = k' = D(G,e) = \max(D(H,e), D(G,e)).$$

T.3: Let $H_1, H_2,...,H_n$ be elements of M_e whose disjunction G is entailed by b&e.

There is at least one H_i such that

$$D(H_i,e) = D(S_e,e)$$

Proof: Since G is equivalent to S_e given b&e,
$$D(G,e) = D(S_e,e)$$
$$D(G,e) = \max(D(H_1,e), D(H_2,e),...,D(H_n,e))$$
By application of T.2.

D.2: Let an investigator who is using rule (X) exercise a degree of caution indexed by k^*, where k^* is greater than the skeptic's value $\underline{k}$.

$d(H,e) = 0$ if and only if $D(H,e)$ is greater than or equal to k^*.

if $D(G,e) < k^*$,

$d(G,e) \lesseqgtr d(H,e)$ if and only if $D(G,e) \gtreqless D(H,e)$.

D.2 explicates the notion of a degree of caution of rejection, $d(H,e)$, that preserves the intuition that degrees of confidence of rejection increase with an increase in the degree of caution (decrease in D-value) required, before a failure to reject sets in. Degrees of confidence of acceptance can now be defined as follows:

D.3: $b(H,e) = d(-H,e)$

T.4*a*: If H is a consistent element of M_e,

$$d(H,e) < d(C_e,e).$$

T.4*b*: If H is any element of M_e other than S_e,

$$b(H,e) < b(S_e,e).$$

Proof of (*a*): $D(C_e,e) = \underline{k}$ by D.1.

If H is any consistent element of M_e,
$D(C_e,e) < D(H,e)$ by condition (v).

Hence, by D.2: $d(H,e) < d(C_e,e)$.

T.5*a*: $d(S_e,e) = 0 \leq d(H,e)$, where H is any element of M_e other than S_e.

T.5*b*: $b(C_e,e) = 0 \leq b(H,e)$, where H is any element of M_e other than C_e.

T.6*a*: $d(HvG,e) = \min(d(H,e), d(G,e))$

T.6*b*: $b(H\&G,e) = \min(b(H,e), b(G,e))$

Proof of (*a*): $D(HvG,e) = \max(D(H,e), D(G,e))$
Let $D(H,e) \leq D(G,e)$
Hence, $D(HvG,e) = D(G,e)$
$d(HvG,e) = d(G,e)$
$d(G,e) \leq d(H,e)$
$d(HvG,e) = \min(d(G,e), d(H,e))$.

T.7: Let $H_1, H_2, ..., H_n$ be elements of M_e exclusive and exhaustive relative to b&e. Let G be their disjunction.

   a: There is at least one H_i such that $d(H_i, e) = 0$

   b: There is at least one H_i such that $b(-H_i, e) = 0$

   Proof of (*a*): By T.3, there is at least one H_i such that $D(H_i, e) = D(S_e, e)$, which is greater than or equal to k^*

   Hence, $d(H_i, e) = 0$ by D.2.

Thus, a deductively cogent caution-dependent acceptance rule has been used to generate a linear ordering of degrees of confidence of rejection and of acceptance. d-values and b-values obey all the presystematic conditions mentioned earlier. Most noteworthy of these is T.6, the rule of disjunction for d-values and conjunction for b-values. Both parts of T.6 indicate quite clearly that degrees of confidence cannot be construed as degrees of subjective probability even in some comparative sense.

7] *Cardinal Confidence*

Let the deductively cogent, caution-dependent acceptance rule that satisfies (i)–(v) of (II) in Section 5 satisfy (vi) as well. In this case, values of the cautionlike parameter are interval-measurable. The function $D(H, e)$ becomes a numerical function of sentences and it is possible to consider differences in D-values. Under these circumstances, $b(H, e)$ and $d(H, e)$ can be redefined as follows:

D.4: $d(H, e) = \dfrac{k^* - D(H, e)}{k^*}$

   if $D(H, e) \leqq k^*$, otherwise 0.

D.5: $b(H, e) = d(-H, e)$

Strictly speaking, dividing by k^* is illegitimate; for interval measurability does not preclude setting $k^* = 0$. However, according to (ii), k (the skeptic's k-value) is the least k-value possible. D.4 and D.5 are to be understood to apply to all values for k^* other than $\underline{k}$ and relative to the choice of $\underline{k}$ as 0 point. Had d(H,e) been defined as the difference between k* and D(H,e), the choice of a 0 point would have been unnecessary. Only the convenience of a normalized measure that restricts d(H,e) to the interval between 0 and 1 has led to division by k*. The limitation of k* to values greater than k̲ is no restriction at all. In the case of the skeptic, there is no point in distinguishing degrees of confidence, since the only sentences that are accepted by the skeptic are deductive consequences of the evidence.

It can easily be shown that D.4 and D.5 preserve all the order properties required by D.2 and D.3 as well as the various other requirements needed to prove the theorems of the previous section. Hence, measurability does not seem to add anything new, unless degrees of confidence are defined relative to a specific acceptance rule.

8] *Potential Surprise*

The British economist, G. L. S. Shackle, has in several publications advocated the use of a measure of uncertainty in decision theory which he calls "potential surprise."[1] Many of Shackle's informal comments about this notion suggest that potential surprise is intended as a measure of what is here called "degrees of confidence of rejection."[2] And an examination of the postulates for potential surprise laid down by Shackle shows that they are reproduced in the theorems proven for d-values in the previous sections.[3]

A detailed critique of Shackle's views will be reserved for another occasion. Note should be taken, however, of two serious deficiencies in Shackle's approach. By failing to reconstruct the

---

[1] The most recent of these is G. L. S. Shackle, *Decision, Order and Time* (Cambridge: Cambridge University Press, 1961). This book contains an extensive bibliography on the notion of potential surprise.

[2] *Ibid.*, pp. 71ff.

[3] *Ibid.*, pp. 80–81, 83. All the axioms (1)–(9), except for the various versions of (7) in Shackle, are either explicit in the formulation given here or are obvious corollaries. (7) can also be proven with the aid of an appropriate definition of conditional d-values. This notion is of small importance here (and Shackle overemphasizes its importance in his own discussion). Extended treatment of it will be given in a critique of Shackle's theory, to be published later.

concept of potential surprise through relating it to acceptance rules, he provides no method by means of which an account of revisions in surprise assignments in the light of new evidence can be undertaken. To be sure, the account of d-measures presented thus far does not go much further than Shackle in this respect; neither d-values nor b-values were defined relative to a specific acceptance rule, but only relative to any acceptance rule that is cogent and caution-dependent. The reason for this approach was to emphasize the extent to which an account of degrees of confidence (potential surprise) has a life of its own and to show that the problem of formulating criteria for revising confidence (surprise) assignments in the light of new evidence can be reduced to the problem of formulating adequate inductive acceptance rules.

This leads conveniently to taking note of a second deficiency in Shackle's approach. Shackle maintains (quite rightly, according to the view adopted here) that construing degrees of belief to be degrees of probability fails to accommodate certain pre-systematic ideas regarding degrees of belief. Shackle overreaches himself, however, in viewing probability and potential surprise as competing measures of uncertainty. As a consequence, he attempts to replace probability by potential surprise in his account of decision-making.[4]

Thus, Shackle seems to rule out the possibility of providing a reconstruction of potential surprise with the aid of the notion of probability; and in doing so, he bars the possibility of using the available theories regarding revision of probability assignments in the light of new evidence for the purpose of giving an account of how surprise assignments are to be revised when the evidence changes.

Observe, however, that if deductively cogent, caution-dependent acceptance rules can be used to produce definitions of d-measures and b-measures, it is at least possible to entertain cogent and caution-dependent rules that are also probability based. To be sure, the applicability of probability-based rules in a large number of situations remains problematical, because of the extensive idealization required. However, Shackle's objections to relating surprise to probability are not along these lines. What he attempts

[4] *Ibid.*, Chapter VII.

to show is that probability values and surprise values cannot be mapped 1 to 1; for 0 surprise (0-d-values) would have to be associated with more than one probability value.

Shackle failed to consider the possibility of relating probability values in a manner which does not require a 1 to 1 correlation yet remains intuitively plausible. An obvious strategy for doing this would be to adopt rule (A) as an inductive acceptance rule and to define degrees of confidence of acceptance and rejection as follows:

D.6: $D(H,e)$ = the maximum value of the q-index of rule (A) for which H is unrejected relative to U_e and b&e. If there is no maximum, $D(H,e) = 0$.

D.7: the degree of confidence of rejection $= d(H,e) =$

$\dfrac{q^* - D(H,e)}{q^*}$, where q^* is the degree of caution actually

exercised.

D.8: $b(H,e) = d(-H,e)$

The effect of D.7 is to generate a many–one correlation of degrees of probability and degrees of confidence of rejection (degrees of potential surprise) assigned to elements of a given ultimate partition U_e and relative to a given degree of caution (where q^* must be positive).

There are, of course, other probability-based cogent and caution-dependent acceptance rules that might serve the same purpose. However, insofar as rule (A) seems appropriate for ideally situated investigators who attempt to replace agnosticism by true belief, rule (A) is the natural candidate for determining rational assignments of degrees of confidence in such cases.

The use of D.6, D.7, and D.8 to construct an account of degrees of confidence succeeds in reducing the problem of revising assignments of degrees of confidence or surprise as the result of variation in evidence to the more familiar problem of revising probability assignments in the light of new evidence. It also removes Shackle's ideas from their splendid isolation by relating them to familiar notions.

The chief question to consider in this connection is the importance of the notion of degrees of confidence or surprise.

Conceding that there is a presystematic notion of degrees of belief and disbelief that was captured by Shackle and elaborated in the account offered here, of what significance is it for an account of rational inductive inference or rational inductive behavior?

Two observations can be made by way of reply. First, when we relate degrees of caution to degrees of probability, it is not only possible to derive confidence assignments from probabilities (together with ultimate partitions and degrees of caution), but, conversely, constraints can be imposed upon probability assignments if confidence assignments are given. Since, on some occasions, it may prove to be the case that agents (presumed to be rational) are clearer regarding their degrees of belief and disbelief—in the sense of degrees of confidence—than they are regarding preferences among gambles, an alternative method to those that are considered in current discussions of subjective probability for obtaining probability assignments might prove feasible. And this method might actually expand the scope of applicability of Bayesian decision theory. Some consideration of this possibility will be undertaken in Chapter XVI.

The other way in which the notion of degrees of confidence is of importance to induction is in the explication of the notion of weight of evidence discussed by Peirce and Keynes. This topic will be considered in the next chapter.

IX

Weight of Evidence

1] *An Alleged Paradox*

Consider an urn that contains 10 balls, of which an unknown percentage are black and the remainder white. A sample with replacement, consisting of 101 draws, is to be made from the urn. The question arises: what is the probability that on the 101st draw a black ball will be obtained (a) relative to the evidence available prior to the first 100 draws, and (b) when the first 100 draws have been made and close to 50 per cent have shown black?

The answer to both questions is that the probability to be assigned to the sentence "On the 101st trial, a black ball will be drawn" is .5.

Now according to subjective interpretations of probability, the only difference that is recognized between the two cases is that the probability assignments are relativized to two different bodies of evidence. There is, in some sense, "more" evidence in case (b) than in case (a), but the acquisition of the additional evidence makes no difference in the risks that an agent would be prepared to take on the hypothesis about the 101st draw, either in connection with practical or cognitive decision problems.

Both Peirce[1] and Popper[2] have argued that examples such as this indicate that there is something wrong with subjectivist interpretations of probability. Surely the difference in the amount of evidence available in the two cases ought to be reflected in different assessments of the prospects for drawing a black ball on the 101st draw. Yet, subjective probability assignments are quite incapable of registering such differences.

John Maynard Keynes, who devoted some attention to the notion of "weight of arguments," insisted upon making a distinction between weight and probability. However, he did not seem to think that differing situations of type (a) and type (b) necessitated the use of an index of weight of evidence.

The conclusion, that the 'weight' and the 'probability' of an argument are independent properties, may possibly introduce a difficulty into the discussion of the application of probability to practice. For in deciding on a course of action, it seems plausible to suppose that we ought to take account of the weight as well as the probability of different expectations. But it is difficult to think of any clear example of this, and I do not feel sure that the theory of 'evidential weight' has much practical significance.[3]

Keynes' failure to think of a clear example in which weight of evidence plays a role in practical applications cannot be attributed to lack of sufficient imagination to be able to envisage illustrations of the sort introduced by Peirce and later by Popper. He does, in point of fact, use urn examples in discussing weight. But instead of introducing these examples as puzzles that necessitate the introduction of a notion of weight of evidence for their solution, he takes for granted the distinction between weight and probability, and uses the urn models to illustrate how weight of evidence can, on some occasions, be measured by the probable error in estimates of the long-run frequencies that result from large-scale sampling with replacement.[4]

[1] C. S. Peirce, *Collected Papers,* Vol. 2 (Cambridge: Harvard University Press, 1932), pp. 420–423.

[2] K. R. Popper, *The Logic of Scientific Discovery* (London: Hutchinson, 1959), pp. 407–410. It is interesting to note that Popper takes Peirce to be an advocate of a subjectivist interpretation of probability who founders on this difficulty. This seems, however, to be a misreading of Peirce's intent.

[3] J. M. Keynes, *A Treatise on Probability* (London: Macmillan, 1921), p. 76.

[4] *Ibid.,* p. 75.

Quite aside from the eminence of Keynes' authority, it is rather difficult to see how the urn example, and others like it, raise any serious problems.

If subjective probabilities are indices of the risks that an agent is warranted in taking, it is, indeed, reasonable to require that probability assignments be based on total relevant evidence at the time of decision. If, at two distinct times, two different bodies of relevant evidence warrant assigning the same probability to a given hypothesis, the two situations are nevertheless obviously distinguishable: the total relevant evidence is different. But as long as the probability assignment to the hypothesis in question remains the same, what difference would this make in the risks that a rational agent should take on these two occasions?

2] *Amounts of Evidence*

According to Keynes, probability measures the "balance" between favorable and unfavorable evidence. Weight of argument or weight of evidence is a "balance, not between the favorable and the unfavorable evidence, but between *absolute* amounts of relevant knowledge and relevant ignorance, respectively."[5] Keynes makes clear in his discussion that by "knowledge" he means the totality of information accepted as evidence. A measure of weight of evidence becomes, for him, a measure of the amount of relevant evidence.

Keynes explicitly mentions his difficulties in finding any important application for the notion of weight of evidence. He does, however, cite one context in which it might be useful.

We may argue that, when our knowledge is slight but capable of increase, the course of action, which will, relative to such knowledge, probably produce the greatest amount of good, will often consist in the acquisition of more knowledge. But there clearly comes a point when it is no longer worth while to spend trouble, before acting, in the acquisition of further information, and there is no evident principle by which to determine *how far* we ought to carry our maxim of strengthening the weight of our argument. A little reflection will probably convince the reader that this is a very confusing problem.[6]

[5] *Ibid.*, p. 71.
[6] *Ibid.*, p. 77.

Keynes takes note of the obvious fact that on some occasions a decision-maker will defer action until further evidence is in. On the other hand, he will sometimes judge additional evidence collection to be pointless. Keynes raises the question: "How much evidence is enough evidence?" He equates this with the question: "How great must the weight of evidence be before further evidence collection becomes pointless?"

If the notion of weight of evidence has any significance in inductive inference, it seems most likely that its importance is to be found in connection with this "confusing" problem. Note, however, that Keynes has made one tacit assumption here, which ought to be scrutinized. He asks *how much* evidence is enough evidence. This presupposes that sufficiency of evidence is a function of absolute amounts of relevant evidence.

Sometimes, however, an increase in the amount of relevant evidence will decrease its sufficiency. A physician might want to find out whether McX has disease D or E, which call for different therapies. Relative to the evidence available to him, he feels justified in diagnosing D. Subsequently, new evidence is obtained that casts doubt on that diagnosis, but without being decisive in favor of E. The amount of relevant evidence has increased; but would it not be plausible to say that the need for new evidence increased after the increase of relevant evidence?

Considerations such as this suggest that it is preferable to view weight of evidence not as a measure of the absolute amount of relevant evidence but as an index of the sufficiency of available evidence. Weight of evidence would then be viewed as of high value when no further evidence is needed and would fall away from that high value as the demand for new evidence increases.

The problem still remains of determining the conditions under which new evidence is needed and when it is pointless; this remains, as Keynes says, a confusing problem. But some partial headway might be made by avoiding Keynes' question-begging assumption that the issue is one of absolute amounts of relevant evidence.

One source of confusion with regard to this topic stems from the fact that the demand for new evidence might be occasioned by a wide variety of needs, depending upon the exigencies of the decision problem under consideration. In order to make the discussion somewhat more manageable, it will be restricted chiefly to a consideration of those conditions under which new evidence is demanded in cognitive decision-making, in general, and in efforts to replace agnosticism by true belief, in particular.

3] *The Skeptic*

Consider an investigator who is interested in replacing agnosticism by true belief. Let him have an initially ultimate partition that consists of four hypotheses: H_1, H_2, H_3, and H_4. Suppose, finally, that he is a skeptic, who uses a value $q^* = 0$.

Relative to his background information b, such a skeptic must be agnostic with regard to the elements of U. For each of these elements is consistent with b. The skeptic accepts as strongest via induction from b the disjunction S of the elements of U.

But given that the skeptic has raised the question to which the relevant answers are the members of the set M generated by U, would it be reasonable for him to look for new evidence and, if so, why? The most plausible answer to offer here is that anyone who is interested in replacing agnosticism by true belief—whether he be skeptic or nonskeptic—would look for new evidence in order to settle the question raised as completely as possible. And it seems plausible to suppose that a complete answer would be obtained when an investigator is in a position to accept as true some element of U.

Thus, one factor that occasions the demand for new evidence on the part of the skeptic is an interest in relief from agnosticism. He wants new evidence in order to be justified in accepting some element of U as true, rather than accepting only the deductive consequences of b.

Prima facie, this suggestion runs counter to the account of the skeptic offered previously, according to which the skeptic did not prefer high content over low content. All true answers were equal in epistemic value, regardless of their content.

Recall, however, that this indifference to content was an evaluation imposed by the skeptic's commitments when he was afforded the opportunity to acquire relief from agnosticism by accepting sentences as true that are not deductively entailed by his evidence. The indifference to content reflects the skeptic's unreadiness to risk error in order to expand his body of beliefs.

But given that the skeptic has foresworn the opportunity to obtain new information via nondeductive reasoning from given evidence, he might still prefer being justified in accepting a highly informative statement as true over being justified in accepting only weaker statements. Suppose, for example, the skeptic has the opportunity to collect evidence. The outcome of such evidence collection will be his having as new evidence either e_1 which entails $-H_1$, e_2 which entails $-H_2$, e_3 which entails $-H_3$, or e_4 which entails $-H_4$. Let it be the case that, relative to his background information b, the skeptic knows that at least and at most one of these results will ensue from the specific method of evidence collection that he has in mind.

The investigator has a decision problem in which he has two options: to remain with the status quo or to follow the evidence-collecting policy.[7] Given his skeptical commitments, the decision problem can be represented according to the matrix in Table 1.

Table 1

States of Nature Specified in Terms of Which Sentence
Will Describe the New Evidence Obtained as a Result
of the Evidence-Collecting Program

	e_1	e_2	e_3	e_4
Status quo	$H_1 v H_2 v H_3 v H_4$	S	S	S
Collect new evidence	$H_2 v H_3 v H_4$	$H_1 v H_3 v H_4$	$H_1 v H_2 v H_4$	$H_1 v H_2 v H_3$

[7] If these observations are sound, it follows that in cognitive decision problems evidence-collection strategies are not alternatives to the various cognitive options that involve accepting elements of M relative to the available evidence. For example, an investigator can suspend judgment and decide to collect evidence or (in the case of nonskeptics to be considered shortly) can reach stronger conclusions and still decide to collect evidence. And not only are evidence-collecting strategies not alternatives to reaching conclusions relative to the available evidence, but they are not equivalent to certain of these conclusions. Some writers (for example, A. Wald, *Statistical Decision Functions* [New York: Wiley, 1950], Chapter 1) suggest that a decision to collect evidence can be viewed as a decision to suspend judgment. This does not seem plausible in connection with cognitive decision problems. The reaching of conclusions is not *deferred* until new evidence is obtained. Rather, new evidence is obtained in order to reach stronger conclusions; or (in the case of the nonskeptic), to check conclusions already obtained. In practical decision-making, it is undoubtedly true that action is deferred until new evidence is obtained; but in the case of belief, commitments made relative to given evidence can always be revised in the light of new evidence.

The outcomes of each of the options are described in terms of which sentence the skeptic will be justified in accepting as strongest in M via induction and deduction from the evidence obtained.

In the case of the skeptic, therefore, the quest for new evidence is occasioned by an interest in replacing an agnosticism that is justified by currently available evidence with a system of beliefs that are justified relative to the evidence hopefully to be obtained, and which, in addition, will relieve the agnosticism. Evidence will be sufficient in the sense that no further evidence is needed when the skeptic has a total body of evidence that entails the truth of an element of U—his initially ultimate partition. In his case, weight of evidence can be measured in terms of the content of the strongest sentence in M whose acceptance is justified by that evidence.

Note that sufficiency of evidence is here relativized to the skeptic's initially ultimate partition, for that partition formulates the relevant answers to the question originally raised. Observe further that the weight of evidence is not a measure of some feature assigned to a hypothesis relative to given evidence, but a feature of the evidence, manifested in the kind of conclusion that is justified by that evidence. However, one could refer to the weight of evidence in favor of (or against) a given hypothesis. In the case of the skeptic, to say that the weight of the evidence is in favor of a given sentence is to say that the evidence justifies accepting that sentence. To say that it is against that sentence is to say that the evidence justifies rejecting it. Of course, the weight of evidence might be neither pro nor con.

4] *The Nonskeptic*

Many of the observations regarding weight of evidence that were made about the skeptic carry over to the nonskeptic as well. He also will prefer having at his disposal evidence that justifies a strong conclusion rather than a weak one; and he will (provided the costs of inquiry are negligible) continue to look for new evidence, until he can justify a strongest consistent relevant answer to his question. The difference between the skeptic and the nonskeptic is a difference in the standards for justifying conclusions. The nonskeptic is prepared to risk error for information. The degree of caution he exercises reflects how much he is prepared to risk. The value assigned to q^* determines his standard of justification; and the quest for new evidence may be viewed as an effort to acquire evidence that will justify stronger conclusions relative to the standard so determined.

However, because q^* is positive for the nonskeptic, he has another motive for acquiring new evidence. In attempting to justify conclusions locally (in the sense discussed in Chapter I), an investigator relies only on those assumptions and procedures that are not questioned by parties to the inquiry. But if two investigators who are engaged in the same inquiry exercise different degrees of caution, the one who exercises the lower degree of caution may not be able to justify his conclusions to the other one.

Consider, for example, a situation in which the total evidence is b&e_5, relative to which the probabilities assigned to the elements H_1, H_2, H_3 and H_4 of the fourfold ultimate partition U are .74, .24, .01, and .01 respectively. An investigator for whom $q^* = 1$ will accept H_1 as strongest via induction. If the other investigator is somewhat more cautious, he will accept $H_1 v H_2$ as strongest. Under these circumstances, both individuals can agree on the propriety of looking for more evidence in the hope that evidence will be found that will yield agreement according to both standards.

Needless to say, even someone whose investigations are conducted in isolation from others will want his conclusions to win the assent of reasonable men. If such a scientific hermit were faced with evidence b&e_5, he too would deem it appropriate to look for new evidence, even if, for him, $q^* = 1$, and he has accepted as strongest a strongest consistent relevant answer to his question. Evidence is sought, not merely to obtain a *definite* answer to a question (as in the case of the skeptic), but to obtain a *decisive* one as well.

When the total available evidence entails the strongest sentence whose acceptance is justified, there is, of course, no need to test that conclusion further. The degree of confidence in that conclusion, like its probability, has, in that case, its maximum possible value. But the demand for new evidence to test a conclusion does not automatically increase with a decrease in probability of that conclusion. To see this, compare total evidence b&e_5 with total evidence b&e$_6$ and total evidence b&e$_7$, according to probability distributions as given in Table 2.

Table 2

	H$_1$	H$_2$	H$_3$	H$_4$
b&e$_5$	.74	.24	.01	.01
b&e$_6$	.74	.25	.005	.005
b&e$_7$	.74	.0867	.0867	.0867

The probability assigned H$_1$ is the same in all three cases. But there are important differences in the significance of new evidence relative to each body of total evidence.

Relative to b&e$_6$, the nonskeptic would look for new evidence for reasons similar to those that motivate the skeptic. Relative to b&e$_6$ he is justified in accepting H$_1$vH$_2$. New evidence would be sought in order to decide which one of the two disjuncts is true.

Relative to b&e$_5$, however, the quest for further relief from agnosticism can no longer be the chief consideration for the nonskeptic. He has found evidence that justifies an element of his initially ultimate partition U; in that sense, he has a complete answer to his question.

Nevertheless, he might very well recognize the need to check his conclusion further. Although he is justified in rejecting H$_2$, it is a close call. The degree of confidence with which he rejects that hypothesis is very low and, hence, the degree of confidence with which he accepts H$_1$ is also low. New evidence would have to be sought in order to justify rejecting all elements of U other than H$_1$ with a higher degree of confidence. To be sure, the new evidence might not lead to such a result. But the need for new evidence when b&e$_5$ is the total evidence is occasioned by the relative lack of *decisiveness* in the warrant for accepting H$_1$ as strongest.

Matters are somewhat better when b&e$_7$ is the total evidence. To be sure, H$_3$ and H$_4$ bear higher probabilities than they do relative to b&e$_5$; but no element of U other than H$_1$ bears a probability near the rejection level of .25. H$_2$, H$_3$, and H$_4$ are all rejected with a degree of confidence equal to .65. Relative to b&e$_5$, on the other hand, H$_2$ is rejected with a degree of confidence equal to .04. The investigator who exercises minimal caution will prefer having evidence b&e$_7$, because such evidence will induce agreement from a far wider range of nonskeptics. Of course, the skeptic will remain unconvinced, just as will highly cautious nonskeptics. To win their agreement, the investigator might continue to look for new evidence. But assuming that, in scientific inquiry, investigators care to justify their conclusions to men who are not excessively skeptical, presumably a threshold of confidence could be reached at which it would be pointless to continue further investigation in order to win new agreement.

These considerations suggest that, in the case of the nonskeptic, weight of evidence or sufficiency of evidence is to be construed as an increasing function of the content of the strongest element of M (generated by the initially ultimate partition U), whose acceptance is warranted by the available evidence and by the degree of confidence with which it is accepted. Weight of evidence so understood is a characteristic of the total evidence relative to an initially ultimate partition and value q* of the q-index of caution.

Whenever there is an occasion to refer to the weight of evidence in favor of an element of M relative to total evidence, such weight of evidence can be interpreted as the degree of confidence of acceptance of the appropriate hypothesis. (The weight of evidence against a hypothesis would then be the degree of confidence of rejection.)

Observe that the weight of evidence can change, according to this account, without the probability that the strongest sentence whose acceptance is warranted will be altered. What will change is the degree of confidence of acceptance; this change will be due to alterations in the probabilities assigned to the elements of U that are contraries to the strongest accepted sentence. Let U be an ultimate partition that contains n elements and let H be an element of U whose acceptance is warranted relative to b&e. If $p(H,e) = k$, then $b(H,e)$ will be a maximum, when each element of U contrary to H has the same probability as every other. That probability will be, of course, $(1-k)/(n-1)$.

Thus, although the weight of evidence in favor of H can initially increase without its probability changing, this variation has its limits. Further increase in weight of evidence or degree of confidence of acceptance must involve an increase in the probability accorded to H. But observe that this is a necessary and not a sufficient condition. Consider the fourfold ultimate partition that consists of H_1, H_2, H_3, and H_4, and total evidence $b\&e_8$ warranting a probability distribution .8, .15, .025, and .025. The weight of $b\&e_8$ in favor of H_1 is not as great as the weight of $b\&e_7$ when $q^* = 1$. Thus, an increase in the probability assigned H_1 must be accompanied by a *uniform* decrease in the probabilities assigned the contrary elements of U, if an increase in the weight of evidence is to be obtained.

5] *Acceptance as Evidence*

To accept H as evidence is not merely to accept H as true but to regard as pointless further evidence collection in order to check on H. Suppose that H's credentials are questioned at some time and that H is neither a necessary truth nor a report of direct observation. Presumably, evidence that does not entail H will have to be introduced, in order to determine whether H is to be admitted or readmitted into the evidential corpus. Relative to evidence e, which does not entail H, and ultimate partition U, there would be some degree of caution relative to which H would not be accepted as true via induction from e. Some nonskeptics and all skeptics would remain unconvinced by arguments on behalf of accepting H as true that were based on e. But an investigator might very well consider it pointless to win assent from the skeptical and the virtually skeptical. His efforts at justification are not for them. When the weight of evidence becomes sufficiently great in favor of H, further evidence collection for the purpose of winning agreement from the more cautious will cease.

Observe, however, that evidence collection will cease only in the context of the particular question under consideration. If H is a relevant answer to some other question that is recognized as legitimate, even though it is not being considered at the moment, an investigator may consider the propriety of looking for new evidence that will support accepting H as true relative to that second question as well.

Although the lottery problem to some extent lacks realism, it can illustrate this point rather well. Suppose someone asks whether ticket 1 will or will not win in a fair million-ticket lottery. If the inquirer uses $q^* = 1$, he should not only conclude that ticket 1 will not win, but should do so with a degree of confidence equal to .999998. This would seem high enough to convince all but virtual skeptics.

Nonetheless, that person can recognize some point in the further acquisition of evidence, even though he himself is not interested in pursuing matters further in connection with his question. Other men, who are not virtual skeptics, may not predict that ticket 1 will not win because they are interested in different questions—for example, which of the million tickets will win. Relative to that question, the appropriate conclusion is agnosticism, even when $q^* = 1$; there, further evidence would surely be desirable. Thus, a hypothesis accepted as true with a very high degree of confidence relative to one question can still be regarded as questionable, because there are other questions recognized as appropriate, and relative to these the hypothesis either is not accepted as true or is accepted with too low a degree of confidence.

Suppose that new evidence is acquired that indicates that the lottery is rigged, after all. The probability of "ticket 1 will win" is .999999. The investigator who has been asking whether or not ticket 1 will win, will change his mind and predict that it will. In doing so, he will agree with the conclusion of those investigators who have been asking which ticket will win. The same answer can be accepted with a very high degree of confidence by those interested in either one of these questions. Not only will agreement be won from all but the virtual skeptic, it will be won from all who raise serious questions to which "ticket 1 will win" is a relevant answer.

To be sure, one can concoct questions relative to which "ticket 1 will win" will fail of acceptance, even on evidence of rigging. But unless the question is recognized by serious investigators as legitimate, there will be little point in further inquiry to settle the matter.

When a given sentence is accepted as true with confidence great enough to settle the doubts of all but virtual skeptics relative to all questions recognized as serious ones, further evidence collection for the purpose of checking on that sentence seems pointless. Under such conditions, one would seem to be justified in accepting the sentence as evidence.

This account of justifying including within the evidence sentences that are supported by an appeal to other evidence depends upon some notion of what is to count as a legitimate question. But no criterion has been offered. Moreover, except for some minimal conditions of consistency and intelligibility, it is doubtful whether any criterion could be constructed strong enough to rule out all but questions considered to be legitimate at a given time.

But it is doubtful whether such a criterion is needed. What counts as evidence is that which is not subject to serious question or recognized to be so subject by anyone whom the investigator might wish to convince of the propriety of his conclusions. Evidence in this sense need not be evident or immune from revision in the future. One way in which revision might take place is as a result of the recognition as legitimate of some question not previously considered legitimate (perhaps not considered at all). What is evidential is accepted as true with great confidence relative to all the questions we care to raise. Perhaps some criterion of the legitimacy of questions is available, although this is doubtful. But such a criterion is unnecessary for the purpose of characterizing evidence in efforts at local justification.

One other feature of the account of evidence just proposed deserves mention. Consider total evidence b&e_6 in Table 2 of Section 4. The degrees of confidence with which H_3 and H_4 are rejected are both .98. This might seem sufficiently high to satisfy all but the virtually skeptical. Assume, for the sake of the argument, that no other serious question is recognized for which H_1vH_2 is a relevant answer. In that case, H_1vH_2 can legitimately be accepted as evidence. Now the total evidence is b&e_6&(H_1vH_2). H_1 and H_2 are the two sole elements of the ultimate partition truncated with respect to the new evidence. The probabilities assigned to these hypotheses are .7475 and .2525 respectively. H_1 should be accepted as strongest with a degree of confidence equal to .495. Thus, the strength of the conclusion reached has been increased by mere bookkeeping. No new observations or theoretical considerations have been introduced at all.

This consequence seems inescapable not only for the account of evidence offered here but for any account that concedes that a sentence can legitimately be accepted as evidence from other evidence that does not entail it. To consider it a difficulty would be to deny the propriety of expanding the evidential corpus by nondeductive inference from what already counts as evidence.

Such a denial renders one vulnerable to the "creeping skepticism" described in Chapter I.

Furthermore, the revisions obtained by mere bookkeeping do not reduce the need for new evidence but only shift the motive for looking for it. Relative to b&e_6, there is no need for new evidence to convince anyone but virtual skeptics as to the propriety of the conclusion reached. But new evidence would be sought to obtain a more definite answer. Relative to b&e_6& (H_1vH_2), which is obtained by mere bookkeeping, the more definite answer is gained; but the demand for evidence to convince bonafide nonskeptics becomes more urgent. The need for new evidence obtained by nonbookkeeping procedures such as experimentation and observation does not disappear. The motive changes but the need for such evidence remains.

6] *Conclusion*

The aim of this chapter has been to indicate one way in which degrees of confidence are important in inductive inference. It has been suggested that the need for new evidence is a decreasing function of the degree of confidence with which the available evidence warrants accepting the strongest sentence justifiably accepted on that evidence. The few details of an account of weight of evidence (understood as an index of the need for new evidence) that have been offered here are neither complete nor immune from further criticism. Hopefully, however, enough has been said to suggest the presence of an important network of questions and the relevance of degrees of confidence to these questions.

X

Confirmation and Acceptance

1] *Application*

The model for replacing agnosticism by true belief and the inductive acceptance rule (A) derived from this model with the aid of Bayes' rule and the rule for ties is designed for ideally situated investigators. The fact that the results can be applied only rarely in real-life situations need not necessarily detract from the value of the theory. The model may prove to be of explanatory significance if it can be used together with other assumptions so as to obtain prescriptions that are applicable (or approximately so) to real-life problems, or if it can be used as an effective critical tool in the evaluation of other approaches to inductive inference. Above all, it will prove to be of interest if it can shed some light on the relations between rational inductive inference and rational inductive behavior.

Consider, for example, some of the textbook problems that are introduced in discussions of induction—namely, inference from an observed sample of a population to another sample (predictive inference), or inference from a sample to the population (inverse inference). Variety, analogy, and sheer numbers in the sample are

presystematically supposed to be relevant to the sorts of inferences that can be made on the basis of the sample. One of the
ways by which a theory of inductive inference can prove its
mettle, even when it is not directly applicable, is by providing a
systematic account of the way in which such factors determine
the legitimacy of inductive inferences. Moreover, if results of
this sort are obtainable from the theory, it may be possible to
compare them with whatever shreds of presystematic precedent
are available, in order to assess the adequacy of the theory—or,
alternatively, to render such precedent more "coherent."

If this strategy is to be followed in connection with rule (A),
that rule should be tolerated for the sake of the argument in
order to find out what its ramifications actually are. Only if its'
more obvious consequences run strongly against presystematic
precedent would there be any point in dismissing rule (A), before
its properties and those of competing procedures have been
thoroughly canvassed.

Complications arise, however, in attempting to carry out such
a program. In order to apply rule (A), it is necessary to specify an
initially ultimate partition and a procedure for assigning probabilities to elements of that partition.[1] It has been assumed that an
ideally situated investigator is able to make such commitments
for himself. However, as the lottery problem illustrates, it is
possible to make choices of ultimate partitions that, together with
rule (A), yield counterintuitive results. And it is to be expected
that certain methods for assigning probabilities to sentences will
also be counterintuitive in this way. The upshot is that any
counterintuitive prescription that is obtained with the aid of rule
(A) may not constitute a mark against that rule and against the
theory that is used to derive it. It might be more appropriate to
blame the method of assigning probabilities, or the choice of an
ultimate partition.[2]

---

[1] The degree of caution must also be specified. However, the complexities
involved in adjusting this parameter are not as great as in the case of the
others.

[2] Needless to say, the relevance of ultimate partitions and probability
measures is predicated on the assumption that the acceptance rule is rule
(A), or some rule which, like it, is probability-based and preserves deductive cogency with the aid of ultimate partitions. Hence, the program outlined here could be rejected in a radical way by maintaining that acceptance rules need not meet these conditions. However, it is to be suspected

2] *Confirmation*

The fact that an exploration of the properties of rule (A) cannot be carried out independently of some consideration of ultimate partitions and methods of assigning probabilities should not be taken to be a difficulty, but instead seized upon as an opportunity. Even if there proves to be no standard system of criteria for assigning probabilities or choosing ultimate partitions that determine in a unique way how to decide on these matters in all situations, rule (A), together with appeals to presystematic precedents, can be used to impose constraints on the choice of probability measures and ultimate partitions. Thus, the value of rule (A) in a systematic account of inductive inference can be assessed in part in terms of its potency as a tool for criticizing various accounts of the manner in which probabilities or degrees of confirmation are to be assigned to sentences.

The suggestion that rule (A) or, for that matter, any inductive acceptance rule that is alternative to it, can be used to judge the adequacy of a theory of inductive or logical probability (theory of confirmation) is diametrically opposed to the approach taken by almost all authors (most notably, Keynes, Jeffreys, and Carnap) who have been engaged in efforts to construct a measure of the degrees of confirmation of hypotheses. The "orthodox" view attempts to construct measures of probability or confirmation so that degrees of confirmation tend to increase or decrease in a manner that reflects factors such as the size of the observed sample, variety of instances, analogy, etc. And critics of the use of such measures generally take their supporters to task for failing to accommodate these factors in a satisfactory way. The outcome is that discussions about the theory of confirmation tend to ignore the way in which variations in confirmation values influence conclusions reached relative to different kinds of evidence. In contrast, the position adopted here insists that the way in which degrees of confirmation vary with changes in the evidence is

---

that any rule that is proposed will be applicable only when certain "parameters" are specified. The moral of the story is that an inductive acceptance rule, like a law of nature, cannot be "tested" in isolation from a congeries of other assumptions.

not decisive for assessing the adequacy of confirmation measures. The adequacy of confirmation measures cannot be judged in isolation from criteria that indicate how degrees of confirmation control the conclusions that are justifiably accepted relative to given evidence.

Consider, for example, the problem of assigning degrees of confirmation to universal generalizations in very large or infinitely large universes. Carnap's procedures (they are typical in this respect) eventuate in the assignment of very small degrees of confirmation to universal generalizations in very large universes and 0 degrees of confirmation in infinite universes.[3] Is this result counterintuitive or not?

No decision can be obtained in this matter if attention is restricted to this result in isolation from acceptance procedures. Presystematic precedent permits universal generalizations sometimes to be justifiably accepted as true when the total evidence includes a large number of confirming instances and no counter-instances. This, in itself, does not indicate whether the degree of confirmation of a universal generalization under such conditions ought to be high or low. That can be decided only relative to some acceptance rule. And if rule (A) is used, it is clear that low probabilities are not necessarily a bar to acceptance.

3] *Variety and Analogy*

Peter Achinstein has contended that the "fundamental problem" of confirmation theory is "to define a function which will recognize the multiplicity of factors relevant in determining a degree of confirmation."[4] Achinstein has in mind, in particular, the number of confirming instances for generalizations, the variety of

---

[3] R. Carnap, *Logical Foundations of Probability* (2nd ed.; Chicago: University of Chicago Press, 1963), pp. 570 ff. Carnap's own treatment of this result agrees with the view taken here in holding that the degrees of confirmation are not decisive. However, he introduces another measure that he does consider crucial—qualified instance confirmation. But, again, it is difficult to assess the merits of measures of qualified instance confirmation in isolation from principles that indicate how such measures are related to rational belief.

[4] P. Achinstein, "Variety and Analogy in Confirmation Theory," *Philosophy of Science*, 30 (1963), 207.

evidence and analogy as factors determining confirmation values. He shares in common with Carnap the view that degrees of confirmation ought to vary with evidence so as to reflect the influence of these factors in the manner suggested by pre-systematic requirements; but he maintains that the conditions of adequacy laid down in *The Continuum of Inductive Methods*[5] for such measures preclude this. In this respect, he reinforces the skeptical doubts raised by Ernest Nagel with regard to the feasibility of measures of confirmation that could accommodate variety as well as the number of confirming instances.[6]

Achinstein cites three requirements which, he maintains, an adequate measure of confirmation ought to satisfy:[7]

(1) When background information is favorable, the addition of large numbers of confirming instances will not sharply augment the degree of confirmation of the hypothesis.

(2) Additional confirming instances that do not add variety to the evidence will not, after a certain point, increase the degree of support for the hypothesis.

(3) The accumulation of confirming instances will at some point completely offset, rather than diminish, the effect of negative background information.

In defense of (1), Achinstein introduces the following example: "If we have evidence that metals such as copper, iron, and zinc can be melted, this provides background support for the hypothesis that rhodium can also be melted. Hence, numerous tests on rhodium will not greatly increase the degree of confirmation of the hypothesis in question."[8]

Nothing in the example or in scientific practice indicates how numerous tests affect the degree of confirmation of the hypothesis that rhodium can also be melted. What the example does illustrate is that, in the face of suitable background information, a large number of confirming instances is not required in order to warrant acceptance of that hypothesis. As long as the degree of confirma-

[5] R. Carnap, *The Continuum of Inductive Methods* (Chicago: University of Chicago Press, 1952), pp. 12–14, 26, 29.

[6] E. Nagel, *Principles of the Theory of Probability* (Chicago: University of Chicago Press, 1939), pp. 68–70.

[7] Achinstein, *op. cit.*, p. 209.

[8] *Ibid.*, p. 209.

tion afforded by a few confirming instances is sufficient to warrant such acceptance, the behavior of the confirmation measure when a large number of additional instances is found does not really matter (provided, of course, that these additional instances continue to warrant acceptance of the hypothesis in question).

Achinstein, himself, almost slips into taking this line when he says, "If, for example, background information strongly supports an hypothesis, then a large number of positive instances is not required; . . ."[9] Required for what? Achinstein nowhere tells us. But it is tempting to answer, ". . . required for accepting the hypothesis."

Similar comments apply to requirement (2). Observation of a large number of white swans and no black swans will not warrant accepting the assertion that all swans are white, especially if all the swans observed are from the same pond. But the observation of swans of many varieties in many climes and conditions might very well justify such a conclusion. Requirement (2) ought to stipulate that n confirming instances that are varied will sometimes warrant a generalization which n unvaried confirming instances will not justify. On the other hand, n unvaried instances never warrant a conclusion in a case where n varied instances fail to provide justification. This, or something like this requirement, seems to be the noncontroversial core of requirement (2)—i.e., once it is admitted that scientists do accept and reject hypotheses. If that admission is not made, nothing about (2) seems immune from doubt. Witness the clash between Carnap's intuitions about variety and Achinstein's.[1]

Similarly, condition (3) ought to be revised to read that negative background information need not prevent our accepting a hypothesis if there is a sufficient accumulation of varied confirming instances. Again, Achinstein's own example and his description of it suggests this condition more strongly than the one he proposes.

For instance, the kinetic theory of gases as originally formulated, and observations of a number of diatomic gases, provided background support for the hypothesis that the specific heat of the diatonic gas chlorine would be a certain value. However, observations of samples

[9] Ibid.
[1] R. Carnap, "Variety, Analogy, and Periodicity in Inductive Logic," Philosophy of Science, 30 (1963), 222.

of chlorine itself indicated a different value for its specific heat. In this case the support of the background information was disregarded after a few tests on samples of chlorine, and full support was given to the hypothesis that the specific heat of chlorine coincides with the observed value.[2]

Achinstein cannot mean by "full support" assignment of a maximum degree of confirmation to the hypothesis in question. According to the most plausible reading, "full support" means "support warranting acceptance." The illustration shows how scientific beliefs are revised in the light of evidence—not how scientific degrees of belief in the sense of subjective probabilities are revised.

Thus, Achinstein's own examples fail to enforce any conditions of adequacy concerning the ways in which number, variety, and analogy influence degrees of confirmation, except insofar as degrees of confirmation determine whether a given hypothesis is to be accepted or not. Achinstein's and Nagel's criticism of Carnap misfires, not because Carnap has in fact succeeded in doing what they assert he has failed to do, but because their standards of adequacy of confirmation measures—like those used by Carnap himself—constitute an unsuitable basis for assessing the merits of various measures of confirmation. If measures of confirmation are to be judged in the light of presystematic precedent, a new beginning must be made. A study of their behavior when used in conjunction with inductive acceptance rules should be undertaken. Such an investigation will involve greater complications than that undertaken by Carnap in, for example, *The Continuum of Inductive Methods*; for the measures of confirmation must be conjoined with acceptance rules and the specification of other factors pertinent to the application of such rules (such as the choice of an ultimate partition and a degree of caution).

In the chapters immediately following this one, an investigation of the sort just sketched will be made. The behavior of measures of confirmation when rule (A) is the acceptance rule used will be considered. The measures of confirmation to be considered will be those discussed by Carnap in *The Continuum of Inductive Methods*. After some discussion, a certain kind of partition will be taken as initially ultimate.

[2] Achinstein, *op. cit.*, p. 209.

Given these commitments, the conditions will be discussed under which evidence warrants accepting universal generalizations, statistical generalizations, and singular predictions. Because of the severe limitations imposed on the languages for which confirmation measures of the sort described in *The Continuum of Inductive Methods* are designed, and because of the fact that the discussion will be predicated upon the adequacy of rule (A) and the ultimate partitions to be used, the conclusions reached can be, at best, tentative. However, the discussion will have served its purpose if it can contribute to an alteration of the terms in which questions in confirmation theory are discussed.

XI

****

Content and
Learning
from Experience

1] *Preliminaries*

In this chapter and in those immediately following, the so-called "λ system" of measures of confirmation discussed by Carnap in *The Continuum of Inductive Methods*[1] will be examined from the point of view described in the previous chapter. Familiarity with Carnap's terminology and approach will be presupposed. The "languages" to be considered here will be the series L_N^1 containing one extralogical atomic predicate (and, hence, two Q-predicates) and the series of languages L_N^3 containing three atomic predicates and eight Q-predicates. Rule (A) will be adopted as the inductive acceptance rule. The degree of caution to be exercised will be that determined by $q^* = 1$ (the minimum permissible degree of caution).

[1] R. Carnap, *The Continuum of Inductive Methods* (Chicago: University of Chicago Press, 1952). Carnap has indicated that his theory has undergone certain important modifications, hints of which are to be found in R. Carnap and W. Stegmüller, *Induktive Logik und Wahrscheinlichkeit* (Wien: 1959) Anhang B VIII. The discussion here will consider only his earlier formulations.

In order to examine the way in which confirmation measures warrant conclusions when evidence is altered in certain ways, an initially ultimate partition will have to be selected. The subsequent sections of this chapter will be devoted to consideration of this matter.

Throughout the discussion in this chapter and the others devoted to Carnap's λ system, it should always be kept in mind that the conclusions reached can be, at best, tentative. Not only are the assumptions concerning a suitable acceptance rule, degree of caution, and ultimate partition open to question, but the languages to be considered are of such simple structure that it remains a moot point whether the situations for which presystematic precedent is legislative can be reproduced to a sufficiently good degree of approximation to provide an adequate assessment of the confirmation measures to be considered. (For example, precedents regarding the role of variety in inductive inference cannot be studied at all in L_N^1 and at best in a very rudimentary way in L_N^3.)

2] *On Measuring Content*

The notion of the amount of content or information conveyed by a sentence has been held to be of importance to inductive inference—most notably by Karl Popper. At this point, however, it becomes important to consider the respects in which the procedure for measuring content used in connection with rule (A) resembles and differs from those usually adopted.

According to the orthodox view (that which is held more or less in common by writers such as Bar Hillel, Carnap, Hempel, Kemeny, and Popper), measuring content is a problem of assigning content values to each sentence of a given language. For present purposes, the "languages" to be considered will be the languages L_N^π (where π is the number of atomic predicates). Here a content measure can be obtained with the aid of a regular measure function $m(H)$ defined over all state descriptions in the language under consideration and all sentences in the language that are logically equivalent to Boolean combinations of these.

Given such a measure function m(H), the content of a sentence in L can be defined as follows:

D.1: $\text{cont}(H) = m(-H)$

Similarly, the content of H relative to total evidence e, where both H and e are in the language and e is consistent, can be defined as follows:

$$D.2: \quad \text{cont}(H,e) = \frac{\text{cont}(Hv-e)}{\text{cont}(-e)}$$

$$= \frac{m(-H\&e)}{m(e)}$$

Given this approach, the problem of measuring content reduces itself to the choice of a regular measure function for the language. In the present context, it suffices to consider the measure functions that belong to Carnap's λ system. That is to say, the content measure is determined by picking a measure function from the same system of measure functions that is used to determine degrees of confirmation.

All of the writers who, to my knowledge, have devised content measures along lines similar to the one just indicated have required (either explicitly or implicitly) that the same measure function be used to generate a measure of content as is used to generate a measure of confirmation. Thus, Karl Popper often uses as a measure of the content of a sentence the logical probability (or degree of confirmation, in Carnap's sense) of the contradictory of that sentence.[2]

One immediate consequence of adopting this requirement is that, if a measure function is considered inadequate for the purpose of measuring confirmation, it is inadequate also for measuring content. Bar Hillel and Carnap have explicitly acknowledged this implication. In particular, they argue that, for purposes of inductive logic, the measure function m† that assigns equal m-values to state descriptions is unsuitable for measuring content because it is unsuitable for measuring degrees of confirmation.[3]

---

[2] K. R. Popper, *The Logic of Scientific Discovery* (London: Hutchinson, 1959), p. 374.

[3] Y. Bar Hillel and R. Carnap, "Semantic Information," *British Journal for the Philosophy of Science*, 4 (1953), 152.

The confirmation measure $c\dagger$ generated by $m\dagger$ has the following property, which Carnap deems counterintuitive. Consider the sentence Q_1a_1 in L_N^2 where N is some large number. Let e be a sentence in that language which asserts that some number n of individuals other than a_1 are Q_1's. $c\dagger(Q_1a_1,e) = c\dagger(Q_1a_1,t)$ (where t is a tautology). This result indicates, according to Carnap, that using $m\dagger$ "means refusing to give any regard to experience, to the results of observations, in making expectations or estimations. This is in gross contrast to what is generally regarded as sound inductive reasoning."[4]

Note first that, as it stands, Carnap's argument is not decisive against $c\dagger$. It is, indeed, the case that values of this confirmation measure assigned to a given sentence change only when the evidence entails the sentence, its contradictory, its contraries, or their contradictories. But this in itself does not indicate that using $c\dagger$ precludes giving "any regard to experience." What is lacking is some indication of how use of $c\dagger$ precludes reaching conclusions from given evidence unless these conclusions are entailed by the evidence. Thus, if $c\dagger$ together with a suitable acceptance rule prohibits accepting Q_1a_1 on total evidence that consists of a large number of Q_1's and no counterinstances, the confirmation measure cum acceptance rule would appear to be deficient.

What is more disconcerting in the present context is the total absence of any justification by Bar Hillel and Carnap for their dismissal of $m\dagger$ as suitable for measuring content on the grounds of its allegedly being unsuitable for measuring confirmation. After all, it is quite conceivable that content measures might be used for measuring content in circumstances where the properties of $m\dagger$ so disastrous (as is claimed) for measuring degrees of confirmation are not at all undesirable. Indeed, Bar Hillel and Carnap acknowledge that this might be the case when content is used in deductive logic.[5] They claim, however, that the use of $m\dagger$ is inappropriate for measuring content in the context of inductive logic. Unfortunately, they provide no account of the role of content measures in induction. Hence, it is quite difficult to discern their meaning. At best, they make appeal to the assumption that the measure function used to generate degrees of con-

[4] Carnap, *The Continuum of Inductive Methods,* p. 38.
[5] Bar Hillel and Carnap, *op. cit.,* p. 38.

firmation ought to be the same as the measure function used to generate a measure of amounts of content.

Suppose that rule (A) were modified to meet this requirement by our changing the method of measuring content used previously. This would mean that every element of the truncated ultimate partition U_e and, hence, of the set M_e would have a content value equal to the degree of confirmation of its contradictory. Let H be any element of M_e. According to results given earlier, the expected epistemic utility afforded by accepting H as strongest via induction from e would equal $c(H,e) - q^*\text{cont}(-H,e) = c(H,e) - q^*c(H,e)$ where $c(H,e)$, the degree of confirmation of H given e—is used in place of the more neutral notion of a probability of a hypothesis.

If $q^* = 1$, the expected epistemic utility of accepting as strongest any element of M_e becomes 0. The rule for ties recommends suspending judgment; i.e., accepting only deductive consequences of e.

If $q^* < 1$ and $c(H,e) < c(G,e)$, the expected epistemic utility afforded by accepting H as strongest must be less than that afforded by accepting G as strongest. Since S_e is the element of M_e that bears the highest confirmation value relative to e, accepting S_e as strongest—i.e., accepting only deductive consequences of e —is recommended.

Thus, if rule (A) is modified by our requiring that the content values of elements of M_e be equal to the confirmation values of their contradictories, then no matter what degree of caution is exercised by an investigator, he will be justified in accepting only the deductive consequences of his total evidence. Learning from experience will be precluded in a sense more clearly counterintuitive than that used by Carnap in criticizing m† as a basis for measuring confirmation.

The upshot is that measure functions used to measure content cannot be the same as those used to measure confirmation. In any event, this stricture seems to apply when content is understood in at least one sense relevant to inductive inference.

According to the position taken here, the amount of content assigned to a sentence is intended to be an index of the relief from agnosticism that is afforded by accepting that sentence as strongest via induction from given evidence. Now if an investigator has restricted the set of relevant answers to his problem in a manner that is representable with the aid of ultimate partitions, the elements of his ultimate partition are the strongest, consistent, relevant answers to his question. Within the context of his problem, there seems to be no basis for discriminating between elements of the ultimate partition with respect to relief from agnosticism. To concede that one such element H affords greater relief than another element G would seem to suggest that G can be analyzed as a disjunction of consistent sentences that are mutually exclusive and yet are relevant answers, counter to the assumption that G is an element of the ultimate partition. Consequently, it seems plausible to require that all elements of an ultimate partition afford equal relief from agnosticism and, hence, should be assigned equal content values.

Thus, for example, if an investigator chooses as ultimate the set of state descriptions in a language L_N^{π}, each state description will be assigned equal content. This means that m† will be used to measure content.

Suppose, however, he chooses the set of structure descriptions as initially ultimate. This means that prior to the acquisition of evidence, elements of the initially ultimate partition receive content values in accordance with the measure function m* determined by the value of the parameter $\lambda = \kappa$ (where κ is the number of Q-predicates and equal to 2^{π}). It is important to keep in mind, however, that m* cannot be used to measure the content of elements of such an ultimate partition truncated with respect to evidence e. Consider a case in which the number N of individuals is 4 and $\pi = 1$. Let the evidence e consist of the sentence $Q_1 a_1$. Finally, let H be the structure description that asserts that exactly three out of the four individuals are Q_1's.

$$m^*(e) = 1/2 \qquad m^*(-H\&e) = 9/20$$

Now if cont(H,e) is defined via m* in accordance with D.2, Section 2, cont(H,e) = 9/10. This result differs from the one obtained according to the procedures that were adopted in obtaining rule (A). According to the theory adopted here, the content of each element of the truncated ultimate partition is equal to that of any other. But in the case under consideration, the elements of the truncated ultimate partition are the structure descriptions consistent with e. These consist of all the structure descriptions except the one that asserts that all four individuals are Q_2's. There are exactly four distinct structure descriptions that meet this requirement. Hence, cont$(H,e) = 3/4$ (since H is equivalent to a structure description).

The reason for the discrepancy between the two procedures for measuring content is not difficult to trace. The evidence e asserts that a_1 is a Q_1. Although it is consistent with hypothesis H, which asserts that three of the four individuals are Q_1's, it is incompatible with one of the disjuncts in the representation of H as a disjunction of state descriptions—to wit, with the state description that denies that a_1 is a Q_1. Thus, when e is the evidence, to accept H as strongest is to assert a disjunction of three state descriptions—not four.

Now, according to the approach adopted here, when the set of structure descriptions is taken as initially ultimate, specific state descriptions are not as a rule relevant answers. Hence, information that a_1, a_2, and a_3 are Q_1's and a_4 is a Q_2 affords no greater relief from agnosticism than information that three out of four of the individuals are Q_1's. As a consequence, even though accepting H in the face of evidence e permits accepting as strongest a disjunction of three state descriptions rather than four, this does not have any effect on the relief from agnosticism afforded by accepting H as strongest.

Another way of seeing the situation is to consider the relief from agnosticism afforded by the evidence e. Although the evidence indicates that a_1 is a Q_1, from the point of view of the investigator who is taking the set of structure descriptions as ultimate, this relieves agnosticism to no greater degree than the assertion that at least one of the four individuals is a Q_1. Hence m(e) should be 4/5 and not 1/2. Similarly, the content of $-$H&e should be equal to the content of the assertion that either 1, 2, or all four individuals are Q_1's. Hence, m($-$H&e) should equal 3/5. Thus, cont$(H,e) = 3/4$.

The outcome of this is that, except in cases where the set of state descriptions is taken as initially ultimate and m† can be used, content cannot be measured by first adopting a measure function from Carnap's λ system and then using D.1 and D.2. Although for any given initially or truncated ultimate partition it would be possible to construct a measure function to be used to measure content, the measure functions used for an initially ultimate partition and its truncations will not be related to one another as D.2 requires.

These results have been obtained by attempting to focus attention on the role of content in inductive inference. Admittedly, the details may have to be revised in the light of further scrutiny. But they do illustrate the chief point of this account—namely, that in determining what an appropriate measure of content should be, one must keep in mind the role that content is supposed to play in the theory of induction being constructed. With the partial exception of Karl Popper, this almost trite point has been neglected by writers who have dealt with the relevance of content to induction.

3] *The Choice of an Ultimate Partition*

As was indicated previously, no attempt will be made to provide criteria for selecting ultimate partitions. However, it is possible in the context of the present discussion to adduce considerations that militate against some partitions and in favor of others as initially ultimate.

Consider, in particular, the proposal that the set of state descriptions for a given language L_N^π be initially ultimate. In this particular case, m†, together with D.1 and D.2, can be used to assign content values. When $\pi = 1$, the total number of state descriptions equals 2^N. If total evidence e is a complete description of s individuals with respect to their Q-predicates, the total number of state descriptions compatible with e will be 2^{N-s}.

According to considerations already introduced, m† cannot also be used to measure confirmation; "learning from experience" via induction would be precluded. This leaves open for consideration the infinite number of measure functions that are determined by the non-negative finite values of the parameter λ.

Let discussion be restricted to cases where the total evidence consists of a complete Q-description of some sample s of individuals from the population N (where the language is L_N^2). Let s_1 be the number of Q_1's in the observed sample of s individuals, and s_2 be the number of Q_2's. If s_1/s is greater than or equal to

1/2, the state description that asserts that the s observed individuals are as the evidence says they are and that the remaining $N-s$ individuals are all Q_1's will receive a greater degree of confirmation than any other state description (unless $s_2/s = s_1/s = .5$, in which case the corresponding state description for Q_2 will also bear maximum confirmation relative to the evidence).

For example, if one million individuals are observed, 50 per cent are Q_1's, 50 per cent are Q_2's, and N is two million; the two hypotheses that assert, respectively, that all the remaining one million individuals are Q_1's and that all the remaining one million individuals are Q_2's would receive higher confirmation values than any other state descriptions compatible with the evidence. This means that, when the state descriptions are regarded as ultimate, neither of these hypotheses would be rejected, according to rule (A). On the other hand, each of the many state descriptions that assert that 50 per cent of the remaining individuals are Q_1's and 50 per cent are Q_2's would be rejected. By suitable adjustment of numbers N and s, this result can be made to hold for any values of λ and q^*. And it is clearly counterintuitive.

The trouble here is that confirmation measures based on nonnegative finite values of λ are all biased in favor of state descriptions that assert homogeneous Q-distributions in the unobserved part of the population and are all against heterogeneity. When the set of state descriptions is taken as initially ultimate and one of these confirmation measures is used, this bias influences inductive inference in the undesirable way just indicated. It is so strong as to preclude accepting heterogeneity in the observed part of the population as evidence that the remaining part of the population is also heterogeneous.

In this case, it seems sensible to suppose that the trouble lies with using the set of state descriptions as initially ultimate. The considerations just adduced indicate that no matter what confirmation measure is taken from Carnap's λ system, so long as state descriptions are taken to be initially ultimate, untoward results ensue.

The impropriety of using sets of state descriptions as initially ultimate will be reinforced in subsequent discussion of direct inference from statistical hypotheses to the outcome of random sampling. At this point, it is interesting to note that this impropriety indicates one reason why standards for choosing initially ultimate partitions are so difficult to find. It might be thought that every investigator who is ideally situated ought to take as ultimate some partition that consists of the strongest, consistent sentences in his language. Ignoring, for the moment, problems that arise in connection with specifying such strongest sentences in the general case, in the case of simple languages of the sort being considered here, this approach proves to be counter-intuitive. In languages L_N^π, the state descriptions are just such sentences; from what has just been said, it is clear that they should not be used as ultimate.

For an investigator who is working with a simple language of the sort under consideration, the obvious alternatives to using the set of state descriptions as initially ultimate are the sets of structure descriptions for a subpopulation of the N-fold population, or structure descriptions that are obtained by using predicates from some division of predicates other than the division into Q-predicates. Unless otherwise indicated, the set of structure descriptions for the total N-fold population will be considered to be initially ultimate. Preliminary justification for this approach may be found in the plausibility of the supposition that an investigator who is using simple languages of the sort that are being considered could use them, if for anything at all, to make inferences from frequencies in observed samples to frequencies in an entire population. And when relevant answers are restricted to specifications of frequency distributions, the structure descriptions constitute the appropriate initially ultimate partition.

Occasionally, reference will be made to inferences from observed frequencies to frequencies in some other subset in the total population. When that is done, explicit mention will be made of the ultimate partition that is being used.

When $q^* = 1$, prior to the acquisition of evidence the rejection level for each structure description will be equal to its measure, according to the measure function m^*, as determined by $\lambda = \kappa$. If evidence is obtained that consists of a complete Q-description of s individuals, the rejection level can then be obtained as follows:

Deduct the s observed individuals from the universe of size N. Consider the structure descriptions for the remaining N−s individuals. Each of these truncated structure descriptions corresponds to a structure description that is compatible with the total evidence. Hence, the rejection level for each structure description compatible with the evidence should be equal to the measure of the truncated structure description that corresponds to it when m^* is used.

Consider, for example, L_4^1. The rejection level for all structure descriptions prior to obtaining evidence is 1/5. Let total evidence assert $Q_1a_1\&Q_2a_2$. There are three structure descriptions compatible with this evidence. Hence, the rejection level is 1/3. But this is the rejection level that one obtains by considering the language $L_2'^1$ in which the two individual constants are a_3 and a_4 and by determining the rejection level prior to obtaining evidence according to m^*.

Given the decisions made regarding the choice of an initially ultimate partition, it is now possible to return to a study of the behavior of the confirmation measures in Carnap's λ system.

XII

Extreme Methods

1] *Introduction*

In *The Continuum of Inductive Methods,* Carnap examines two "extreme" methods of induction and finds them wanting. These are the methods for assigning confirmation values that are based on the measure functions obtained by assigning to the parameter λ the values 0 and ∞. These two methods will also prove inadequate from the viewpoint adopted here. But in spite of the similarity in conclusion reached, the difference in the grounds for rejecting the two extreme methods should prove instructive.

2] $\lambda = \infty$

The measure function that results from letting $\lambda = \infty$ is m†; it has already been discussed. Carnap's complaint to the effect that using this method does not allow for recognition of learning from experience was criticized on the grounds that the criteria for determining whether evidence was a teacher ignored acceptance rules.

Suppose, however, that c† generated by m† is used in conjunction with rule (A), when $q^* = 1$ and the set of structure descriptions is the initially ultimate partition. The prior confirmation of all state descriptions is equal. Consequently, the prior degrees of confirmation of structure descriptions increase with the number of state descriptions that are disjuncts in these structure descriptions. As a consequence, those structure descriptions that assert that all individuals possess a single Q-property will bear lowest prior confirmation; they will be rejected prior to the acquisition of evidence. Those structure descriptions, on the other hand, that assert that the universe is maximally heterogeneous with respect to Q-properties will not be rejected.

For example, let the number N of individuals be 5 and the number of Q-predicates be 2. Prior to the acquisition of evidence, the rejection level is 1/6. The prior confirmation values of each of the six structure descriptions is given in Table 1.

Table 1

Prior Confirmation Values
for Structure Descriptions in L_5^1

Structure description in terms of percentage of Q_1's	Prior confirmation
0	$\frac{1}{32}$
20	$\frac{5}{32}$
40	$\frac{10}{32}$
60	$\frac{10}{32}$
80	$\frac{5}{32}$
100	$\frac{1}{32}$

It is clear that in this case, rule (A) warrants concluding that either 2 or 3 out of the 5 individuals are Q_1's.

This result does not in itself suffice to determine the adequacy of c†. At best it suggests that a person who uses this confirmation measure is committed at the outset of inquiry to the view that the world is relatively heterogeneous.[1]

Suppose now that new evidence is obtained which asserts that two individuals a_1 and a_2 are both Q_1's. The truncated ultimate partition consists of the four structure descriptions that are compatible with the assertion that at least 40 per cent of the individuals are Q_1's.

---

[1] That is, heterogeneous with respect to Q-properties.

The degrees of confirmation relative to the new evidence are given in Table 2.

Table 2

*Confirmation Values for Structure Descriptions
Relative to Evidence $Q_1a_1 \& Q_1a_2$*

Structure descriptions	Confirmation
40	⅛
60	⅜
80	⅜
100	⅛

Rule (A) would recommend in this case concluding that either 60 or 80 per cent of the individuals are Q_1's. This is, indeed, a modification of the conclusion that was arrived at prior to obtaining the evidence. And the modification is not due simply to deductive considerations.

However, in one important respect, nothing is learned from experience, except by way of deduction. If attention is restricted to the individuals that have not been observed, the conclusion that is warranted according to rule (A) is that either 1/3 or 2/3 of these are Q_1's. In other words, a conclusion that implies as much heterogeneity as is deductively compatible with the evidence is thus justified. This holds true even though the observed sample is entirely homogeneous with respect to Q-properties. Indeed, had the new evidence consisted of an assertion that one of the two observed individuals was a Q_1 and the other a Q_2, the Q-distribution among the remaining unobserved individuals would have been assumed to be the same as it had been relative to the homogeneous sample.

This result is not due to the smallness of the sample size. Even if 1 million individuals had been observed to be all Q_1's and only 3 individuals in the universe had been unobserved, the conclusion about these 3 individuals would have been exactly the same.

This result is strongly counterintuitive. It seems plausible to require that conclusions reached regarding the distribution of Q-properties in the unobserved portion of the universe will reflect in some measure the distribution of Q-properties in the observed portion. But the use of c† precludes learning from experience in this way and hence this confirmation measure ought to be abandoned.

3] *The Straight Rule*

The second extreme method, in which $\lambda = 0$, is called "the straight rule" by Carnap. When the total evidence specifies that s_i out of s individuals have the Q-property Q_i, the degree of confirmation accorded by this method to the hypothesis that the next individual is a Q_i is s_i/s. As a consequence, this measure is not a regular confirmation measure; for when all individuals have a single Q-property Q_i, the degree of confirmation assigned to the hypothesis $(x)Q_ix$ is 1, even though this hypothesis is not entailed by the evidence. Nonetheless, the measure is "quasi-regular" in the sense that the confirmation values that are assigned hypotheses according to this measure are limits of the series of regular confirmation values that are assigned as the positive values of λ decrease towards 0.[2]

The prior confirmation values of all structure descriptions other than those that assert that all individuals share a given Q-property in common are 0; these hypotheses of perfect homogeneity bear equal prior confirmation of $1/\kappa$ where κ is the number of Q-predicates. Whereas m† is biased in favor of heterogeneity, the straight rule is biased in favor of homogeneity.

Consider a language L_N^1 where N is arbitrarily large but finite. Let the total evidence consist of a sample of s individuals and let s_i of these individuals be Q_i's (where i is 1 or 2). According to the straight rule, the degree of confirmation of a hypothesis that asserts that a given individual not in the sample is a Q_i will be s_i/s.

When the straight rule is used together with rule (A), where $q^* = 1$ and structure descriptions constitute the initially ultimate partition, the following results obtain:

T.1: The sentence $(x)Q_ix$ is justifiably accepted relative to evidence asserting that $s_i/s = 1$ as long as $1 \leqq s$. (Proof here is obvious.)

---

[2] See R. Carnap, *The Continuum of Inductive Methods* (Chicago: University of Chicago Press, 1952), p. 42.

T. 2: When s_i/s is positive but less than 1, the conclusion that the relative frequency with which Q_i's appear in the unobserved portion of the population is within some interval around s_i/s is justifiably accepted.

The width of the interval can be reduced by increasing the size s of the observed sample.[3]

T.2 is a very attractive result; it conforms to whatever shreds of presystematic precedent are available. T.1, however, is strongly counterintuitive. It allows investigators to generalize too rapidly from the evidence available to them. Even on the basis of a single confirming instance, a universal generalization can justifiably be accepted as true. For this reason, the straight rule seems to be unsuitable for incorporation into a theory of inductive inference. Nonetheless, its virtues should not be ignored. Although the straight rule will be discarded, therefore, it will not be forgotten.

[3] Proof of T.2 is too lengthy to offer here. However, the assertions are correct for all languages L_N^π.

XIII

Generalization

1] *Large Worlds*

The difficulties that confront use of the straight rule and m†
suggest that, if measure functions from Carnap's λ system are to
be used to measure confirmation, finite positive values of λ
should be considered. For present purposes, it will prove useful
to examine "inductive methods" (in Carnap's sense) that are obtained by considering the positive finite values of a parameter C
such that $\lambda = C\kappa$ (where κ is the number of Q-predicates in the
language under consideration).

Before exploring these measures further, however, some attention should be devoted to a problem that rule (A), as it has been
stated, cannot handle. Rule (A) is applicable in cases where the
initially ultimate partition is finite. When the set of structure
descriptions is initially ultimate, that fact precludes considering
inferences where the universe is either infinite, or finite but of
indefinitely large (or unknown) size.

2] *Inference Sequences*

Consider a language L^π, which contains π atomic (one-place) predicates and an infinite number of individual constants, arranged in some alphabetical order. Let the languages L_N^π be obtained from L^π by deleting all but the first N individual constants and restricting the universe of discourse to the individuals referred to by these constants.

For each language in the sequence L_N^π, specify an initially ultimate partition U^N. In addition, let each language in the sequence be associated with a definite confirmation measure c^N. The sequence of triples $<L_N^\pi, U^N, c^N>$ will be called an "inference sequence."

An investigator who uses L^π and wishes to reach conclusions via induction from evidence e (stated in L^π), which specifies the Q-distribution among a finite sample of individuals, would be in a position to use rule (A) relative to every element of the inference sequence. And, in some instances, there will be sentences in L^π such that there is an N' associated with a $U^{N'}$ and $c^{N'}$ such that for every N greater than N', these sentences will be rejected according to rule (A) relative to the total evidence and $<L_N^\pi, U^N, c^N>$. It seems reasonable to require that just such sentences be rejected in L^π.[1]

In the subsequent discussion, inference sequences will be restricted to those in which U^N is the set of structure descriptions in L_N^π. This requirement is plausible where relevant answers are those that specify relative frequencies of Q-predicates in the population.

In addition, Carnap would require that the confirmation functions c^N all be determined by the same value of λ. For the present, this requirement will also be adopted. It will be discussed at greater length subsequently.

Given these decisions, rule (A) can be used to determine what

[1] Keep in mind that the hypotheses under consideration are satisfiable in finite universes, if they are satisfiable at all.

to accept and what to reject, even in the case of indefinitely or infinitely large worlds of the sort under consideration.

3] *Universal Generalizations*

Let C (for language L^1) bear a value greater than 1. Suppose the investigator has total evidence expressed in the sentence Q_1a_1. It would be unreasonable to expect that $(x)Q_1x$ be justified on such evidence (the fact that the straight rule allows this is one of its chief defects), but such evidence ought not, surely, justify rejecting this sentence. Yet, when the confirmation measure is determined by C > 1, this will happen.

For example, let C = 2 and let the evidence assert that the s individuals $a_1, a_2, ..., a_s$ are Q_1's. Let n = N−s, where N is the total number of individuals in the universe of discourse. In L_N^1, the truncated ultimate partition contains n+1 structure descriptions. Hence, the rejection level when $q^* = 1$ is $1/(n+1)$. It can be shown that the degree of confirmation of the sentence $(x)Q_1x$ in L_N^1 is equal to $\dfrac{(s+2)(s+3)}{(s+2+n)(s+3+n)}$.[2]
Let $1/(n+1)$ equal that degree of confirmation. The equation reduces to n = s²+3s+1. Let the value of the solution be n*. It is positive. When n is less than n*, rule (A) recommends not rejecting $(x)Q_1x$ (which is not the same as accepting it). But for every value of n greater than n*, rule (A) recommends rejection of that hypothesis. Since n increases with N, it follows that there is a value of N such that, for every value greater than it, rule (A) recommends rejecting $(x)Q_1x$ relative to evidence that asserts that s out of a definite set of s individuals are all Q_1's. Hence, in universes of indefinitely or infinitely large size, $(x)Q_1x$ would be rejected, no matter how large s (the number of confirming instances) might be. This is clearly counterintuitive.

This result can be generalized to obtain for any value of C

[2] The degree of confirmation accorded to the hypothesis in question is, in accordance with Carnap's formula, equal to $\dfrac{(s+2)}{(s+4)}$ x ... x $\dfrac{(s+n+1)}{(s+n+3)}$, which equals $\dfrac{(s+2)(s+3)}{(s+2+n)(s+n+3)}$.

greater than 1 and any value of π. It constitutes good grounds for refusing to choose such values of C.

In the case where $C = 1$ (and $\pi = 1$), the confirmation measure c^*, which Carnap has frequently suggested to be suitable, is obtained. For this value of C, as well as for all values less than this, it can be shown that evidence that asserts that all observed individuals are Q_1's never warrants rejecting the hypothesis that all individuals in the universe are. The degree of confirmation of that hypothesis will be $(s+1)/(s+n+1)$. When s is positive, there is no positive value of n that satisfies the equation $(s+1)/(s+n+1) = 1/(n+1)$—i.e., the left-hand term is always greater than that on the right when s is positive.

Observe that this holds true no matter how large N and, hence, n, might be. As a consequence, $(x)Q_1x$ will not be rejected, even in indefinitely or infinitely large universes. This is so in spite of the fact that the degree of confirmation of that hypothesis converges to 0 as N increases to infinity. This point accentuates the basic difference between the approach adopted here and that usually adopted in discussions of measures of confirmation. The result that universal generalizations bear degrees of confirmation that converge to 0 as N approaches infinity has been thought to be damaging to the use of logical probabilities as measures of degrees of confirmation. Even Carnap has admitted this by taking as the index of the degree to which universal generalizations are supported by evidence, not the degrees of confirmation of these generalizations but either their instance confirmation or qualified instance confirmation.[3]

From the standpoint adopted here, the crucial question is not what degrees of confirmation are assigned to such hypotheses, but what conclusions about their truth or falsity are warranted by different kinds of evidence, when a confirmation measure together with an acceptance procedure is adopted. The results obtained thus far indicate that, even though a universal generalization might bear 0 confirmation in an infinite universe, it will not be rejected on evidence that consists entirely of confirming instances when C is 1. This result also obtains when C bears some positive value less than 1.

The crucial point to keep in mind here is that the fact that a

---

[3] R. Carnap, *The Logical Foundations of Probability* (2nd ed.; Chicago: University of Chicago Press, 1962), pp. 571–574.

hypothesis has a very low degree of confirmation or probability is not sufficient to warrant its rejection. Its probability must be compared with that of its competitors. (This holds true, strictly speaking, only for elements of the ultimate partition.) In very large universes, all structure descriptions will bear very low probabilities relative to the evidence. But when $C \leqq 1$ and the evidence consists of a sample of individuals homogeneous with respect to some Q-property Q_1, the structure descriptions that assert that all or almost all individuals in the universe have Q_1 will bear higher degrees of confirmation than those that assert that many do not. In large finite universes, therefore, heterogeneity (relative to evidence of the sort described) will be rejected in favor of homogeneity.

These considerations suffice to weed out values of C greater than 1 from among the parameters that are eligible for determining an appropriate confirmation value. Unfortunately, the positive values of C less than or equal to 1 that do remain suffer from deficiencies which, if not as seriously objectionable as those belonging to values of C greater than 1, are, nonetheless, quite serious.

It has just been noted that universal generalizations that are confirmed by some positive number s of confirming instances are not rejected according to the procedure adopted here, provided that $C \leqq 1$. But, except when $C = 0$ (the straight rule), it will also be true that no universal generalization can be accepted relative to such evidence in indefinitely or infinitely large universes, no matter how large or how varied the sample might be.

To see this, note that when s individuals are all observed to be Q_1's (where there are only two Q-predicates) and $C = 1$, the degree of confirmation assigned to the hypothesis that k/n of the remaining n individuals ($n = N-s$ where N is the size of the universe) are Q_1's is:

$$\binom{n}{k} \frac{s+1}{s+k+1} \times \frac{1}{s+k+2} \times \ldots \times \frac{n-k}{s+n+1}$$

$$= \frac{s+1}{s+k+1} \times \frac{k+1}{s+k+2} \times \ldots \times \frac{n}{s+n+1}$$

$$= \frac{k+1}{s+k+1} \times \ldots \times \frac{n}{s+n} \times \frac{s+1}{s+n+1}$$

Now in any universe of size N″, such that a hypothesis that asserts that exactly ak/an of the individuals are Q_1's, the degree of confirmation of that hypothesis will be in accord with the result just given, except for the fact that k will be replaced by ak and n by an. That hypothesis will be rejected in such a universe just in case that degree of confirmation is less than $1/(an+1)$. But this means that in such a universe the following holds:

$$\frac{ak+1}{s+ak+1} \times \dots \times \frac{an}{s+an} \times \frac{an+1}{s+an+1} < \frac{1}{s+1}$$

Observe, however, that the left-hand term can be restated as follows:

$$Z_{an}^{ak} = \frac{ak+1}{an+2} \times \dots \times \frac{ak+s}{an+s+1}$$

As a increases, Z_{an}^{ak} approaches $(k/n)^s$.

Thus, if $(k/n)^s < 1/(s+1)$, there is an a′ such that for every a greater than a′, $Z_{an}^{ak} < 1/(s+1)$. Let $N' = s+a'n$. For every N greater than N′, the hypothesis that k/n individuals as yet unobserved are Q_1's will be rejected.

Conversely, assume that there is an N′, such that the hypothesis that k/n individuals not in the observed sample are Q_1's is rejected and remains rejected for every N greater than N′. Let $a'n = N'-s$. $Z_{a'n}^{a'k} < 1/(s+1)$, and so is Z_{an}^{ak} for every a greater than a′. Hence, $(k/n)^s$ is less than or equal to $1/(s+1)$.

This argument can be summarized in the following theorem:

Let s individuals be observed all to be Q_1's (where there are two Q-predicates), C = 1 and $q^* = 1$. Let H be the hypothesis that exactly k/n of the unobserved individuals are Q_1's. H will be rejected in some universe of size N and in all universes of greater size, if $(k/n)^s < 1/(s+1)$ and only if $(k/n)^s \leqq 1/(s+1)$.

No matter how large s might be, a ratio k/n less than 1 can be found such that $(k/n)^s$ is greater than $1/(s+1)$. Hence, no matter how large the number of instances of Q_1's that have been observed (without observed instances of Q_2's), the hypothesis that at least one unobserved individual is not a Q_1 cannot be ruled out. To be sure, as s increases, the set of uneliminated relative frequencies is restricted to an interval of values very close to and including unity–i.e., such evidence warrants concluding that all or almost all individuals in the universe are Q_1's, where the "almost" converges to "all" as the number of confirming instances increases.

The trouble here is, of course, that no matter how large the finite sample of s observed confirming instances might be, the conclusion that all individuals are Q_1's can never be justifiably adopted. This result remains true even when C is less than 1, provided that it is positive. However, as C decreases toward 0, a sample of fixed size s will warrant accepting a conclusion that asserts that the relative frequency with which Q_1's appear is in a smaller interval including unity. As has been mentioned previously, when $C = 0$ (the straight rule), the universal generalization is accepted, even on one confirming instance.

These results pose the following problem. Presystematically, it seems plausible to suppose that at least sometimes the set of confirming instances is large enough to warrant accepting universal generalizations. This requirement is satisfied by the straight rule. Unfortunately, the straight rule permits too rapid generalization from confirming instances–e.g., even on the basis of a sample of one instance. However, when C is positive, no finite number of confirming instances will suffice, provided that N is made sufficiently large. To be sure, when N is known to be some definite size and the number of individuals in the observed sample is given, it is always possible to find a positive value of C, such that the conclusion that all individuals are Q_1's is warranted. But where the value of N is unknown or is considered to be infinite, it is impossible to find a value of C that will warrant such a conclusion, no matter how large s might be.

4] *Fitting Sequences*

The difficulty just mentioned could be used to cast doubt on the inductive acceptance procedures that have been proposed here. However, it could also be the case that something is wrong with the confirmation measures in Carnap's λ system. And it is not too difficult to identify one source of difficulty in Carnap's requirements for measures of confirmation.

One of the conditions of adequacy imposed by Carnap in *The*

Continuum of Inductive Methods is that the degree of confirmation of a singular sentence relative to evidence that describes a finite number of individuals not mentioned in the hypothesis ought to be independent of the size N of the universe.[4] This requirement, C.6, is tantamount to demanding that inference sequences $<L_N^\pi, U^N, c^N>$ be such that the value of C that determines c^N be independent of N. Such sequences are obtained with the aid of what Carnap calls "fitting sequences" of confirmation measures c^N.[5]

The inference sequences considered thus far have been required to meet condition C.6, and it is easy to place the blame on this requirement for the difficulties that have been encountered. Observe that if C is allowed to be a *decreasing* function of N taking all positive values less than or equal to 1, one can generate inference sequences such that, on a sample of s confirming instances, $(x)(Q_1 x)$ can be justifiably accepted even in infinite universes.

As has just been noted, for any finite value of N, there is a positive value of C such that $(x)(Q_1 x)$ is justifiably accepted on a fixed number s of confirming instances. If s remains fixed and N is increased, smaller and smaller values of C are required to justify acceptance. Clearly the function $C = C(N)$ will depend on how large s must be, before acceptance is considered to be justified in indefinitely large universes. This matter will not be considered here. The crucial point to note is that by rejecting C.6—the requirement of fitting together—it is possible to accommodate the view that universal generalization is sometimes legitimate, without allowing such generalization to be made as rapidly as the straight rule would permit.

The procedure just suggested bears an interesting relationship to the straight rule. The limiting value of the degree of confirmation of any hypothesis, in an inference sequence of the sort just characterized, would be identical with its degree of confirmation according to the straight rule, when the requirement of fitting together is obeyed. However, in a universe of finite size N, the degree of confirmation will be different (although, when N

---

[4] R. Carnap, *The Continuum of Inductive Methods* (Chicago: University of Chicago Press, 1952), p. 13.
[5] Carnap, *Logical Foundations of Probability*, pp. 290–292, 309–311.

is very large, the difference will be small). Thus, when the evidence consists of s individuals, all of which are Q_1's, the degree of confirmation of $(x)(Q_1x)$ will converge to 1—not 0—as N increases. But for any finite value of N (greater than s), it will always be smaller than 1. What is more important, however, the function $C(N)$, which is used to generate the series of confirmation measures c^N for the inference sequences, can be so constructed as to preclude justifying the accepting of universal generalizations on evidence that is too slight. By preventing $C(N)$ from decreasing too rapidly as N increases, small samples will prove insufficient to warrant accepting universal generalizations. This is true even though the limit of the series of confirmation values that are assigned to such generalizations is 1.

The suggestion that the requirement of "fitting together" be abandoned—i.e., that confirmation values be a function of the size of the universe—is a radical one within the context of discussions of the theory of confirmation. Carnap is correct in claiming for this view the authority of the orthodox literature on probability theory.[6] However, the entire literature has shared with Carnap the view that measures of probability are to be evaluated by considering how probabilities vary with alterations in evidence, the size of the universe, and other such parameters. Yet presystematic precedent deals with how conclusions concerning what to accept are altered by shifts in these parameters. And it seems clear that universal generalizations are sometimes justifiably accepted on the basis of finite evidence, even when the investigator has no clear idea of the size of the universe of discourse. This precedent is much stronger than any presystematic ideas concerning the requirement of fitting together.

It might be objected that this approach neglects the role of judgments of uncertainty in practical decision-making. One of the consequences of making C a function of N is that singular sentences do not receive a unique confirmation value relative to given evidence. How can confirmation values be used for giving advice on practical decisions?

[6] Carnap, *The Continuum of Inductive Methods*, p. 13. Jaakko Hintikka, however, has recently suggested abandoning "fitting together" for reasons different from those offered here. "Towards a Theory of Inductive Generalization," *Proceedings of the 1964 International Congress for Logic, Methodology and Philosophy of Science* (Amsterdam: North Holland, 1964), pp. 278–279.

Given that the largest value of $C(N)$ is 1, it is clear that, if the number of observed individuals that are Q_1's (in L^1) is s_1 in a sample of size s, the degree of confirmation of the hypothesis that the next individual is a Q_1 will fall in the interval between $(s_1+1)/(s+2)$ and s_1/s. As the sample size increases, the interval becomes narrower, approaching s_1/s. In effect, therefore, the consequence of abandoning the requirement of fitting together is that confirmation assignments become "imprecise" when the evidence is slight, and sharper with an increase in evidence. This result is surely compatible with real-life situations in which probability assignments, when they are made at all, cannot be held to be precise. The view taken by confirmation theorists that the "vagueness" in real-life situations is something that can—at least in principle—be eliminated by an adequate theory of confirmation is not self-evidently false. But it is not self-evidently true, either. The considerations adduced here suggest that there may be good theoretical grounds for supposing that limitations on precision in assigning confirmation values ought to be imposed, if an account of measures of confirmation is to do justice to all the problems that it should be able to handle. Vagueness in probability judgments might not, after all, be due entirely to human frailty.

In any event, if all the familiar obstacles to the application of confirmation theories of the Carnapian variety in real-life situations were to be removed, it is clear that the emendation proposed here would not radically hinder the use of such theories in using Bayes' rule. Even when the sample size s is fairly small, the interval within which probability assignments fall will not as a rule make much difference in the policies recommended.

5] *Variety*

Consider a language L_N^3 with eight Q-predicates where $C(N) = 1$. For purposes of illustration, let $N = 10$. Assume further that 8 of the 10 individuals have been examined and all prove to be confirming instances of the hypothesis H: $(x)(P_1 \rightarrow P_2)$. (P_1, P_2, and P_3 are the three atomic predicates.) As Achinstein observes, Carnap's confirmation measures require that the degree of confirmation of H relative to such evidence be the same, no matter how varied the evidence is. In the case under consideration, it will be 105/136. Results similar to this lead Achinstein to conclude that Carnap's measures cannot accommodate the role of variety in inductive inference.[7]

Consider, however, the case in which the thirty-six structure descriptions that are compatible with the evidence are taken as elements of the truncated ultimate partition. When the eight confirming instances all attribute the same Q-predicate to the 8 observed individuals, the degree of confirmation of the hypothesis that one of the remaining 2 individuals has a specific Q-property different from it will be 9/136—which is greater than 1/36. This Q-property could be one that yields a counterinstance to H. Thus, H cannot justifiably be accepted according to rule (A), even when $q^* = 1$.

Suppose, however, that of the six Q-predicates compatible with H, none is true of more than 2 of the 8 individuals in the observed sample. The degree of confirmation of a hypothesis that asserts that one of the 2 unobserved individuals has a Q-predicate incompatible with H can be no greater than 3/136, which is less than 1/36. H will, therefore, be accepted, since structure descriptions that assert that both individuals are exceptions will bear still lower confirmation values.

In this rather simple situation, variety in the sample of confirming instances does appear to make a difference in whether or not H can justifiably be accepted. The difference does not depend on the total degree of confirmation assigned to H or to its contradictory. It depends, rather, on the distribution of confirmation values over the elements of the truncated ultimate partition. When there is great variety in the sample, each such structure description that is incompatible with H will bear a confirmation value below the rejection level. This is not true when the sample is unvaried. The difference is masked if we consider the total probability of all structure descriptions that are incompatible with the hypothesis—which is the same in both cases.

It should be possible to construct a function $C(N)$ such that the sequence of confirmation measures c^N permits acceptance of universal generalizations in indefinitely large universes on varied

[7] P. Achinstein, "Variety and Analogy in Confirmation Theory," *Philosophy of Science,* 30 (1963), 210–212.

evidence of definite size, without permitting this when the evidence is unvaried. This problem, however, will not be considered here.

6] *The Paradox of Confirmation*

Suppose that the 8 individuals in the observed sample discussed in Section 4 are all instances of individuals that lack the property P_1. There are four Q-predicates that are compatible with this requirement and also compatible with H. If these Q-properties are distributed evenly in the sample, H will be accepted. But, then, so will $G = (x)(P_1x \rightarrow -P_2x)$. The reason for this is that $(x)(-P_1x)$ will be accepted as true.

On the other hand, suppose that the 8 observed individuals are all P_1's and none are counterinstances of H. There are only two Q-predicates that could be true of individuals in the sample in the case. It can be shown that the sample is not sufficiently varied to accept H.

The only way in which H can be accepted and G rejected is if some of the confirming instances are cases in which P_1 is applicable and others are cases in which it is not. This explains, on the one hand, why white handkerchiefs are needed as confirming instances of "All ravens are black," without being sufficient for establishing such a hypothesis as true and, at the same time, ruling out "No ravens are black." Instances of nonravens are needed in order to ensure that confirming instances are sufficiently varied to warrant accepting the conclusion that all ravens are black. But large numbers of nonravens will not rule out the hypothesis that there are no ravens.[8]

7] *Statistical Generalization*

According to the straight rule, a sample of s individuals containing s_iQ_i's supports the conclusion that the relative frequency with

---

[8] Note that one observation of a raven suffices to rule out "There are no ravens," but not "There are no unobserved ravens." For an approach similar to the one suggested here, see Sidney Morgenbesser, "Goodman on the Ravens," *Journal of Philosophy*, 59 (1962), 493–495.

which Q_i appears in the total population will be in an interval around s_i/s. The interval will decrease with an increase in s (where s_i/s is held constant).

A similar observation holds for when C is positive and less than or equal to 1, except that, when s_i/s is greater than $1/\kappa$, where κ is the number of Q-predicates, the interval will be around a value somewhat less than s_i/s. The discrepancy is reduced as C decreases (as N increases), and as s increases.

If we make C a decreasing function $C(N)$ of N, the desirable features of the straight rule can be preserved, without its questionable properties.

8] *Conclusion*

The discussion undertaken in this chapter and in the preceding two is not intended to present definitive results, but to argue for a new approach in the assessment of measures of degrees of confirmation. Several obstacles stand in the way of presenting anything more than conjectures at this stage of the discussion.

First, rule (A) and the machinery required for its application are in need of further scrutiny.

Second, mathematical problems of considerable difficulty would have to be solved before the behavior of rule (A), together with various measures of confirmation, could be studied even in the case of fairly simple languages.

Finally, the extension of theories of confirmation to very rich languages still awaits fully adequate solutions.

In any event, enough has hopefully been said to suggest that the usual procedure of examining the behavior of confirmation measures in isolation from rules of acceptance leads up blind alleys, and that taking rules of acceptance seriously does promise some hope for an escape. Nonetheless, in the face of the formidable obstacles still remaining to the construction of any adequate theory of confirmation, it is desirable to consider the way in which rule (A) can be used to shed light on inductive inference, without the aid of theories of logical probability or confirmation. The following chapters are devoted to various aspects of this matter.

XIV

****

Statistical Probability

1] *Introduction*

The probabilities required for applying rule (A) are assigned
to sentences. When a rational agent assigns a certain probability
to a sentence, that probability indicates the risks that the agent is
prepared to take in acting as if the hypothesis were true (relative to the evidence available to him). It is the agent's "subjective" probability for that hypothesis.

One major obstacle to the application of rule (A) in real-life
situations is the difficulty in determining with any degree of precision the (subjective) probability assignments of agents. The
work of Ramsey, De Finetti, and Savage has shown how the
subjective probabilities of a rational agent can be related to his
preferences, and how knowledge about preferences among acts
and consequences can be used to derive information about probability assignments. However, in many situations, an agent will
be just as unclear with regard to his preferences as he is with
regard to his subjective probabilities.

One possible way to bypass this problem is to devise some
standardized method for assigning probabilities to sentences relative to given evidence. If such a procedure becomes available,

the subjective probabilities of the agent or investigator are then of small importance. What becomes crucial is the probability distribution warranted by the evidence. For the purpose of evaluating inferences, not the probabilities that are assigned by the agent but the probabilities that he ought to assign are now relevant.

Carnap's theory of measures of degrees of confirmation is an effort to devise a standardized method for assigning probabilities to sentences in a manner that will bypass the idiosyncrasies of the agent. However, as has already been observed, his theory is not applicable in most real-life situations; even in the simple cases that have been studied, the problem of selecting a standardized measure of confirmation remains unsolved.

There are, however, situations that occur frequently in science, in which it does appear possible to assign probabilities to sentences in a standardized way. Such cases arise when the total evidence contains statistical hypotheses that specify statistical probabilities of outcomes of (repeatable) tests. Thus, men are often in a position to judge (as part of their evidence) that a given coin is fair. This information seems to enforce assigning a probability of .5 to the sentence "On the next toss, the coin will land heads."

In this chapter, an interpretation of statistical probabilities will be outlined, in terms of the relations of such probabilities to relative frequencies and to inductive probabilities.[1] In subsequent chapters, rule (A) will be applied to the problem of making predictions about relative frequencies from information about statistical hypotheses.

2] *Dispositions*

Karl Popper has hinted at an interpretation of statistical probabilities as dispositions or propensities of certain kinds.[2] Accord-

[1] "Inductive" probabilities are probabilities assigned to sentences. They may be subjective probabilities—i.e., the probabilities assigned by agents. Or they may be probabilities that ought to be assigned according to some standard method (as in the theory of confirmation).

[2] K. R. Popper, "The Propensity Interpretation of Probability," *British Journal for the Philosophy of Science,* 10 (1959–60) and "The Propensity Interpretation of the Calculus of Probability and the Quantum Theory," *Observation and Interpretation,* S. Körner, ed. (London: Butterworth Scientific Publications, 1957).

ing to such a "propensity interpretation," statistical probabilities are not to be confused with relative frequencies. The chief difficulty with developing such an approach is that the notion of a disposition or propensity has itself received several interpretations. In the present section, an account of disposition predicates will be offered that seems important and suitable for constructing a qualified propensity interpretation of probability.[3] Subsequently, this notion of dispositionality will be applied to statistical probability attributions in an effort to provide some indication of the relationships between statistical probabilities, relative frequencies, and inductive probabilities.

The epithet "dispositional" has in the past often been a term of opprobrium. "Has dormitive powers" is dispositional; it appears to be deficient for purposes of description and explanation precisely because it is dispositional. The account of dispositionality to be outlined here identifies dispositional status in terms of the kinds of problems that are occasioned by the use of predicates that have that status.

The problem of dispositionality is not to be found in the non-observational status of disposition predicates. Assuming that within given contexts a rough and ready distinction can be made between the observational and the non-observational, many non-observational terms lack the deficiencies of "has dormitive powers," even though their connections with "the observation language" are more tenuous. It is far easier to test for the presence of dormitive powers than it is to determine the spin of an electron.

Nor is the problem of dispositionality found in the dubious ontological commitments that are often associated with the use of such predicates. One can avoid reference to unactualized possibles in the case of "has dormitive powers" by taking the parts of the predicate to be syncategorematic. "Has-dormitive-powers" makes no reference to powers; "is-disposed-to-dissolve-upon-immersion-in-water" makes no reference to dissolvings, either actual or merely possible.

[3] For a review of some alternative accounts of dispositions and a discussion of the position taken here, see I. Levi and S. Morgenbesser, "Belief and Disposition," *American Philosophical Quarterly*, 1 (1964), 221–232.

The trouble with disposition predicates resembles (as Quine has suggested[4]) the trouble with *ceteris paribus* clauses. Frequently, it will be observed that certain conditions (to be called, somewhat metaphorically, "test-conditions") are more or less regularly followed by certain other conditions (to be called "test-outcomes"). The regularity may or may not be one for which no exception has been observed. However, some grounds exist for suspecting that the test-conditions are followed by the test-outcomes in question, only if certain other conditions are realized. The state of knowledge at a given time may not warrant the specification of these conditions. In such cases, one might say that test-conditions T are invariably followed by test-outcomes O *ceteris paribus*. The "ceteris paribus" clause is in effect a place-holder for those unspecified conditions that, were they adequately characterized, would convert the generalization into an adequate lawlike sentence.

Sometimes the available evidence warrants reaching a somewhat stronger conclusion. Certain systems may be observed to behave according to regular patterns that are not exhibited by other systems. Salt dissolves in water when it is immersed; wood does not. This difference in the behavior of salt and wood is to be attributed—so it is suspected—to some as yet inadequately characterized property of salt. Moreover, sugar and salt seem to share this characteristic (a conjecture that may prove to be mistaken in the light of subsequent inquiry).

In situations such as this, disposition predicates are used instead of *ceteris paribus* clauses. Some things dissolve in water *ceteris paribus*, while others do not *ceteris paribus*. Obviously, the *ceteris paribus* clause in the two cases is a place-holder for two different conditions. Whatever is water-soluble dissolves in water when immersed. "Is water-soluble" is a place-holder for certain conditions that are inadequately characterized by available theories. Wood and salt differ in that the latter is, and the former is not, water-soluble. "Is water-soluble" is used here to mark that difference in a manner that will hopefully be replaced

---

[4] W. V. Quine, *Word and Object* (New York: Wiley; Mass.: Technology Press, 1960), p. 225.

by a more adequate characterization in the light of subsequent inquiry.

Many writers have observed that disposition predicates are often associated with "bases" to which such predicates are "reduced."[5] The basis of a disposition is a specification of those conditions that the disposition term characterizes inadequately. No effort will be made here to lay down conditions for being the basis of a disposition. That would require introduction of some criterion for distinguishing between those descriptions that are inadequate characterizations of certain conditions and those that are adequate. Such a criterion, it is to be suspected, would have to be relativized to commitments about the kinds of theories and theoretical predicates that are suitable for purposes of fundamental or "deep" explanation. Because of this relativity, whether or not a predicate is to count as dispositional depends in part on theoretical commitments. Thus, whether or not motive-attributions are dispositional depends upon whether an investigator considers explanations that contain motive-predicates to be in need of further explanation in terms of some more "fundamental" theory (e.g., a physiological theory).

Given this (all too brief) account of dispositionality, three distinct kinds of disposition predicates can be listed:

(i) *Problem-raising disposition predicates:* No basis has yet been specified, but the need for such a basis is recognized.

(ii) *Mystery-raising disposition predicates:* No basis is specified, no basis is held necessary, but the predicate is still considered dispositional. This situation arises when dispositions are appealed to for purposes of explanation, and are held to be perfectly adequate for that purpose (as in the case of "has dormitive powers").

(iii) *Non-problematic disposition predicates:* A basis has been specified. In this case, the disposition predicate can be taken as an abbreviation of an adequate description of the basis.

[5] C. D. Broad, *Mind and Its Place in Nature* (New York: Harcourt, Brace, 1925), pp. 430–440; and C. L. Stevenson, *Ethics and Language* (New Haven: Yale University Press, 1940), pp. 46–53.

3] *Subjunctive Dispositions*

One of the chief features of the place-holder account of disposition predicates is that, except for the fact that they are considered inadequate descriptions for conditions that relate test or initial conditions to outcomes by law, they are not distinguishable qua dispositional in any important respect from non-dispositional theoretical terms. Whether or not a term like "has temperature k" is considered dispositional is independent of procedures for measuring temperatures, of whether the predicate can be "unpacked" into some conditional form—subjunctive or otherwise—of how it is interpreted relative to some privileged "observation language" and whether it is non-occurrent or characterizes an event. Attempts to distinguish dispositional from non-dispositional predicates in terms of this sort have often been proposed; but they either convert every non-observational, non-occurrent term into a dispositional term—thereby trivializing the distinction—or else they fail to take into account the two features of disposition predicates that are recognized by the place-holder view and reasonably well entrenched in presystematic precedent—to wit, that dispositionality is a defect and that the defect can be lifted only by providing disposition predicates with bases.

Suppose someone insists that "has temperature k" is dispositional. This need not imply that the notion of temperature lacks articulation within a theory that possesses good empirical backing (although it could). The attribution of dispositionality may reflect a commitment to the reduction of thermodynamics to statistical mechanics. In a situation such as this, "temperature" is treated as a place-holder in thermodynamic laws, as well as in the laws that characterize the behavior of thermometers.

Recall, however, that when dispositionality is attributed to a predicate, it usually seems appropriate to ask: Relative to what is the disposition that is characterized by the predicate a disposition? According to the place-holder account, this question is a request for an indication of those laws (or law-sketches) in which the disposition predicate performs its place-holder role. In the case of "has temperature k," one could say that the disposition attributed is a disposition for volume to change in a certain way when pressure is altered, for thermometers to behave in certain ways when they are attached to systems that have the temperature, etc. "Has temperature k" can figure in characterizations of antecedent conditions in a great many generalizations as the result of its integration within thermodynamics. If it is considered dispositional, it describes a disposition to a great many things.

Compare "has temperature k" with "is water-soluble." Because of certain linguistic conventions, the dispositional status is more plainly marked for "is water-soluble" than for "has temperature k." However, one can envisage the construction of a theory in which "is water-soluble" is a theoretical primitive. In such an eventuality, one would have the same sort of option between treating "is water-soluble" as dispositional and refusing to do so that one has in the case of temperature. Moreover, water-solubility (if it is still held to be dispositional) would become a disposition to a great many things.

But no matter how the status of "is water-soluble" might change during the course of scientific inquiry, this term illustrates one of several linguistic devices employed to mark off dispositional from non-dispositional predicates. "Is water-soluble" is at least *prima facie* a disposition predicate; what is more, it is *prima facie* a disposition to dissolve in water.

There are several other linguistic devices for constructing disposition predicates that not only indicate that the predicate is at least *prima facie* dispositional, but specify, at least in part, what its place-holding function is. "Is disposed to dissolve in water when immersed in water under conditions C" is an application of just such a device.

Another such device is the use of subjunctive conditionals. Consider, for example, "is such that, if it were immersed in water under conditions C, it would dissolve." This expression is a disposition predicate. As such, it is a place-holder for certain conditions and should be read as follows:

"is-such-that-if-it-were-immersed-in-water-under-conditions-C-it-would-dissolve."

Hyphenation here is intended to emphasize the fact that qua place-holder, the parts of the expression have no more significance than the "cat" in "catalogue." This is not to say that the structure of the predicate has no significance. It indicates, first, that the predicate is a place-holder; and, second, that it is a place-holder for some complex theoretical predicate D, such that the following is a true lawlike sentence:

"For every x, if x is D then whenever x is immersed in water under conditions C, x dissolves."

Disposition predicates of subjunctive conditional form will be called "subjunctive disposition predicates" in what follows. They are of some importance here because, according to the "propensity" interpretation of statistical probability to be proposed, probability attributions resemble subjunctive disposition predicates very closely in certain respects. To repeat, these respects are:

(i) that the predicates are place-holders that demand reduction to bases.

(ii) that the structure of the place-holding predicate indicates in some detail what that place-holding function is.

4] *Statistical Probabilities*

Consider the following three statements:

(a) This coin is well balanced.
(b) This coin is fair.
(c) The statistical probability of obtaining heads up on a toss of this coin is .5 and of obtaining tails up is .5.

Leaving aside knotty problems of synonymity, it is clear that these three sentences are at least truth-functionally equivalent. Indeed, there is a rough analogy between the way in which these three sentences are related to one another and sentences or sentence sketches of the following sort:

(a') This piece of salt has such and such microstructure.
(b') This piece of salt is water-soluble.
(c') This piece of salt is such that, if it were immersed in water under conditions C, it would dissolve.

According to the account given previously, a description of the microstructure of the piece of salt would provide a basis to which "is water-soluble" could be reduced, thereby rendering it non-problematic. Assuming that "is well-balanced" is shorthand for some description of the physical structure of the coin, "is well-balanced" becomes a reduction basis for the predicate "is fair" in essentially the same way.

Both (b′) and (c′) attribute a disposition to the piece of salt, but (c′) specifies the disposition in a more "determinate" fashion —i.e., the place-holding function of the disposition predicate is more precisely stated. According to the proposal being made here, the statistical probability predicate in (c) is a place-holder like "is fair," in (b) which indicates more explicitly what its place-holding function is. How does it do so?

First, it specifies "test-conditions" of a certain kind, just as subjunctive disposition predicates do. Unlike the latter, however, it does not single out a specific "test-outcome" as the one that invariably results from the test in the presence of the condition that is the basis of the disposition. Rather, it indicates a range of possible outcomes (e.g., heads up and tails up) and assigns certain numbers to them. The customary procedure at present is to construe the possible outcomes of a set called a "probability set" or "sample space," and associate with subsets of the sample space a probabilistic set measure.[6]

Observe that, when either a finite or a countable number of possible outcomes is envisaged, one can construe the probability set as the set of predicates that describe these outcomes. The probability is not strictly speaking assigned to the two possible outcomes of tossing the coin, but to the unit sets of which these outcomes are sole members or of which the predicates that describe these outcomes are sole members.

The significance of these probability measures is that, when they are given, it is possible to infer, from the presence of the probability disposition of a system (the coin) and from the fact that the coin will be tossed a large number of times, a conclusion about the relative frequencies with which the outcomes will occur in the series of tests. Thus, in the case of the coin, the statistical probability attribution licenses inferences according to rules of which the following is a very rough approximation:

[6] A. N. Kolmogoroff, *Foundations of the Theory of Probability* (New York: Chelsea, 1950), pp. 3–4.

Given that the statistical probability of obtaining heads is .5 and tosses are stochastically independent (another disposition of the coin), then one can infer from the fact that the coin will be tossed in a certain way a large number of times, that the relative frequency with which the coin will land heads up will be very close to .5.

Note here one important difference between probability dispositions and the subjunctive dispositions described previously. The subjunctive disposition predicate indicated that the predicate was a place-holder for a basis in a certain universal lawlike sentence. The place-holding function that is explicitly indicated in probability attributions is not of this sort. Not only is the fairness of a coin not related by law to a specific kind of outcome of a specific kind of test, but it is not related by law to a relative frequency distribution for outcomes of a specific kind of test. One could not reformulate the rule of inference stated above as a lawlike sentence of the following form:

For any x, if x is a coin such that the statistical probability of obtaining heads on a toss of the coin is .5, and such that tosses are stochastically independent, then whenever the coin is tossed a large number of times, the relative frequency with which it lands heads up is very close to .5.

Whether this sentence may be considered lawlike or not, it is false. Thus, if a coin deemed fair were to be tossed a million times, it could land heads up every time and still be fair. The inference-ticket formulation of the relationship between the statistical probability attribution and the prediction of frequencies would not be vitiated—but the formulation as a "law" would be. The reason for this is that the rule of inference is an inductive rule—indeed an inductive acceptance rule; the rule may be perfectly legitimate even though it sometimes licenses false conclusions from true premises.

In the case of subjunctive dispositions of the sort discussed in the previous section, whether the connection between test and test-outcome is formulated as a law or in inference-ticket form is a matter largely of taste; for the rule of inference is required to satisfy the conditions demanded of a consistent set of rules for deductive inference—to wit, it may not license inferences from true premises to a false conclusion. This means that the conditions for the adequacy of the inference-ticket are the same as the truth conditions for the corresponding universal generalization.

This does not hold in the case of inductive inferences. The correlation between statistical probabilities and predictions of frequencies has to be stated in terms of rules of inference. There are no true lawlike statements that correlate one with the other.

One further qualification must be introduced into this "propensity" account of statistical probability. Insofar as statistical probability attributions are treated as dispositional, a demand is made that bases be sought to which such attributions can be reduced. If all statistical probability attributions were subjected to this demand, the statistical notions used in quantum mechanics would require reduction to bases in some more fundamental theory. It is at least a moot point whether such a demand is warranted. As a consequence, although it seems to be true in most cases that statistical probability attributions are dispositional, in that reduction to bases is considered legitimate, it would be unwise to impose this requirement in all cases. When statistical probability attributions are not treated in this way, they are not, according to the account given here, to be considered dispositional but as attributions of theoretical terms, which bear relations to frequencies that are specifiable in terms of certain rules of inductive inference. As a consequence, the interpretation of statistical probabilities suggested here is not, strictly speaking, a propensity interpretation but a qualified propensity interpretation.[7]

[7] Thus, Popper's contention that a propensity interpretation is useful in understanding quantum mechanics is at least misleading. Popper seems to equate the set of disposition terms with the set of theoretical terms (*Conjectures and Refutations* [New York: Basic Books, 1962], pp. 118–119) although the distinction between observational and theoretical (and, hence, non-dispositional and dispositional) is made a question of degree. Treating statistical probabilities as dispositions or probabilities in this sense is hardly news. Authors such as Kolmogoroff, Cramer, Braithwaite, and Nagel have at least considered the possibility of treating statistical probability attributions as theoretical. Now the account of disposition terms given here is intended to distinguish them from other theoretical terms. Not only is there presystematic backing for this approach, the distinction itself is interesting. But according to the interpretation of dispositions in general and probability dispositions in particular that has been proposed here, statistical probabilities can be dispositions just in those cases where a commitment is made to re-

The main problem to be considered is the character of the inductive acceptance procedures that license inferences from statistical probabilities to frequencies. This is the problem of "direct" inference. Criteria for direct inference are of interest for several reasons. First, they are relevant to evaluating statistical prediction and explanation. In addition, the propensity interpretation of statistical probability remains incomplete without such criteria. The very applicability of statistical probability requires inductive acceptance procedures. Otherwise, there would be no criteria that related statistical hypotheses to predictions about frequencies. Recognition of this is explicit in R. B. Braithwaite's contention that statistical hypotheses require some sort of "partial" interpretation via "rejection rules."[8] Aside from the differences between the rules to be considered here and those proposed by Braithwaite, there is one fundamental respect in which the position taken here disagrees with his.

According to Braithwaite, the rejection rules are to be understood as rules for action.[9] Rejection rules, as understood in this book, are rules that determine what ought to be believed or disbelieved in senses not reducible to actions or dispositions to action. Predicting the outcome of a series of tosses of a coin is not the same as placing a money bet on the outcome or deciding on a course of action relative to some practical objective. The prediction may be considered an "act" or "decision to act," in the metaphorical sense in which cognitive acts are recognized. Insofar as statistical hypotheses may be said to receive a partial interpretation in terms of statements about frequencies of out-

---

duce the probability attribution to bases. This commitment is not made in quantum mechanics. Hence, statistical probabilities in quantum mechanics can be treated as dispositions only at the expense of making them mystery-making. To be sure, this does not preclude according non-dispositional theoretical status to probabilities in quantum mechanics. If this is all Popper intends to do, then calling such probabilities "propensities" is surely misleading.

[8] R. B. Braithwaite, *Scientific Explanation* (Cambridge: Cambridge University Press, 1955), pp. 151–153. Braithwaite's rejection rules are concerned with criteria for rejecting statistical hypotheses on given data about observed frequencies. The "partial interpretation" of statistical hypotheses to be offered here is obtained with the aid of rules legitimizing inferences from statistical hypotheses to conclusions about relative frequencies.

[9] *Ibid.* This may not be a fair interpretation of Braithwaite, but it is surely suggested by his remarks.

comes of "tests," that interpretation should surely be in terms of the conclusions whose acceptance is warranted on the basis of statistical assumptions—not in terms of the practical acts thereby warranted.

5] *Relative Frequency*

The qualified propensity account of statistical probability just sketched differs in certain important respects from many frequency interpretations. Although statistical probability attributions are related via inductive acceptance procedures to statements about relative frequencies, and in that sense may be said to be "partially interpretable" in terms of such frequencies, they do not entail predictions about relative frequencies.

Many frequency interpretations of probability, like the qualified propensity account, may be understood as applications of the theory of probabilistic measures on sets to certain sample spaces. Note, however, that the sample spaces generally used in statistical applications are sets of possible outcomes of tests of certain kinds, and statistical probabilities are assigned to subsets of these possible outcomes. It may be possible to avoid a dubious ontology of possible outcomes in some cases by shifting to sets of predicates. Ontology, however, is not the central concern here. The point is that the sample space is not the set of actual trials of a given test. A coin may be fair if it is never tossed, if it is tossed once, if it is tossed 100 times and lands heads each time. No coin has ever been tossed an infinite number of times; to say that the probability is equal to what the limit of relative frequency would be, were it to be tossed an infinite number of times, seems to be nothing but an indication that, in general, probability attributions are disposition attributions of a certain sort, which may be recast in subjunctive form. Moreover, adequate rephrasal in subjunctive terms is hardly worth the small illumination it might shed upon the significance of statistical probability.

There is some temptation to construe the sample space used for statistical probabilities in terms of frequencies of a different sort. Consider an urn that contains 10 balls, 3 of which are black and 7 white. Suppose that the following "test" is used. The urn is thoroughly shaken, a ball is drawn, its color is noted and then the ball is returned. Under these conditions, it seems reasonable to conclude that the statistical probability of obtaining a black ball on a single draw is .3, and that, in a series of draws, the outcomes of separate draws are stochastically independent. This suggests that the statistical probability is to be interpreted in terms of the relative frequency, not with which black balls are actually drawn, either in the short or long run, nor with which they would be drawn, were draws made, but rather with which black balls are present in the urn.

There is a sense in which this frequency "interpretation" is legitimate in the case of the urn and in situations resembling it. The urn with its contents is a "system" of a certain kind. A statistical hypothesis that assigns a statistical probability distribution to outcomes of draws from the urn in effect attributes a certain statistical disposition to the urn. An interpretation of the hypothesis in terms of the relative frequency with which white and black balls are present in the urn is tantamount to specifying the basis of the probability disposition. The "interpretation" is a "reduction" in the sense in which an "interpretation" of temperature as mean kinetic energy is. It cannot be taken as a synonymity preserving translation, but amounts to a theoretical or empirical hypothesis that relates the structure of the urn and its contents to the outcomes of certain experiments.

Observe that not all probability disposition attributions are reducible to bases of this sort. In the case of a fair coin, there is nothing resembling the urn with its contents that can be shaken up and sampled with replacement. A basis is specified in terms of the physical structure of the coin in a way that may make no reference at all to relative frequencies. Consequently, an attempt to impose a standard frequency "interpretation" with the aid of urns can succeed in at best that metaphorical sense in which Braithwaite treats his Briareus model.[1]

Insofar as statistical probabilities are measures on sets, therefore, they are measures on sets of possible outcomes. In some special cases, the unit sets that have single possible outcomes as their sole members may be accorded equal probability. In that kind of situation, the statistical probability of obtaining one possible outcome from a certain subset of possible outcomes may

[1] Braithwaite, *op. cit.*, pp. 112–133.

be construed as a relative frequency in an attenuated sense—although hardly in the sense that any frequentist would accept. But such probability distributions would be the exception rather than the rule. Statistical probability attributions do not in themselves entail relative frequencies of outcomes of tests or relative frequencies of the appearance of certain traits in certain populations (although such frequencies may provide bases for statistical dispositions).

XV

****

Direct Inference

1] *Practical Certainty*

The formulation of criteria for direct inference is of importance, as was noted in the last chapter, for three reasons. First, such criteria are, in effect, criteria for evaluating statistical predictions and explanations; second, they provide a partial interpretation of statistical hypotheses in terms of frequencies. Finally, they offer an opportunity for examining rule (A) in situations in which that rule can be applied to real-life problems.

In *Mathematical Methods of Statistics*, Harald Cramer introduces the following principle for relating statistical probability attributions to predictions of relative frequencies:

> Whenever we say that the probability of an event E with respect to an experiment Œ is equal to P, the concrete meaning of this assertion will thus simply be the following: In a long series of repetitions of Œ, it is practically certain that the frequency of E will be approximately equal to P.—This statement will be referred to as the frequency interpretation of the probability P.[1]

[1] H. Cramer, *Mathematical Methods of Statistics* (Princeton: Princeton University Press, 1945), pp. 148–149.

Cramer's labeling of this interpretation as "the frequency interpretation of probability" seems to be something of an act of piety. He admits earlier that probabilities are theoretical magnitudes that are not completely interpretable as relative frequencies.[2] What Cramer has done is to provide a rule for making predictions about relative frequencies on the basis of statistical hypotheses.

Note that Cramer assumes that "experiment" Œ is random. For the present, it is sufficient to note that, if an experiment is random and the statistical probability of obtaining E as an outcome on a single trial is P, the statistical probability of obtaining two occurrences of E on two trials is $P \times P$, and that for n occurrences of E on n trials is P^n.

On these assumptions, it can be deduced from the principles of mathematical probability (which such statistical probabilities are supposed to satisfy) that the statistical probability of obtaining a relative frequency close to P for outcome E in a large number of trials is approximately 1. This conclusion is not, of course, a prediction with regard to the relative frequency with which E will occur in a large number of trials. It is, rather, another theoretical assertion, which attributes a characteristic to the "system" that can be repeatedly subjected to the experiment Œ. This characteristic is deducible from the initial statistical probability attribution (together with the assumption of the randomness of the experiment or test).

Thus, this result from the theory of mathematical probability will not in itself suffice to yield Cramer's practical certainty principle. In order for it to do so, another principle must be invoked.

(P)   If the statistical probability of obtaining an outcome E of an experiment Œ is very close to 1 (how close will be left open), it is practically certain that the outcome will be E.

When a test or experiment Œ is repeated several times, the n-fold series of trials can be viewed as another test of a more complicated variety, whose possible outcomes are the relative frequencies with which the possible outcomes of single trials of Œ occur. With this understanding, the principle just enunciated, together with Bernoulli's theorem, generates Cramer's practical certainty rule.

[2] *Ibid.*, pp. 145–148.

How is "practically certain" to be interpreted? Observe that practical certainty is attached to a hypothesis about the outcome of a specific trial of a given experiment (which trial may itself consist of repeated trials of another experiment). Keeping this in mind, four possible interpretations are worth considering:

(1) H is practically certain (where H is a sentence) if the evidence warrants acting on H relative to all practical objectives.

(2) H is practically certain if the evidence warrants acting on H relative to virtually all objectives that might be contemplated.

(3) H is practically certain if H is accepted as true.

(4) H is practically certain if H is accepted as true with a high degree of confidence.

Interpretation (1) does not appear appropriate; for even if the statistical probability of outcome E of test Œ is very high, acting as if E will occur, as the result of one specific trial, may be unwarranted relative to certain objectives, because of the risks involved.

Interpretation (2) amounts to saying that H is practically certain if the inductive probability of H is very close to 1. When this interpretation is incorporated into rule (P), that rule reads:

(P′)   If the statistical probability of obtaining an outcome E of an experiment Œ is very close to 1, the inductive probability that E will occur on a specific trial will also be close to 1.

Now P′ does appear to be plausible; in subsequent developments, a principle that implies its truth will be adopted. But, as it stands, it does not provide the link that is required between statistical hypotheses and predictions about relative frequencies. For that purpose, procedures must be provided for deciding what predictions to accept as true, or to accept as true with great confidence. Hence, attention must be directed to interpretations (3) and (4). When practical certainty is understood in one or the other of these senses, Cramer's principle amounts to an inductive acceptance procedure of the following sort:

(P″)   When the statistical probability of obtaining outcome E of an experiment Œ is very close to 1, then the hypothe-

sis predicting that E will result on a specific trial can be
legitimately accepted as true (accepted as true with
high confidence).

This principle is inadequate, for reasons already given. The
lottery problem shows that a high probability cannot be sufficient for acceptance.

It seems, therefore, that Cramer's practical certainty principle
for drawing inferences from statistical hypotheses to relative frequencies will not do the job for which it was apparently designed.
Yet there is an important truth in Cramer's approach. Under certain circumstances (which may be considered "normal"), it does
seem plausible to assert that, when the statistical probability of
obtaining an outcome E of a test Œ is close to 1, it is practically
certain in senses (2), (3), and (4) that E will occur on a
specific trial.

In order to indicate the conditions under which this assertion
is true for interpretation (2) of practical certainty, further consideration is necessary of the relations between statistical and
inductive probability. Discussion of this matter will be undertaken in the next section. A method will be introduced for assigning inductive probabilities to hypotheses about the outcome of a trial of a given "test" or "experiment." With the aid of
this method, it will prove possible to utilize rule (A) in order to
determine what conclusions about relative frequencies can be
obtained from statistical hypotheses. The result should, hopefully,
constitute a surrogate for Cramer's practical certainty principle;
it escapes the difficulties that are found in the use of that principle, while still preserving its important truth.

2] *Statistical and Inductive Probability*

Consider an urn with 10 balls, 3 of which are black and the remainder white. One test or experiment on the urn may consist of
mixing the contents of the urn thoroughly, drawing a ball, noting
its color, and then returning the ball to the urn. Other tests may
be constructed in which this test is repeated a certain number
(n) of times.

The urn and its contents constitute a system that has a known
structure, which is the basis of a probability disposition. Relative

to the test of sampling 1 ball from the urn, the probability disposition is articulated as a statistical probability distribution over the two possible outcomes of testing (obtaining 1 white ball and obtaining 1 black ball). The statistical probabilities assigned to these two possible outcomes are equal to the relative frequencies with which white balls and black balls are present in the urn.

If the test is repeated n times, another hypothesis is also brought into play—to wit, that the outcomes of separate tests are stochastically independent, so that, for example, the statistical probability of drawing a black twice on two draws is $.3 \times .3 = .09$. Again the basis for this disposition lies in the structure of the urn and the composition of its contents, as well as in the way it is tested (which ensures that before each draw the contents are the same as before the last draw and are thoroughly mixed).

Let a sample of n draws with replacement be contemplated. The set of possible outcomes of an arbitrary test of this kind would be the 2^n permutations of r black balls and n-r white balls, in which r takes all values from 0 to n. The statistical probability of such an outcome of an arbitrary trial of n-fold sampling with replacement is $.3^r \times .7^{n-r}$.

It seems reasonable to assume (and it is usually assumed by those who recognize the intelligibility of inductive probabilities) that the inductive probability of obtaining such an outcome on a specific trial will be equal to the statistical probability of obtaining an outcome of that type on an arbitrary trial, *provided that no relevant information is known about the specific trial to be made other than that it is a trial of an experiment of the type just described.* This proviso is required by the condition that inductive probabilities be assigned to hypotheses relative to the total relevant evidence available.

The procedure used here may be reformulated as follows:

> If Œ is an experiment on a system Z, E is a possible outcome of the experiment, the statistical probability of obtaining E on an arbitrary trial of Œ is P, t is a specific occasion upon which Œ is conducted on Z, and nothing else relevant to predicting the outcome of the experiment on that occasion is known, then the inductive probability of obtaining E on occasion t is P.

This rule imposes a constraint upon measures of inductive probability, no matter what other conditions they are supposed to satisfy. It correlates the basis of the probability disposition via the statistical characterization of that disposition with inductive probability distributions over possible outcomes of various tests.

Some advocates of the importance of subjective probability, most notably Bruno de Finetti, have argued that statistical probabilities are unnecessary for purposes of statistical inference. Part of De Finetti's argument involves showing that assignments of probabilities to hypotheses that specify relative frequencies of outcomes on future trials can be obtained from assignments of subjective probabilities to outcomes of each of the future trials, without the intervention of statistical probabilities.[3] Similarly, he shows how assignments of probabilities to relative frequencies in future trials can be obtained from information about relative frequencies in past trials without introducing statistical probabilities.[4] In effect, he concludes that, for purposes of direct inference and predictive inference, all that needs to be considered are subjective probabilities and relative frequencies.

In this connection, it might prove instructive to consider the importance of this thesis, as De Finetti sees it:

It is not without reason that we have considered ourselves obliged to proceed in this way. The old definition cannot, in fact, be stripped of its, so to speak, "metaphysical" character; one would be obliged to suppose that beyond the probability distribution corresponding to our judgment, there must be another, unknown, corresponding to something real, and that the different hypotheses about the unknown distribution . . . would constitute *events* whose probability one could consider. From our point of view these statements are completely devoid of sense, and no one has given them a justification which seems satisfactory, even in relation to a different point of view. If we consider the case of an urn whose composition is unknown, we can doubtless speak of the probability of different compositions and of probabilities relative to one such composition; indeed, the assertion that there are as many white balls as black balls in the urn expresses an objective fact which can be directly verified, and the conditional probability, relative to a given objective event, has been well defined. If, on the contrary, one plays heads or tails with a coin of irregular appearance, . . ., one does not have the right to consider as distinct hypotheses the

[3] B. de Finetti, "Foresight: Its Logical Laws, Its Subjective Sources," *Studies in Subjective Probability*, H. Kyburg and H. E. Smokler, eds., H. Kyburg, trans. (New York: Wiley, 1964), pp. 113–118.
[4] *Ibid.*, pp. 118–147.

suppositions that this imperfection has a more or less noticeable influence on the "unknown probability," for this "unknown probability" cannot be defined, and the hypotheses that one would like to introduce in this way have no objective meaning. The difference between these two cases is essential, and it cannot be neglected; one cannot "by analogy" recover in the second case the reasoning which was valid in the first case, for this reasoning no longer applies in the second case. . . .[5]

De Finetti's position seems to be that, in urn-type problems, the composition of the urn, whether known or unknown, constitutes an intelligible "objective" condition of the urn, relative to which subjective probabilities of outcomes of trials of certain experiments on the urn can be determined. He would not say (although he admits that in situations of this sort it would be harmless to do so) that these objective conditions are characterized by statistical probabilities; for one can appeal directly to descriptions of the contents of the urn which, in his view, are more intelligible.

In the case of a coin of irregular appearance, De Finetti holds that "one does not have the right to consider as distinct hypotheses the suppositions that this imperfection has a more or less noticeable influence on the 'unknown probability.'" But what is it that bars one from having this right? Apparently, the fact that, unlike the case of the urn, differences in the physical structure of the coin are not adequately correlated with different subjective probability distributions over outcomes of tests on the coin. De Finetti wants, therefore, to bypass reference to conditions we know not what in assigning subjective probabilities to these outcomes.

De Finetti's approach is analogous to one that would bypass reference to the characteristics of sugar while asking whether it will dissolve if immersed in water under certain conditions (temperature, pressure, etc.). Evidence for a prediction of this sort might be based on previous tests with sugar; it could be argued that one can pass from these previous tests directly to the prediction, without having to refer to solubility or to the microstructural basis for solubility. Similarly, De Finetti wishes to go from the knowledge of relative frequencies of heads in past tosses to

[5] *Ibid.*, pp. 141–142.

subjective probabilities for such relative frequencies in future tosses, without reference to statistical hypotheses or to other descriptions of the characteristics of the coin.

This interpretation of De Finetti's position suggests that his view that the notion of statistical probability is expendable in science is a variant of the thesis that is embodied in Carl Hempel's statement of the "theoretician's dilemma." This asserts that, if the terms and general principles of a scientific theory establish connections among observable phenomena, then they are expendable for the purpose of establishing such connections.[6] Statistical probability attributions are theoretical hypotheses that are used (on many occasions) for relating statements about observable relative frequencies. Assuming that De Finetti has shown that statistical probabilities are expendable for that purpose, it does not follow that they are expendable for all purposes of scientific theorizing. Scientists are often concerned, for example, to provide explanations of observable phenomena. Now explanation does indeed involve the provision of systematic accounts of the ways in which phenomena are interrelated, but scientific explanation is often expected to satisfy other conditions as well. Its laws or theories are often required to be of certain forms, to involve the use of certain kinds of predicates rather than others, etc. It is far from clear that the requirements have remained the same throughout the history of science—witness differences in attitudes toward action-at-a-distance principles in explanation. In any event, the concession to De Finetti does not imply that statistical probabilities are expendable for purposes of explanation, any more than other similar concessions would imply expendability of other theoretical terms for that purpose.

Observe, however, that, according to the propensity account of statistical probability proposed here, statistical probability attributions are expendable when adequate bases can be provided for the probability disposition. In many instances, statistical probability attributions are place-holders for more adequate theoretical descriptions of conditions that are used in explaining and predicting mass phenomena. This means, in particular, that statistical probability attributions are eliminable in urn-type cases, in which bases can be specified in terms of the contents of the urn.

<hr>

[6] C. G. Hempel, "The Theoretician's Dilemma," *Minnesota Studies in the Philosophy of Science*, 2 (1958), 49–50.

On the other hand, in the case of a coin of irregular appearance, no basis has been provided for the probability disposition. Statistical probability attributions in such a situation play the role of place-holders for better descriptions of the characteristics of the coin that will explain its behavior in coin-tossing games. As place-holders, the statistical probability attributions are inadequate descriptions; there are indeed grounds for dissatisfaction with their use. But the situation is not to be remedied by ignoring them, in the manner suggested by De Finetti. Rather, investigations that provide bases (and in that respect reduce the coin example to an urn case) should be attempted. Reference to the statistical probability of the coin's landing heads up on an arbitrary toss is "metaphysical" in a pernicious sense, only if the probability disposition is mystery-making (like "dormitive powers"). As was pointed out, the trouble with "has dormitive powers" lies in its use in explanation not as a place-holder, but as a theoretical term that does not require reduction to a more adequate basis. Taken as "problem-raising dispositions," however, statistical attributions in the coin-type case are far from expendable. Inadequate though they may be, nothing else has been found to serve the explanatory function that is served by these attributions. De Finetti's procedures do permit the elimination of such attributions—but at the cost of eliminating one of the first steps towards adequate explanation.

In short, De Finetti has reversed the true status of statistical hypotheses in urn- and coin-type contexts. Statistical probabilities are indeed expendable in urn-type cases, even for purposes of explanation, but this is so precisely because a basis can be provided for the probability disposition. In the case of coins, such bases are lacking and, until their introduction, explanation must hobble along with the statistical probability attributions.

If these comments have any force, the view advocated by Carnap and Nagel, among others, that two conceptions of probability are relevant to science can be defended in the face of the results obtained by De Finetti. As a consequence, the rule for associating statistical with inductive probabilities imposes significant methodological constraints on the manner in which inductive probabilities are assigned to sentences.

One final comment is in order before rule (A) is brought to bear on problems of direct inference. The rule for deriving inductive from statistical probabilities requires that nothing that is relevant to predicting the outcome of a specific trial of a given experiment, be known except the statistical probabilities of the possible outcomes of such an experiment. This application of the total relevant evidence requirement to the case of direct inference is often expressed by saying that the experiment should be a random one. Whether or not a given trial is random depends on the available evidence. In some situations, there are certain procedures that tend to ensure randomness. Problems involved in devising criteria for ascertaining whether the total relevant evidence requirement is met will be ignored. In subsequent developments, it will be assumed that this requirement is satisfied.

3] *The Choice of an Ultimate Partition*

In the following discussion, rule (A) will be applied to only one kind of direct inference. A system is given on which a repeatable experiment Œ, which has two possible outcomes on each trial, is to be conducted some finite number (n) of times. The statistical probability of obtaining one of the two outcomes E on an arbitrary trial is p; that of obtaining $-E$ is $1-p$. Any two trials in the series are taken to be stochastically independent. The problem is to predict the relative frequency with which E occurs in the n trials to be conducted.

A concrete illustration of such a problem would be random sampling with replacement from an urn containing a fixed number s of balls, k of which are black and s-k white. The statistical probability of obtaining a black ball on a single draw would be k/s. Hence, if a single draw is about to be made, the inductive probability assigned to the hypothesis "A black ball will be drawn" will be k/s. The statistical probability to be assigned to obtaining some number r of black balls and n-r of white balls in some definite order in an arbitrary n-fold sample with replacement would be $p^r(1-p)^{n-r}$ where $p = k/s$. Hence, the inductive probability of obtaining r black and $n-r$ white balls in that order in a specific n-fold sample with replacement would also be $p^r(1-p)^{n-r}$.

Similarly, inductive probabilities can be assigned to hypotheses that will predict that, on a specific n-fold test with replacement, r balls will be black and the remainder white (without indicating order). That probability will be $\binom{n}{r} p^r (1-p)^{n-r}$.

Bernoulli sequences of the sort under consideration supply those cases in which Cramer's practical certainty principle, insofar as it is applicable, ought to apply. That is to say:

> When n is very large, the prediction that r/n lies in a small interval around p ought to be accepted (with a high degree of confidence).

One way in which the propriety of using rule (A) can be tested is by determining whether this germ of truth in the practical certainty principle (where "practical certainty" is understood in senses (3) and (4) of Section 1) is certified by rule (A). In order to do this, however, an ultimate partition must be selected. It seems plausible to suppose that only two partitions deserve serious consideration in this context.

(i) The 2^n possible ways in which black and white balls might appear in an n-fold sample with replacement, where possible outcomes are distinguished both by the number of black balls and the order in which they appear.

(ii) The $n+1$ possible relative frequencies of black balls in the n-fold sample with replacement.

In the following two sections, it will be shown that type (i) ultimate partitions violate the practical certainty requirement, whereas type (ii) partitions obey it. In the light of the discussion of Carnap's theory of confirmation, this result is not surprising. And it reinforces a point that could be defended independently —to wit, that in statistical explanation and prediction, what is to be explained or predicted is relative frequencies, without specification of the order of outcomes of trials.

4] *Type (i) Partitions*

Suppose that in making direct inferences an investigator takes all possible outcomes of n-fold sampling with replacement from the urn to constitute the ultimate partition, under which possible outcomes are distinguished from one another, not only with respect to the relative frequency with which black balls appear in the sample, but also with respect to the order with which they appear. Such a type (i) ultimate partition corresponds to using the set of state descriptions as ultimate in a Carnapian scheme. The rejection level will be $q^*/2^n$ (for there are 2^n distinct possible outcomes). The probability of an element of the ultimate partition entailing that r out of the n balls drawn are black will be $p^r(1-p)^{n-r}$, where p is the probability of obtaining a black ball on a single draw. Rule (A), therefore, implies adoption of the following procedure.

Let H be one of the $\binom{n}{r}$ elements of the ultimate partition that entail that r out of the n balls drawn are black. Reject H if and only if $p^r(1-p)^{n-r} < q^*/2^n$.

The inequality that specifies the necessary and sufficient condition for rejection can be restated in terms of logarithms as follows:

(a) $r\log p+(n-r)\log(1-p) < \log q^*+n\log.5$

Condition (a) can be restated as follows:

(β) $r(\log p-\log(1-p))+n\log(1-p) < \log q^*+n\log.5$

(γ) $r(\log p-\log(1-p)) < \log q^*+n(\log.5-\log(1-p))$

There are three cases to consider.

Case (1): p = .5. All of the logarithms involved must be nonpositive. (This will be true for all cases.) The left-hand side of the inequality (γ) will be equal to 0 and the right-hand side to $\log q^*$, which is nonpositive. Hence, (γ) must be false. When p = .5, therefore, complete suspension of judgment is recommended.

Case (2): .5 < p. Both $\log p-\log(1-p)$ and $\log.5-\log(1-p)$ are positive. Hence, (γ) is equivalent to the following:

(δ) $\dfrac{r}{n} < \dfrac{\log q^*}{n(\log p-\log(1-p))} + \dfrac{\log.5-\log(1-p)}{\log p-\log(1-p)}$

Case (3): p < .5. Here (γ) reduces to:

(ϵ) $\dfrac{\log q^*}{n(\log p-\log(1-p))} + \dfrac{\log.5-\log(1-p)}{\log p-\log(1-p)} < \dfrac{r}{n}$

These considerations lead to the following theorem:

T.1: When a type (i) partition is ultimate, then an element H of the ultimate partition that asserts that r/n of the balls drawn are black will be rejected if and only if one of the following two conditions obtains:

> $p < .5$ and condition (ϵ) obtains
> $p > .5$ and condition (δ) obtains

When $q^* = 1$, $\log q^*$ is, of course, equal to 0. Conditions (δ) and (ϵ) are especially simple in this case.

It is also clear that an element of the ultimate partition that implies that r/n balls drawn are black will be rejected if and only if all other elements that imply the same relative frequency are likewise rejected. Hence, the consequences of using type (i) partitions as ultimate can be explored by considering which relative frequencies are rejected, given p and q^*.

In order to proceed, it is necessary to introduce two inequalities:[7]

When p is greater or less than .5, $p(1-p) = p-p^2 < .25$

When p is greater or less than .5, $p^p(1-p)^{1-p} > .5$

When $p = .5$, this inequality becomes an equality.

In virtue of the first inequality, $\log p + \log(1-p) < 2\log.5$ when $p \neq .5$.

Hence, $\log p - \log.5 < \log.5 - \log(1-p)$

Hence, $\log p - \log.5 + \log.5 - \log(1-p) < 2(\log.5 - \log(1-p))$

Hence, $\log p - \log(1-p) < 2(\log.5 - \log(1-p))$

Hence, if $p \gtreqless .5$, $\dfrac{\log.5 - \log(1-p)}{\log p - \log(1-p)} \gtreqless .5$

This allows enunciation of the following theorem:

T.2: When $q^* = 1$, $p < .5$, and a type (i) partition is ultimate, all hypotheses that assert that the relative frequency

---

[7] To prove the second inequality, take the derivative with respect to p of $p\log p + (1-p)\log(1-p)$. It is negative when $p < .5$, 0 when $p = .5$, and positive when $.5 < p$. Hence, $p\log p + (1-p)\log(1-p)$ receives its minimum value when $p = .5$ and that minimum is $\log.5$.

with which black balls are drawn is greater than or equal to .5 are to be rejected.

Similarly, for $.5 < p$.

In virtue of the second inequality, the following are true:

$$p\log p - p\log(1-p) + \log(1-p) > \log.5$$
$$p(\log p - \log(1-p)) > \log.5 - \log(1-p)$$

Hence, when $.5 < p$, $p > \dfrac{\log.5 - \log(1-p)}{\log p - \log(1-p)}$. When $p < .5$, $p < \dfrac{\log.5 - \log(1-p)}{\log p - \log(1-p)}$. Taken together with T.1, this yields the following theorem:

T.3: When $q^* = 1$ (and *a fortiori* when it is less than 1), and a type (i) partition is ultimate, the hypothesis that the relative frequency with which black balls are drawn is p is not rejected.

When $p \geqq .5$, and $q \geqq p$, $p^{nq}(1-p)^{n(1-q)} \geqq p^{np}(1-p)^{n(1-p)}$.

Taken together with T.3, this allows the following theorem:

T.4: Given the conditions of T.3, all hypotheses that assert that the relative frequency with which black balls are drawn is greater than p where $p > .5$ or less than p where $p < .5$ are not rejected.

From these theorems, it is clear that the use of a type (i) partition as ultimate and minimum caution recommends suspension of judgment regarding the outcome of sampling when $p = .5$; when p differs from .5, it recommends concluding that the relative frequency with which black balls appear in the sample lies within an interval from 1 to $p - e > .5$ when $.5 < p$, and from 0 to $p + e < .5$ when $p < .5$.

The value of e is a function of the value of p alone and not of the size of the sample. When $q^* < 1$, the conclusion warranted is, of course, weaker. Here, however, an increase in sample size results in an interval estimate of the relative frequency in the sample that more and more closely coincides with the interval estimate that is warranted when $q^* = 1$.

It should be clear from these results that type (i) partitions are inappropriate for use as ultimate partitions when direct inferences are made. If a coin that is known to be fair is tossed 1 million times, it would seem reasonable to predict that the coin will land heads approximately half of the time. Yet, the result of choosing a type (i) ultimate partition is complete agnosticism.

If the coin is biased with a probability of .7 that it will land heads on a single toss, it seems reasonable to predict that, in 1 million tosses, it will land heads approximately 7 out of 10 times. Yet, when a type (i) partition is chosen as ultimate, the prediction warranted is that the relative frequency will lie in the interval from 1 to .7−e where .7−e is some value greater than .5 but less than .7.

The rejection of type (i) partitions as ultimate in direct statistical inference is reinforced by the observation that, in making predictions of relative frequency, one relative frequency is usually taken to be as informative as another; when type (i) partitions are ultimate, however, predicting a relative frequency of .5 is far less informative than predicting a relative frequency of .99.

This leads naturally to the consideration of type (ii) partitions as ultimate. The consequences of using such partitions will be explored in the next section.

5] *Type (ii) Partitions*

Consider the consequences of adopting a type (ii) partition as ultimate. The elements of this partition consist of the $n+1$ hypotheses that specify the possible relative frequencies with which black balls can occur in an n-fold sample with replacement. The probability of that element of the ultimate partition asserting that the relative frequency is r/n will be $\binom{n}{r} p^r (1-p)^{n-r}$ and the rejection level will be $q^*/(n+1)$.

According to the Bienayme-Tchebycheff inequality, the probability that $|r/n-p| > e$ (where e is some small positive number) is less than $p(1-p)/ne^2$. For any n, let k be the smallest positive integer such that $\dfrac{k}{n+1} \geqq \dfrac{p(1-p)}{ne^2}$. It is easy to see that there is some value of n for any pair of values of p and e such that for all greater values of n, $k \geqq (p(1-p)/e^2) + 1$.

Let n bear some value such that the total number of relative frequencies that are possible in an n-fold sample lying within the interval $0 \leq r/n < p-e$ is greater than k, and the total that lies within the interval $p+e < r/n \leq 1$ is greater than k. When $p \leq .5$, n can be any number larger than $k/(p-e)$, and when $.5 \leq p$, n can be any number larger than $k/(p+e)$.

Under the conditions specified, the probability that r/n will fall in one of the two tails is less than $k/(n+1)$. Now if $q^* = 1$, any prediction that the relative frequency of black balls is r/n (for some specific value of r) will be rejected if and only if the probability of that prediction is less than $1/(n+1)$.

As a consequence, at most k among the more than 2k predictions in the two tails can go unrejected. (Actually, inasmuch as the probabilities decrease as s/n moves away from p, fewer than k of these hypotheses will go unrejected.) Since the binomial distribution is approximately symmetrical when n is fairly large, it can be established that, for large n, at most k/2 hypotheses in each tail will go unrejected. Hence, the prediction is warranted (when $q^* = 1$) that $p-e-k/2n \leq r/n \leq p+e+k/2n$.

This argument justifies the following assertion:

Let δ be any small positive number, e be positive and less than δ, k the least integer greater than or equal to $(p\,(1-p)/e^2)+1$, and n such that $e+(k/2n) \leq \delta$, then for every n′ greater than n, $p-\delta \leq r/n' \leq p+\delta$ can be justifiably accepted as an interval estimate of the relative frequency with which black balls (positive instances) will occur in a random n-fold sample with replacement, provided that $q^* = 1$.

The argument can be generalized to hold for any positive q^* less than or equal to 1. Consequently, when δ is small but fixed, the degree of confidence with which the interval estimate of the relative frequency is accepted increases with n.

These considerations permit the enunciation for acceptance of two "laws of large numbers":

For very large n, the prediction that r/n will fall in a small interval around p can be justifiably accepted. The interval can be reduced by increasing n. The value of q^* employed can be reduced by increasing n (and holding the size of the interval constant).

For very large n, the prediction that r/n will fall within a very small interval around p can be accepted with a high degree of confidence. The degree of confidence will approach the maximum if the interval is kept fixed and n allowed to increase to infinity.

These results show that, when a type (ii) partition is chosen to be ultimate, Cramer's practical certainty principle (as modified in Section 3) is satisfied. Applying rule (A) in direct inference, together with a type (ii) ultimate partition, does lead to recommendations that accord with presystematic considerations.

Before concluding this section, it might be useful to consider a numerical application of the argument. Let $\delta = .1$ and $e = .09$. When $p = .3$, $k = 26$ (which is the smallest integer greater than or equal to $\frac{.3 \times .7}{.09^2} + 1$). In order for δ to be greater than or equal to $e + (k/2n)$, n must be greater than 1,300. According to the proof, this shows that when n is greater than 1,300, r/n is greater than or equal to .2 and less than or equal to .4.

Actually, n can be reduced considerably by using the normal approximation to the binomial distribution, rather than the Tchebycheff inequality. Thus, when $n = 100$, the probability that $|r/n - .3|$ is greater than .1 is approximately .0278. When $q^* = 1$, the rejection level is $1/101 = .0099$. Hence, at most two hypotheses in the tails can go unrejected, one at each tail. Hence, the prediction that r/n is greater than or equal to .19 and less than or equal to .41 can be accepted. If one increases n to 144, similar procedures allow one to assert that r/n lies in the interval from .2 to .4.

It should be kept in mind that the results obtained here do not determine the strongest conclusions that are warranted when type (ii) partitions are ultimate. The problem of providing an algorithm for doing this remains to be solved. As in the other applications of rule (A), the central question here is not the total probability of the strongest conclusion that can be justifiably accepted. Although it will be true that this probability is very high, the crucial question is whether there is a hypothesis that predicts a specific relative frequency outside of the interval whose probability is not sufficiently low to warrant rejection.

6] *Long and Short Runs*

Consider an urn that contains 1 million balls, all but 1 of which are black. If a single draw is to be made from the urn, the probability that the ball drawn will be black is .999999. It seems reasonable to predict that the ball drawn will be black, and rule (A) recommends such a conclusion—provided that q^* is not extremely low and the ultimate partition contains as elements "the ball drawn will be black" and "the ball drawn will not be black." (Observe that this partition can be construed as a type (ii) partition for the case where $n = 1$.)

Suppose, however, that the draw from the urn is considered as 1 of 1 billion draws from the urn in a billionfold sample with replacement. Even if $q^* = 1$, rule (A) will fail to recommend predicting that the ball drawn on the specific draw under consideration will be black; for when a type (ii) partition is used relative to a billionfold sample with replacement, rule (A) will recommend predicting that the relative frequency with which black balls will appear lies in a very small interval around .999999, an interval sufficiently small to rule out the prediction that all balls drawn will be black. Since no conclusions can be obtained as to which draws will yield nonblack balls, agnosticism regarding the specific draw under consideration will be recommended. (Strictly speaking, predictions with regard to the outcomes of specific draws are not even relevant answers.)

The outcome is that rule (A) recommends predicting that a black ball will be drawn on trial n for each n from 1 to 1 billion. On the other hand, it also recommends concluding that at least 1 of the draws in the very same sample will yield a white ball. These results do not detract from the merits of rule (A). Indeed, they seem to conform with presystematic intuitions about the matter. The virtue of rule (A) in this connection is that it accommodates these intuitions, avoids the apparent contradiction in them, and preserves deductive cogency as a requirement for rational inductive inference.

By relativizing the scope of deductive cogency to the choice of an ultimate partition (that is, to a decision concerning what is to count as a relevant answer), the theory proposed here explains away the apparent inconsistency as being due to a shift in ultimate partitions. The prediction that a black ball will be drawn the nth time is justified relative to an ultimate partition that consists of the two hypotheses: "a black ball will be drawn the nth time" and "a nonblack ball will be drawn the nth time." When the ultimate partition consists of the billion and one hypotheses that specify a possible proportion of black balls in 1 billion draws, the conclusion that a black ball will be drawn the nth time is not only unjustified but is not even, strictly speaking, a relevant answer.

Unlike the lottery problem originally considered in connection with deductive cogency, situations of which the urn example is typical illustrate cases in which investigators may and often do exploit two or more ultimate partitions in reaching conclusions from given evidence. In the million-ticket lottery, it seems clear that most people would regard as ultimate the millionfold partition that consists of sentences of the form "ticket x will win." Evidence for this stems from the intuitive plausibility of the recommendation to suspend judgment as to the outcome of a fair lottery. But in the case of predictions concerning sampling from the urn, an investigator might very well reach conclusions with regard to the short and the long run, that could not, by being taken together, form a deductively consistent and closed body of sentences.

The statistical interpretation of the law of entropy seems to provide an illustration in science of the use of two distinct ultimate partitions, one for the short run and one for the long run. Consider a closed system that consists of a piece of metal in a bath of water. Suppose this system to be maintained for a long period of time, and consider the behavior of the metal-in-water-bath at intervals of equal length during this period. If asked whether the water will freeze and the metal turn red hot during some specific interval $\triangle t$, every expert would agree in answering negatively. They would do so no matter which interval was under consideration. Yet, if the experts were adherents of a statistical interpretation of the law of entropy, they would also maintain that, if the period during which the metal-in-water-bath is maintained is sufficiently—i.e., astronomically—long, there will be some interval during that period at which the water will indeed freeze while the metal turns red hot.

These conclusions when taken together do not form a consistent body of beliefs. According to Kyburg's position, inconsistency is to be avoided by abandoning the requirement of deductive closure. The position taken here is that deductive closure can be preserved in a modified form by restricting its scope of application to conclusions reached relative to an ultimate partition. Conclusions about short and long runs that seem to conflict do not do so in actuality, because they are reached "from different points of view"—i.e., when different kinds of answers are considered to be relevant.[8]

7] *Conclusion*

The attempt to apply rule (A) to direct inference, in which the problem is to predict the outcome of n independent trials of an experiment with two possible outcomes, whose probabilities are p and 1−p, indicates that rule (A) does lead to plausible results—provided that the ultimate partition is of type (ii)—i.e., consists of hypotheses that predict the relative frequencies of positive outcomes in the n trials.

This result does not obligate the investigator to take as ultimate the n+1 hypotheses about the relative frequencies in n trials. He can consider the m+1 hypotheses that predict the relative frequencies in some m-fold subset of these n trials. In particular, he can take as ultimate the partition that consists of the two possible outcomes of a specific trial. The elements of this partition will not as a rule be relevant answers, according to the "long run" ultimate partition. Since there seem to be situations in science, in which conclusions are reached from the same evidence and the same theoretical considerations, both for the long and the short run, grounds can be offered for concluding that there are limits to the constraints that can be imposed on the choice of ultimate partitions. These limits seem to preclude the specification of a unique ultimate partition relative to given evidence. From the point of view of the theory of inductive inference being proposed

---

[8] See T. Ehrenfest-Afanassjewa, "On the Use of the Notion 'Probability' in Physics," *American Journal of Physics*, 26 (1958), 388–392, especially 389–390.

here, therefore, there seems to be no hope of eliminating the relativization of deductive cogency requirements to the choice of ultimate partitions. It does seem possible to suggest constraints upon such choice in a piecemeal fashion, but these constraints are not strong enough to entail unique choices in every case.

XVI

✳✳✳✳✳✳✳✳✳✳✳✳✳✳✳✳✳✳✳✳✳✳✳✳

Inverse Inference

1] *Introduction*

Central though the problem of direct inference may be for providing an interpretation of statistical probability and for indicating the structure of statistical explanation and prediction, the chief concern of theories of statistical inference has been with the problem of inverse inference. Relative to certain background information b, it is accepted as true that one and at most one of a given list of statistical hypotheses is true. A random experiment is conducted; the evidence thereby obtained is then used to reach a conclusion concerning which of the statistical hypotheses is true.

In line with the discussion in the chapters immediately preceding, consider a situation in which it is known that a given urn contains 10 balls, each of which is either white or black. The problem is to ascertain on the basis of an n-fold random sample with replacement what the percentage is of black balls in the urn.

One procedure that has suffered varying fortunes throughout the history of statistical theory (it is now on the upswing) is to use Bayes' rule. This requires a specification of the prior probability distribution over the eleven hypotheses that specify the possible relative frequencies of black balls in the urn. This information, together with the conditional probability distributions over the possible outcomes of sampling relative to each of these eleven hypotheses (the "likelihoods" of each of the hypotheses relative to each possible outcome of sampling), can be used with the aid of Bernoulli's theorem to compute the conditional probabilities of each of the eleven hypotheses relative to each of the possible outcomes of sampling.

The result obtained via this procedure after sampling is a probability distribution over the eleven hypotheses regarding the composition of the urn relative to the data (and background information). This is not, of course, the same as specifying which hypotheses among the 2^{11} relevant answers (it is being assumed that the eleven hypotheses that specify distinct relative frequencies of black balls in the urn form the ultimate partition) is justifiably accepted as strongest. However, rule (A) can be applied to yield an answer here.

The difficulty with employing Bayesian methods in inverse inference is that judgments concerning prior probabilities are often difficult to come by. The theory of confirmation that is put forward by Jeffreys and Carnap has not been sufficiently well developed to provide a standardized method. Efforts to elicit subjective commitments to probability assignments from information about the investigator's choice behavior will often falter, as the result of lack of clarity concerning the investigator's or agent's preferences.

In this chapter, an attempt will be made to elicit probability assignments for hypotheses from an investigator's epistemic commitments and preferences. Rather than taking an investigator's preferences among practical options and outcomes as the basis for obtaining subjective probability assignments, an appeal will be made to his beliefs and to the degrees of confidence with which he holds them. It is to be suspected that, at least on some occasions, men are clearer about what they believe (accept as true) and their degrees of confidence, than they are about their preferences among various risky alternatives. If beliefs can be used to obtain probability assignments prior to experimentation, then the scope of applicability of Bayesian techniques in real-life situations might conceivably be extended.

No claim is being made here concerning the precise extent to which the proposals made will enlarge the domain of applicability of Bayesian techniques of inverse inference. That will require further exploration. Nor is it being maintained that the proposals introduced here are in conflict with the methods of Ramsey, De Finetti, and Savage for deriving probability commitments. They are intended to supplement such procedures in various ways. Regardless of whether or not they do successfully extend the scope of Bayesian methods of inverse inference, they should indicate some interesting respects in which rational inductive inference and rational inductive behavior are related to one another from a critical cognitivist point of view.

2] *Deriving Probability from Belief*

Suppose an investigator is interested in finding out the proportion of black balls in an urn (containing 10 balls) on the basis of an n-fold sample with replacement. He is committed to using rule (A) with minimum caution (where $q^* = 1$) and takes the 11-fold partition specifying the possible proportions of black balls in the urn as ultimate. He is not clear at the outset, however, what prior probabilities to assign to elements of the ultimate partition.

Whether or not he can assign probabilities, he may very well have an opinion prior to sampling concerning what the true composition of the urn is. For example, he may actually believe that one half of the balls are black.[1] Or he may be quite clear that he is utterly agnostic. In either event, his commitments to rule (A), a minimum degree of caution, and the ultimate partition provide a basis for arguing that he is obligated to assign prior probabilities in certain ways and not in others.

Thus, if the investigator is agnostic about the contents of the urn, he is obliged to assign equal prior probabilities to each element of his ultimate partition; for it is only in this way that he is justified—according to rule (A)—in his agnosticism, given that he exercises minimum caution.

---

[1] Remember that his acceptance of that hypothesis as true is not tantamount to his accepting it as evidence. During the 1964 presidential campaign, many people believed that Goldwater would lose, yet would not have used their belief as evidence for other inferences—in any event, they considered that belief to be deserving of further test.

On the other hand, if he believes that one half of the balls are black, he is committed to assigning a prior probability greater than 1/11 to the hypothesis that one half of the balls are black and probabilities less than 1/11 to the remaining ten hypotheses.

In the second case, the amount of information that is obtained regarding the prior probability distribution is quite small. And had the investigator exercised greater caution—i.e., had q^* been less than 1—agnosticism would not have yielded the unique probability distribution just indicated.

Thus, an investigator's prior beliefs about elements of the ultimate partition give, in general, only very slight information regarding the prior probability distribution.

3] *Deriving Probability from Confidence*

Observe, however, that in many situations an investigator can tell not only what he believes and disbelieves prior to acquiring evidence, but also the degrees of confidence with which he believes or disbelieves those things. To be sure, he may not be able to specify numerical values for degrees of confidence. But he can often distinguish (in Shackle's language) between those events by whose occurrence he would be very much surprised and those by whose occurrence he would be relatively slightly surprised. I do not believe that Goldwater will run again for President in 1968; I do not believe that Nixon will run, either. But I would be somewhat less surprised if the latter happens than if the former does.

Information about an investigator's degrees of surprise (degrees of confidence of rejection) can be used together with rule (A) and the theory of degrees of confidence attached to it, to obtain stronger determination of prior probability assignments.

For the present, the unrealistic assumption will be made that an investigator is able to assign numerical values to the degrees of confidence with which he rejects elements of his ultimate partition prior to further evidence collection. In later sections, this assumption will be weakened in various ways in order to render the proposals more applicable.

Suppose that the investigator who is concerned to ascertain the proportion of black balls in the urn accords the prior assignments of degrees of confidence of rejection to elements of his ultimate partition as in Table 1.

Table 1

Relative Frequencies	0	.1	.2	.3	.4	.5	.6	.7	.8	.9	1
Prior Degrees of Confidence of Rejection	.9	.7	.2	.1	0	0	0	.1	.2	.7	.9

Consider the hypothesis that none of the balls is black. This is rejected with a degree of confidence of .9. If $q^* = 1$, the maximum q-value relative to which that hypothesis goes unrejected is obtained from the following equation:

$$1 - q = .9$$

Hence, $q = .1$.

Now when $q = .1$, the rejection level will be $1/110 = .0091$. This means that any hypothesis that is rejected for any q-value greater than .1, but goes unrejected at that value, must bear a probability of .0091. This is the prior probability to be assigned to the hypothesis that none of the balls in the urn is black.

Suppose the investigator held himself to be exercising a degree of caution less than 1. The formula to be used to determine the maximum q-value relative to which the hypothesis goes unrejected that no balls in the urn are black is $(q^* - q)/q^* = .9$. Thus, if $q^* = .5$, $(.5 - q)/.5 = .9$. Hence, $q = .05$. The probability to be assigned to the hypothesis is, by reasoning identical to that offered before, equal to $.05/11 = .0045$. Table 2 gives the prior probability assignments to the elements of the ultimate partition relative to the confidence of rejection assignments given in Table 1 when $q^* = 1$, .5, and .1.

Table 2
Elements of the Ultimate Partition

q^*	0	.1	.2	.3	.4	.5	.6	.7	.8	.9	1
1	.009	.027	.073	.082	x	x	x	.082	.073	.027	.009
.5	.005	.014	.036	.041	x	x	x	.041	.036	.014	.005
.1	.001	.003	.007	.008	x	x	x	.008	.007	.003	.001

4] *The Quasi-Laplacian Rule*

Although the procedure just described suffices to determine unique probabilities for rejected elements of the ultimate partition, it does not do so, except in special cases, for unrejected elements. What can be obtained is the total probability that can be assigned to unrejected elements. This total probability is 1 minus the sum of the probabilities that are assigned to the rejected elements. In the example under consideration, the total probability that is assigned to the unrejected hypotheses which assert that the relative frequency of blacks in the urn is either .4, .5, or .6 is .718 when $q^* = 1$, .808 when $q^* = .5$, and .962 when $q^* = .1$.

Observe that there are two situations in which the total probabilities assigned to unrejected elements can be uniquely determined: when $q^* = 1$ and no element is rejected, and when one and only one element goes unrejected. Furthermore, even when unique assignments cannot be obtained, assignments of intervals of probability values can be made to unrejected elements; for no element that is unrejected can bear a probability less than q^*/n, where n is the number of elements of the ultimate partition, and no unrejected element of the ultimate partition can bear a probability greater than $T-(q^*m)/n$, where T is the total probability that is assigned to unrejected elements and $m+1$ is the total number of unrejected elements. Thus, when q^* or m is relatively large, the upper bound of the interval will tend to approach the lower bound.

In spite of the fact that the procedure for obtaining prior probabilities from prior assignments of degrees of confidence would be sufficiently precise for many applications, there are situations in which the intervals of probability that are assigned to unrejected elements would be too large. Thus, in the example described in Tables 1 and 2, when $q^* = 1$, the interval of probability assigned to each unrejected element of the ultimate partition would have .091 as lower bound and .536 as upper bound.

In order to escape such imprecision, it is desirable to introduce additional constraints on probability assignments. In some situations, it might be possible to utilize information about an agent's preferences among risky alternatives, after the usual fashion of subjective-probability theorists. However, some consideration seems in order of situations in which the appeal to such factors is unavailing.

Another possible procedure obtains if the investigator is able to consider as ultimate another partition of the same domain of possibilities. For example, in the case under discussion, he might be able to articulate his prior opinions relative to the ultimate partition, which consists of the two hypotheses that state that the number of balls in the urn is 0 or even and the number of balls in the urn is odd. Suppose that when $q^* = 1$ he is able to state that he is agnostic regarding these two alternatives. This would obligate him to assign probabilities of .5 to each of these two hypotheses. Since probability assignments have been supposed to remain constant when ultimate partitions are changed (provided that the total evidence remains constant), this commitment can be used to determine more narrowly probability assignments to the unrejected hypotheses in the original 11-fold partition. There are five hypotheses that assert that an odd number of balls are black; only the one that asserts that 5 are is unrejected. The total probability assigned to the rejected ones is .112. In order to make a total probability of .5, the proposition that asserts that exactly half of the 10 balls in the urn are black must be assigned a probability of .388. The remaining two unrejected hypotheses, which specify that even numbers of balls (4 and 6) are black, share between them a total probability of .330. The previous indeterminateness in probability assignments is substantially decreased.

The main complaint to be leveled against this approach is that it seems rarely to be the case that men can declare the degrees of confidence with which they accept or reject hypotheses relative to more than one ultimate partition. The most obvious situation in which this does appear to take place is one in which long- versus short-run predictions are contemplated. But in the problems of inverse inference under consideration, this does not seem to be true.

This leads to consideration of still a third procedure, which amounts to a generalization of the classical principle of indifference or insufficient reason. Where an investigator, prior to data collection, does not find in his background information any grounds for discriminating between elements of his ultimate partition that he fails to reject, he should give them equal weight. In anticipation of subsequent developments, this principle will be strengthened so as to require assignment of equal probabilities to all the elements of an ultimate partition that are rejected with the same degree of confidence. (Unrejected elements are rejected with the same 0 degree of confidence.) This rule will be called the "quasi-Laplacian rule."

The quasi-Laplacian rule is not to be understood as obligatory. If an investigator can utilize information about his preferences among risky alternatives, or can exploit his degrees of confidence relative to several different ultimate partitions, in order to derive probability assignments, he should do so. The quasi-Laplacian rule is intended to cover cases in which the investigator admits that he is incapable of making discriminations between elements of his ultimate partition on the basis of his other commitments. The rationale for proceeding in this way is that, when an investigator is incapable of making discriminations among hypotheses with respect to probability, belief, betting, etc., the entire burden of providing the grounds for making distinctions should rest with the evidence to be collected.

5] *Degrees of Caution*

Throughout the discussion of direct inference in the previous chapters and of inverse inference here, it has been taken for granted that the investigator could determine the degree of caution which he was exercising relative to a given problem. Now it does not appear entirely absurd to suppose that he can distinguish between utter skepticism and minimal caution. But even an investigator who thoroughly understood and accepted rule (A) as a legitimate criterion for rational inductive inference might be hard put to specify a numerical value between 0 and 1 for the degree of caution that he exercises.

Such an investigator could, however, ascertain in a rough and ready way what degree of caution he exercises in cases of direct inference, for which the probability distribution over outcomes of sampling is known. For example, an investigator who obeys the requirements of rule (A) (or commits himself to obeying them) might declare that he believes that, on 10 tosses of a fair coin, heads will show anywhere from 3 to 7 times. This means that he rejects the hypothesis that 2 out of 10 tosses will show heads. On the assumption that the coin is fair, this hypothesis bears a probability of .0439. The maximum value of q for which this hypothesis goes unrejected would be $11 \times .0439 = .4829$. Hence, the value of q^* must be greater than .4829 and less than or equal to 1.

Had the number of tosses of the coin been larger, say 100, it would have been possible to obtain a much sharper determination of the degree of caution exercised.

The procedure presupposes that the investigator can declare what he believes to be true (and false) in situations in which elements of his ultimate partition can be assigned definite probability values. For present purposes, it does not matter whether what the investigator declares himself to believe are truly his beliefs. For purposes of evaluating inferences, as a rule, the investigator's expressly declared commitments are usually what are taken into account. And it does not seem too far-fetched, even in real life, for an investigator to express himself in the manner indicated.

But what about situations in which the probability distribution over the elements of the ultimate partition is not given? In such cases, an investigator could be asked to commit himself on the following matter: Is the degree of caution that he is exercising equal to the degree of caution that would warrant predicting that a fair coin tossed 100 times will land heads at some point between 30 and 70 times? No investigator could reasonably be expected to give a definite answer to such a question; but he could be expected to indicate whether his degree of caution is approximately equal to that involved in the coin-tossing case. By varying the interval around 50 for the strongest prediction of the outcome of coin tossing, it should be possible to elicit a commitment to a degree of caution that falls within an interval sufficiently narrow for most purposes.

6] *Degrees of Confidence*

Substantially the same procedure can be used in order to ascertain the degrees of confidence with which an investigator rejects elements of an ultimate partition prior to testing. For the sake of simplicity, let the degree of caution exercised be indexed by $q^* = 1$. Let H be an element of an ultimate partition that is rejected prior to experimentation. In order to ascertain the degree of confidence with which it is rejected, ask the following question: Is that degree of confidence roughly equal to the degree of confidence with which the prediction is rejected, when $q^* = 1$, that none of the 100 tosses of a fair coin show heads, that 1 toss lands heads, that 2 tosses land heads, etc.

On the basis of such comparisons, it is possible to obtain a numerical value for the degree of confidence of rejection of H or, at any rate, an interval of such values.

Observe that the comparisons involved here are not direct comparisons of probability. The investigator is not asked whether he considers H to be as probable as obtaining x heads on 100 tosses of the fair coin. The comparisons are between degrees of confidence of rejection. Hypotheses rejected relative to one ultimate partition with the same confidence as hypotheses rejected relative to another may nonetheless bear different probabilities, for the probability assignments are also a function of the number of elements of the ultimate partition.

In situations in which an investigator is able to make the sorts of comparisons demanded in this and the previous section, it becomes possible to utilize the procedures of Section 4 in order to obtain numerical values for prior probabilities for elements of an ultimate partition.

The distinctive feature of this method is its reliance upon an investigator's ability to compare his beliefs and disbeliefs and the degrees of confidence with which he has them. No appeal is made to direct judgments of probability, except for reference to probability distributions over possible outcomes of tossing a coin that is known to be fair. And the investigator is not required to make judgments about preferences among risky alternatives (except insofar as accepting a sentence via induction is a risky alternative).

The theoretical interest of this approach is that it allows the use of Bayesian routines on the basis of an assessment of what an agent believes to be true rather than of how he chooses to act. Its possible practical advantage is in extending the scope of Bayesian theory to cover cases in which it is easier to ascertain a person's beliefs than it is his practical utilities. Obviously, the proposed procedures deserve closer examination and refinement than has been offered here. Hopefully, it has at least been shown that the notion of degrees of confidence of rejection (Shackle's notion of potential surprise) does have sufficient importance for accounts of inductive inference to warrant further consideration.

XVII

Belief
and Action
Revisited

1] *Evidence and Action*

A *discredited scientific* theory is rarely discarded in its entirety.
If it has, in its time, proven successful in accommodating wide
ranges of data, the new theory which replaces it preserves some
of its features. Proponents of scientific revolutions are obligated
to account for the partial successes of the systems they overthrow.

Much the same is true of philosophical doctrines that have
proceeded through history with little challenge. The naive cognitivist model for belief and action is as old as Aristotle and as
new as Gilbert Ryle. Various aspects of the relations between
belief and action have, indeed, been subject to considerable
philosophical debate. But the features attributed in Chapter I
to the naive cognitivist model have rarely, until recently, been
questioned. Surely there must be some truth to the doctrine, or
at least some good reason why the deficiencies in the model have
escaped the attention of philosophers for so long. Critics of naive
cognitivism should be able to accommodate within their own
theories the legitimate insights that are found in that view.

A germ of truth is not difficult to find. Although belief that H is not equivalent to regarding H as evidence, belief that H is a necessary condition for accepting H as evidence. The naive cognitivist model for belief and action is substantially a correct one— provided the belief involved is evidential. One qualification must be made. A man can be justified in acting as if H were true, even though H is not part of his evidence. Nonetheless, if he does take H as evidence, he should adopt the policy that is best when H is true. This is so, no matter what his objective may be. Relative to evidence that includes H, the probability that H is 1. Relative to that evidence, therefore, there is no risk whatsoever in betting on the truth of H.

This concession would be of small importance if evidence were restricted to the incorrigibly evident. But in the context of local justification, evidence can include statements which, when their evidential status is called into question, are justified by nondeductive inference from other evidence. What constitutes evidence in ordinary decision problems will cover a wide range of sentences, including highly theoretical assumptions. The portion of an agent's beliefs at a given time that are evidential will, in general, be considerable. Naive cognitivism does provide, in this respect, a good first approximation to the truth.

To be sure, if all beliefs were evidential, skepticism would threaten not only global but local justification. A necessary condition for justifying the acceptance of a nonevident sentence as evidence is to accept it as true on other evidence. Because such acceptance involves risks that may be different from those involved in practical decision-making, the naive cognitivist model for belief and action breaks down.

Even here the breakdown is not complete. To accept a sentence H as true relative to evidence e and ultimate partition U is not necessarily to decide that further inquiry is pointless. Only when H is accepted as evidence is this so. According to the account tentatively offered in Chapter IX, H can be justifiably accepted as evidence when the degree of confidence with which H is accepted is very high relative to other evidence and relative to all questions deemed legitimate at the time. This can happen only if (but not necessarily if) its probability is very high.

Thus, inquiry tends to continue until (in what is now unfashionable jargon) "hypotheses" become "theories" and then "laws," or until conjectures and tentative conclusions are firmly established. Although at any given time many of the conclusions reached are not evidential and, hence, not susceptible to naive cognitivist analysis, the investigator in pursuit of the interests of science obtains results that are evidential and which can, therefore, provide the basis for decision-making without risk.

2] *Determinism and Action*

Writers in the naive cognitivist tradition have often identified the contribution of scientific inquiry to practical deliberation as consisting of the laws established by that inquiry on the basis of which predictions can be made that are relevant to policy-making. Contributions of this sort are, indeed, made. Given a lawlike sentence L that is so well supported by the evidence as to be justifiably taken as evidential in its own right, predictions can be deduced from L, provided that suitable assumptions about initial conditions are added. If the initial conditions are themselves evidential, the predictions are acceptable as evidence. Decisions based on them are made without risk.

But predictions are often based on statistical assumptions. Even when these assumptions are accepted as evidence, the predictions themselves are not evidential. Suppose the evidence asserts that individuals who have been inoculated with a particular vaccine stand a 90 per cent chance of immunization from polio. Given this statistical assumption, it might be legitimate to predict that Jones, having been inoculated with the vaccine, will not succumb to polio. But that prediction may, nonetheless, lack evidential status. Consequently, in deciding how to act, one should attend to the odds, not to the prediction.

The plausibility of naive cognitivism stems, in part, from the image of the scientist as providing deterministic laws so well established that they are beyond question. One way in which the breakdown of the naive cognitivist conception of the relation between belief and action comes to light is through recognition that predictions—even "scientific" ones—are often based on statistical assumptions. Reflection on the philosophical import of this fact has developed only relatively recently. It is not too surprising, therefore, that the ramifications of the classical models of belief and action have taken so long to be appreciated.

3] *Science and Action*

Thus, some concessions can be made to the naive cognitivist point
of view. A rational agent ought to act in the manner that is best
relative to his goals, when a sentence he accepts as evidence is
true. But this "put up or shut up" model is unsatisfactory in cases
where decision-making involves risks.

Behavioralism, however, is no better off. According to this
point of view, science is the handmaiden of practice. The aim and
raison d'être of scientific inquiry is to accumulate evidence and
to base probability assignments on that evidence, in order to
provide advice to practical decision-makers. But, as was argued
in the first chapter, behavioralism implies a form of creeping
skepticism that eventuates in an evidential base which consists
of the evident. Such a base is not only too poor to meet the demands for knowledge, it is quite insufficient for the needs of real-
life decision-makers. If science is the handmaiden of practice, in
the sense that behavioralism implies, it is a rather ineffective one.

However, behavioralism is not entailed by the deficiencies of
naive cognitivism. An account of inductive inference has been
outlined in this book that relates criteria for legitimate inference
to the ends of scientific inquiry, with the aid of principles that
are applicable to any problem in which a rational agent must
choose between alternative policies in order to attain given ends.
This has been done without reducing belief to action, or cognitive
ends to practical ones.

On this account, science does contribute to the formation of
rational policy in the manner suggested by behavioralists. However, the evidence and the probabilities that are supplied to
decision-makers are not the end-products of inquiry, but by-
products, produced in the course of the pursuit of the special ends
of science itself. Science is not a handmaiden of practice, but a
partner; it contributes advice to decision-makers while pursuing
its own objectives.

Individuals and institutions strive to attain many objectives. At
times, these ends conflict; at other times, they complement one
another. Philosophers legitimately ask questions about the relative
importance of different ends, including the cognitive objectives of

scientific inquiry. But disparagement of cognitive ends (even when there are grounds for it) ought not to disguise itself by reducing these ends to practical ones.

Truth, information, explanation, simplicity are desiderata that are different from wealth, love, security, health, peace, etc. They ought to be recognized as such. Such recognition is enhanced by showing how the ends of inquiry control the legitimacy of inferences. In this book, some first, tentative steps have been taken in that direction.

Selected Bibliography

This list includes, in addition to all items to which reference is made in the text, other entries relevant to the topics covered.

Achinstein, Peter. "Variety and Analogy in Confirmation Theory," *Philosophy of Science*, 30 (1963), 207–221.

Bar Hillel, Yehoshua. Discussion notes in *The British Journal for the Philosophy of Science*, 6 (1955), 155–157; and 7 (1956), 245–248.

———. "An Examination of Information Theory," *Philosophy of Science*, 22 (1955), 86–105.

———, and Rudolph Carnap. "Semantic Information," *The British Journal for the Philosophy of Science*, 4 (1953), 145–157.

Braithwaite, R. B. *Scientific Explanation*. Cambridge: Cambridge University Press, 1953.

———. "Belief and Action," *Aristotelian Society Supplementary*, 20 (1946), 1–19.

———. "The Nature of Believing," *Proceedings of the Aristotelian Society*, 33 (1932–1933), 129–146.

Brandt, Richard, and Jaegwon Kim. "Wants as Explanations of Actions," *Journal of Philosophy*, 60 (1963), 424–435.

Broad, C. D. *Mind and Its Place in Nature*. New York: Harcourt, Brace, 1925.

Carnap, Rudolf. "Replies and Systematic Expositions," in P. A. Schilpp, ed., *The Philosophy of Rudolf Carnap*. La Salle, Ill.: Open Court, 1963. Pp. 966–998.

———. "Variety, Analogy and Periodicity in Inductive Logic," *Philosophy of Science*, 30 (1963), 222–227.

———. *Logical Foundations of Probability*, 2nd ed. Chicago: University of Chicago Press, 1962.

———. "The Aim of Inductive Logic," in E. Nagel, P. Suppes, and A. Tarski, eds., *Logic, Methodology and Philosophy of Science*. Stanford, Calif.: Stanford University Press, 1962. Pp. 303–318.

———. Discussion note in *The British Journal for the Philosophy of Science*, 7 (1956), 243–244.

———. *The Continuum of Inductive Methods*. Chicago: University of Chicago Press, 1952.

———, and Wolfgang Stegmüller. *Induktive Logik und Wahrscheinlichkeit*. Wien: Springer, 1959.

Carter, C. F., G. P. Meredith, and G. L. S. Shackle. *Uncertainty and Business Decisions*. Liverpool: Liverpool University Press, 1962.

Chernoff, Herman, and Lincoln E. Moses. *Elementary Decision Theory*. New York: Wiley, 1959.

Chisholm, Roderick M. *Perceiving: A Philosophical Study*. Ithaca, N.Y.: Cornell University Press, 1959.

Churchman, C. West. "Science and Decision Making," *Philosophy of Science*, 23 (1956), 248–249.

———. *Theory of Experimental Inference*. New York: Macmillan, 1948.

Cramer, Harald. *Mathematical Methods of Statistics*. Princeton, N.J.: Princeton University Press, 1945.

Davidson, Donald. "Actions, Reasons and Causes," *Journal of Philosophy*, 60 (1963), 685–700.

Dewey, John. *Reconstruction in Philosophy*. New York: Beacon, 1948.

Ehrenfest-Afanasjewa, Tatiana. "On the Use of the Notion 'Probability' in Physics," *American Journal of Physics*, 26 (1958), 388–392.

De Finetti, Bruno. "Foresight: Its Logical Laws, Its Subjective Sources," in H. Kyburg and H. E. Smokler, eds., *Studies in Subjective Probability* (trans. by H. Kyburg). New York: Wiley, 1964. Pp. 97–158.

Goodman, Nelson. *Fact, Fiction and Forecast*. Cambridge: Harvard University Press, 1955.

Hacking, Ian. *Logic of Statistical Inference*. Cambridge: Cambridge University Press, 1965.

Hempel, Carl G. "Deductive-Nomological vs. Statistical Explanation," *Minnesota Studies in the Philosophy of Science*, 3 (1962), 98–169.

———. "Inductive Inconsistencies," *Synthese*, 12 (1960), 439–469.

———. "The Theoretician's Dilemma," *Minnesota Studies in the Philosophy of Science*, 2 (1958), 37–98.

Hintikka, Jaakko. "On a Combined System of Inductive Logic," *Acta Philosophica Fennica*, 18 (1965), 21–30.

———. "Towards a Theory of Inductive Generalization," *Proceedings of the 1964 Congress for Logic, Methodology and Philosophy of Science*. Amsterdam: North Holland, 1965. Pp. 274–288.

Jeffrey, Richard C. *The Logic of Decision*. New York: McGraw-Hill, 1965.

———. "Valuation and Acceptance of Scientific Hypotheses," *Philosophy of Science*, 33 (1956), 237–246.

Keynes, John M. *A Treatise on Probability*. London: Macmillan, 1921.

Kolmogoroff, A. N. *Foundations of the Theory of Probability*. New York: Chelsea, 1950.

Kyburg, Henry. "Probability, Rationality, and a Rule of Detachment," *Proceedings of the 1964 Congress for Logic, Methodology and the Philosophy of Science*. Amsterdam: North Holland, 1965. Pp. 301–310.

———. "Recent Work in Inductive Logic," *American Philosophical Quarterly*, 1 (1964), 249–287.

———. "A Further Note on Rationality and Consistency," *Journal of Philosophy*, 60 (1963), 463–465.

———. "Logical and Fiducial Probability," *Bulletin of the Interna-*

tional Statistical Institute, Proceedings of the 34th Session. Ottawa: 1963.

―――. *Probability and the Logic of Rational Belief.* Middletown, Conn.: Wesleyan University Press, 1961.

Lehrer, Keith. "Knowledge and Probability," *Journal of Philosophy,* 61 (1964), 368–372.

Levi, Isaac. "Deductive Cogency in Inductive Inference," *Journal of Philosophy,* 62 (1965), 68–77.

―――. "Hacking Salmon on Induction," *Journal of Philosophy,* 62 (1965), 481–487.

―――. "Belief and Action," *The Monist,* 48 (1964), 306–316.

―――. "Corroboration and Rules of Acceptance," *The British Journal for the Philosophy of Science,* 13 (1963), 307–313.

―――. "On the Seriousness of Mistakes," *Philosophy of Science,* 29 (1962), 47–65.

―――. "Decision Theory and Confirmation," *Journal of Philosophy,* 58 (1961), 614–625.

―――. "Must the Scientist Make Value Judgments?" *Journal of Philosophy,* 57 (1960), 345–357.

―――, and Sidney Morgenbesser. "Belief and Disposition," *American Philosophical Quarterly,* 1 (1964), 221–232.

Luce, R. D., and H. Raiffa. *Games and Decisions.* New York: Wiley, 1957.

Morgenbesser, Sidney. "Goodman on the Ravens," *Journal of Philosophy,* 59 (1962), 493–495.

Nagel, Ernest. "Carnap's Theory of Induction," in P. A. Schilpp, ed., *The Philosophy of Rudolf Carnap.* La Salle, Ill.: Open Court, 1963. Pp. 785–825.

―――. *The Structure of Science.* New York: Harcourt, Brace, 1961.

―――. *Principles of the Theory of Probability.* Chicago: University of Chicago Press, 1939.

Neyman, Jerzy. " 'Inductive Behavior' as a Basic Concept of Philosophy of Science," *Review of the International Statistical Institute,* 25 (1957), 7–22.

―――. *Lectures and Conferences on Mathematical Statistics and Probability.* Washington: 1952.

―――. "Basic Ideas and Some Recent Results of the Theory of Testing Statistical Hypotheses," *Royal Statistical Society,* 105 (1942), 292–327.

―――, and E. S. Pearson. "The Testing of Statistical Hypotheses in Relation to Probabilities a priori," *Proceedings of the Cambridge Philosophical Society,* 29 (1932–1933), 492–510.

Peirce, C. S. *Collected Papers,* 2. Cambridge: Harvard University Press, 1932.

Popper, Karl R. *Conjectures and Refutations.* New York: Basic Books, 1962.

―――. *The Logic of Scientific Discovery.* London: Hutchinson, 1959.

246]   Selected Bibliography

————. "The Propensity Interpretation of Probability," *The British Journal for the Philosophy of Science*, 10 (1959), 25–42.

————. "The Propensity Interpretation of the Calculus of Probability and the Quantum Theory," in S. S. Körner, ed., *Observation and Interpretation*. London: Butterworth, 1957.

————. Notes in *The British Journal for the Philosophy of Science*, 5 (1954), 143–149; 6 (1955), 157–163; 7 (1956) 244–245, 249–256.

Quine, W. V. *Word and Object*. New York: The Technology Press and Wiley, 1960.

Ramsey, F. P. *The Foundations of Mathematics and Other Logical Essays*. New York: Humanities Press, 1950.

Rudner, Richard. "The Scientist qua Scientist Makes Value Judgments," *Philosophy of Science*, 20 (1953), 1–6.

Savage, Leonard J. *The Foundations of Statistics*. New York: Wiley, 1954.

————, and others. *The Foundations of Statistical Inference*. New York: Wiley, 1962.

Schick, Frederic. "Consistency and Rationality," *Journal of Philosophy*, 60 (1963), 5–19.

Shackle, G. L. S. *Decision, Order and Time*. Cambridge: Cambridge University Press, 1961.

————. *Expectation in Economics*, 2nd ed. Cambridge: Cambridge University Press, 1952.

Sleigh, Robert C. "A Note on Some Epistemic Principles of Chisholm and Martin," *Journal of Philosophy*, 61 (1964), 216–218.

Stevenson, C. L. *Ethics and Language*. New Haven, Conn.: Yale University Press, 1940.

Von Neumann, John, and Oskar Morgenstern. *Theory of Games and Economic Behavior*. Princeton, N.J.: Princeton University Press, 1947.

Wald, Abraham. *Statistical Decision Functions*. New York: Wiley, 1960.

————. *On the Principles of Statistical Inference*. South Bend, Ind.: University of Notre Dame Press, 1942.

Weyl, Hermann. *Philosophy of Mathematics and Natural Science*. Princeton, N.J.: Princeton University Press, 1949.

INDEX

A Note on the Type

The text of this book is set in Caledonia, a typeface designed by W(illiam) A(ddison) Dwiggins for the Mergenthaler Linotype Company in 1939. This new typeface was inspired by the Scotch types cast about 1833 by Alexander Wilson & Son, Glasgow type founders, and Dwiggins chose the Roman name for Scotland—Caledonia. There is a calligraphic quality about this face that is totally lacking in the Wilson types. Dwiggins referred to an even earlier typeface for this "liveliness of action"—one cut around 1790 by William Martin for the printer William Bulmer. Caledonia has more weight than the Martin letters, and the bottom finishing strokes (serifs) of the letters are cut straight across, without brackets, to make sharp angles with the upright stems, thus giving a "modern face" appearance.

W. A. Dwiggins (1880–1956) was born in Martinsville, Ohio, and studied art in Chicago. In 1940 he moved to Hingham, Massachusetts, where he built a solid reputation as a designer of advertisements and as a calligrapher. He began an association with the Mergenthaler Linotype Company in 1929, and over the next twenty-seven years designed a number of book types for that firm; of especial interest are the Metro series, Electra, Caledonia, Eldorado, and Falcon. In 1930, Dwiggins first became interested in marionettes, and through the years made many important contributions to the art of puppetry and the design of marionettes.

Typography and binding design by
LEON BOLOGNESE